D1602256

REAL WAGES AND EMPLOYMENT
Keynes, Monetarism and the Labour Market

In this book Andrès Drobny examines the foundations of the Monetarist counterrevolution against Keynesian economics. He distinguishes between two approaches, concentrating on their respective views of the importance of relative prices in business cycles. As he shows, the core of the Monetarist critique centres on the natural rate hypothesis and the associated view that periodic fluctuations in employment arise as a result of counter-cyclical movements in real wages. He argues that the success of Monetarism stems from the fact that prominent Keynesian analyses of business cycles accept the view that real wage levels in the main determine aggregate employment levels. He proposes an alternative disequilibrium model of the demand for labour which produces Keynesian-type conclusions while simultaneously being immune to the Monetarist critique.

Drobny derives models of the demand for labour based on the Keynesian and Monetarist approaches which produce conflicting propositions between real wages, output and employment. These propositions are subjected to a battery of tests for Granger-causality using post-war data. His comparison reveals many of the implicit assumptions underlying both the Monetarist and orthodox Keynesian theories.

Dr Drobny has lectured in Economics at the universities of Cambridge and London. He is currently Chief Economist of Bankers Trust Company, London.

REAL WAGES AND EMPLOYMENT

Keynes, Monetarism and the Labour Market

ANDRÈS DROBNY

R
ROUTLEDGE
London and New York

First published 1988 by Routledge
Reprinted 1989
11 New Fetter Lane, London EC4P 4EE
29 West 35th Street, New York, NY 10001

Printed and bound in Great Britain by
Antony Rowe Ltd, Chippenham, Wiltshire

British Library Cataloguing in Publication Data
Drobny, Andrès
  Real wages and employment.
  Keynes, monetarism and the labour market.
  1 Personnel. Remuneration. Econometric
  models
  I. Title
  331.2′1′0724
  ISBN 0-415-00386-5

Library of Congress Cataloging in Publication Data
Drobyn, Andrès.
    Real wages and employment: Keynes, monetarism, and the labour
  market / Andrès Drobny.
        p. cm.
    Based on the author's thesis (Ph. D.) — Kings College, Cambridge.
    Bibliography: p.
    ISBN 0-415-00386-5
    1. Classical school of economics. 2. Keynesian economics.
  I. Title.
  HB94.D76   1988
  330.15′3–dc19   88-23879
                                                              CIP

dedicado a mi papa y mama

CONTENTS

PREFACE

This book is based on my Ph.D. presented to King's College, Cambridge. It is the product of my background in economics at two institutions with dramatically different analytical traditions. At the London School of Economics I developed a knowledge and appreciation of choice-theory particularly within what I define in the book as the neoclassical tradition. I also developed at that time a dissatisfaction with the explanation of business cycles and economic crises provided by this tradition. I subsequently moved to King's College, Cambridge, where my dissatisfaction with neoclassical theory was nurtured, and where I was encouraged to read the works of Keynes and Kalecki. I developed there an appreciation of aggregative economic reasoning and class-based models of economic analysis. This book therefore constitutes an attempt to bridge some of the gap between the two schools of thought or, more precisely, to obtain a better understanding of the differences between the schools.

A great many individuals have influenced me during this process. Most notable are Gene Savin, my Ph.D. supervisor who introduced me to the topic of employment fluctuations; David Currie who has read my work critically and sympathetically; Meghnad Desai for critical comments and suggestions; and Maurice Peston who helped me organise my thoughts on Keynesian economics in particular. I have an enormous debt to these four. I would also like to thank my colleagues at Queen Mary College, London, for offering their help and advice, and for putting up with me during the process of writing the book. Special thanks go to Joan McSweeney for typing the orginal draft of the book in such good spirits. Finally, thanks go to my good and close friends Alan Speight, John Wells and Nigel Mason for encouraging me, talking to me and helping me (almost) keep my sanity during this process.

Andrès Drobny
August 1987

LIST OF FIGURES AND TABLES

FIGURES

TABLES

Part One

THE IMPORTANCE OF RELATIVE PRICES IN COMPETING

MACROECONOMIC THEORIES

There is, therefore, no ground for the
belief that a flexible wage policy is
capable of maintaining a state of
continuous full employment... The
economic system cannot be made self-
adjusting along these lines.
Keynes (1936, p.267)

Chapter One

THE DECLINE OF THE KEYNESIAN ERA - AN OVERVIEW

The end of the long boom was accompanied by a
collapse of confidence in Keynesian theory and
policy proposals. A prominent Keynesian recently
described these developments by pronouncing that
'Keynesian economics has now reached middle age'
(Akerlof, 1979, p.219). Keynesian macroeconomics,
centred on demand management policies designed to
produce rapid and stable rates of output growth and
high employment levels, is in some senses the
establishment now under heavy attack from two well-
articulated schools of thought advocating a return
to laissez faire policies by the state.
Macroeconomics during the Keynesian era was a
subject concerned with the efficient exercise of
state control or influence over key macroeconomic
variables. Today it has become a dismal science
emphasising the factors on the supply side of the
economy which impair, or totally inhibit, the
state's ability to manage the capitalist economy
using macroeconomic tools.
     The first and more established school
confronting Keynesianism is monetarism, popularised
by Milton Friedman. In a recent assessment of
monetarism, Laidler (1981) describes its key
characteristics as including (1) the 'view that
fluctuations in the quantity of money are the
dominant cause of fluctuations in money income';
(2) that the division of money income fluctuations
between prices and real income are analysed using
the expectations-augmented Phillips curve model,
the structure of which is based on Friedman's
(1968) natural rate hypothesis; and (3) an
antipathy to macroeconomic activism which
characterised the Keynesian era (p.1).[1] A
further characteristic of monetarism not emphasised
in Laidler's assessment is the view advanced by

3

Friedman (1968, 1975) and Laidler himself[2] that
microeconomic policies designed to remove so-called
'structural rigidities' in labour markets are the
most effective weapons against unemployment. The
key role assigned to monetary policy by monetarists
is to provide for the 'maintenance of long-run
price stability' (Laidler, 1981, p.21). Providing
the conditions for the maintenance of high levels
of employment is, in monetarist theory, a role for
microeconomic policies.

During the 1970s a new school in
macroeconomics known as new classical economics
further developed the arguments of the monetarists.
Led most notably by Lucas (1972, 1981), new
classical economists introduced rational
expectations into Friedman's natural rate
hypothesis to develop a coherent individual market-
based theory of aggregate movements (Lucas, 1972).
This theory suggests that systematic macroeconomic
(i.e. fiscal and monetary) policies cannot alter
the level of output and the unemployment rate in
capitalist economies (the 'policy ineffectiveness
proposition').[3] Although differences in emphasis
and opinions do exist between monetarists and new
classicals (and indeed within the schools of
thought as well - see Chapter Three below), their
shared antagonism to Keynesian macroeconomic
activism has led some commentators such as James
Tobin (1980) and Frank Hahn (1980) to classify them
under the single heading of monetarist.[4]

Further, the theoretical basis of both schools
lies in the natural rate hypothesis which implies
that aggregate supply is the binding constraint on
output and employment in capitalist economies. The
natural rate hypothesis is derived from a method of
analysis which Coddington (1986) calls
'reductionist', where observed market phenomena are
explained on the basis of individual choices. The
choice-theoretic foundations of the natural rate
hypothesis implies that the monetarist analysis of
the labour market is conducted in terms of
equilibrium states where relative prices play the
crucial role of reconciling the choices and
competing desires of individuals in the market
place. Thus since Friedman (1975) claims that
'every economic theorist from Adam Smith to the
present' would claim that labour demand and supply
depend on the real wage rate (p.15), he defines the
natural rate of unemployment as that rate 'which
has the property that it is consistent with

equilibrium in the structure of <u>real</u> wage rates' (Friedman, 1968, p.8).

The reductionist nature of the natural rate hypothesis also implies that fluctuations in the level of employment over the business cycle must be explained as the outcome of individual choices.(5) The various monetarist and new classical <u>explanations</u> for these fluctuations key on systematic shifts in the supply of labour in generating real wage movements which induce inverse movements in the observed level of employment. Aggregate demand exerts an <u>indirect</u> influence on the level of employment in these models by altering the real wage rate. Both sets of theories single out real wage movements as the critical factor in generating fluctuations in employment.

1. THE ERA OF MONETARIST POLICIES

Recent trends in policy making have mirrored these theoretical developments. Governments are today orienting their policies towards supply-side management in contrast to Keynesian demand-side management (as expounded, for example, by Beveridge, 1944). According to Buiter and Miller (1981), the election of the Thatcher government in 1979 was the critical turning point in policy making in the UK. They argue that 'a central plank of the new government's platform was to strengthen the supply side of the economy' (p.315). The government abandoned the use of fiscal and monetary policies to maintain high and stable employment levels. The medium-term financial strategy launched in March 1980 formally committed the government to a five-year target of reducing the rate of growth of the money supply with an aim to reducing, if not eliminating, inflation. Fiscal policy was designed to accommodate this restrictive monetary policy without placing an 'undue' burden on interest rates. A further role for fiscal policy was to relax the supply constraints on the economy by reducing the volume of the state's command over resources and by reducing and redistributing tax burdens. In direct contrast to the Keynesian era of demand management, the resulting levels of output and employment were in the main left to be determined by the private sector.

The key to the employment-unemployment problem, according to the government, is the level of real wages paid by firms. Workers today are

being directly threatened by governments either to
reduce real wages and living standards or face high
and perhaps increasing unemployment. Early in her
first term of office, Margaret Thatcher proclaimed:
'We have no alternative but to accept a reduction
in the standard of the country's living if
investment and employment are going to recover.'[6]
     The current Chancellor of the Exchequer, Nigel
Lawson, recently provided a concise summary of the
Thatcher government's strategy in his Mais Lecture
delivered on 18 June 1984. It is a remarkable restatement of the monetarist policy position as laid
out by Friedman (1968). Lawson argues that:

> It is the conquest of inflation, and not
> the pursuit of growth and employment,
> which is or should be the objective of
> macroeconomic policy. And it is the
> creation of conditions conducive to
> growth and employment... which is or
> should be the objective of microeconomic
> policy.
>
>   (p.5-6)

     Lawson's analysis of UK unemployment also
shows his faith in monetarist theory. He argues
that the high and rising unemployment rate in
Western Europe as compared with the recent and
dramatic fall in unemployment in the United States
is due to the fact that over the past ten years
'the workers of Western Europe have seen their real
earnings rise... over the same period their
American counterparts have been prepared to accept
a small reduction in real earnings' (p.18). It is
the alleged rise in real wages and not the
government's deflationary macroeconomic policies
which, according to Lawson, generated what Buiter
and Miller (1981) have gone as far as to call a
'depression' in the UK economy (p.318).

2. A PLAN

This book investigates and examines the foundations
of the monetarist counter-revolution against the
Keynesian orthodoxy and argues that post-Keynesian
analysis provides an appropriate response. The
argument is conducted in three parts. Part One
describes the foundations of the analysis which
underlies both the monetarist and new classical
attack on Keynesian theory. Our contention is that

these developments centre on the natural rate
hypothesis and the associated view that periodic
fluctuations in employment (business cycles) arise
as a result of counter-cyclical movements in real
wages.[8] The monetarist theory of business cycles
and inflation relies on this mechanism. Further,
we argue that the failure of Keynesians to respond
adequately to the monetarist counter-revolution
arose from a tradition of Keynesians relying on a
particular model, the neoclassical-Keynesian
synthesis, as first elaborated by Modigliani
(1944), in conducting analyses of the workings of
the modern capitalist economy and the effects of
macroeconomic policies on its performance. The
widespread use of this model, which accepts the
view that real wages determine the level of
employment, left the Keynesian tradition ill-
equipped to defend its theories and associated
policy prescriptions from the new wave of
criticisms.

The analysis in Part One is geared towards
answering two particular questions concerning the
successful monetarist (and new classical) counter-
revolution. The first is why, after so many years
of dominance in macroeconomic analysis, did the
Keynesian theory prove to be so fragile under the
weight of the monetarist critique? To examine this
question we first re-examine the nature of Keynes'
own critique of the 'classical' view that the
market mechanism contains strong self-equilibrating
forces. This is discussed in Chapter Two. Much
attention is given to certain questions left
unanswered in Keynesian theory. The second
question, discussed in Chapter Three, is how the
monetarist and new classical theories were able to
rehabilitate the classical theory in such a way
that it is immune to certain problems posed
originally by Keynes. We also examine in this
chapter certain important differences between
monetarist and new classical theory.

Part Two presents a more detailed and formal
analysis of two alternative views of labour market
behaviour. The object in this part of the book is
to pare down the complex and wide range of
arguments between Keynesians on the one hand, and
classicists, monetarists and new classicists on the
other, to their bare essentials as regards the
aggregate real wage-employment relationship. The
analysis centres on alternative views of the
determinants of the demand schedule for labour.

Our main theme throughout Part Two is best

understood as the 'importance of being unimportant'. This does not relate directly to one of Marshall's four laws, but does refer to the subject of these laws - the derived demand for factors of production.(9) The particular subject in Part Two is the cyclical movement in real wages and their alleged influenced on key macroeconomic variables, particularly output and employment. A common feature of monetarist and new classical models of the business cycle is the counter-cyclical movement in the real wage rate and its importance in generating movements in output and employment.

Our discussion in these chapters focuses on a comparison between two fundamentally different approaches to cyclical fluctuations as regards the labour market and the corresponding role attributed by each approach to real wage movements. We differentiate in rather stark terms between models positing a direct interaction between real wages and employment and those based on a direct output-employment relationship at the aggregate level.(10) Static versions of these models are considered in Chapter Four. The demand for labour schedules of both approaches is derived from a choice-theoretic framework. This analysis brings to focus the distinguishing characteristics of the two approaches and in particular highlights their main differences. These differences are interpreted in terms of traditional income and substitution effects, and form the basis for the empirical investigation reported in Part Three of the book. However, as our main topic concerns the cyclical relationship between real wages and employment, we develop and examine dynamic versions of the labour demand schedules in Chapter Five. These equations are richer in detail and in particular incorporate rational expectations into the analysis.

The empirical investigations reported in Part Three are designed to examine the extent of support provided by UK data for the two approaches discussed in Parts One and Two. Chapter Six sets out our empirical methodology, which is based on non-structural time series models originally developed by Granger (1969). Chapter Seven reports the results of applying a battery of tests for Granger-causality running from real wages and real materials prices to employment. These results are therefore relevant for assessing the empirical validity of classical-type models premised on a direct interaction between real wages and

employment.   In Chapter Eight we examine the
performance   of   alternative   post-Keynesian   type
output-employment   models,   and   proceed   to   test
between these alternatives using a nested version
of   the   Granger   methodology.   Concluding comments
are presented in Chapter Nine.

Before   proceeding   to   our   analysis,   a   few
caveats are needed.   Throughout our discussion the
analysis will centre on the working of the market
mechanism   in   the   labour   market.   We   will
consistently   abstract   from   institutional
considerations   which   obviously   influence   the
workings   of   the   market   mechanism,   and   will   in
general refrain from a discussion of developments
in product markets.[11]   We adopt unquestioningly
the   traditional   Keynesian   assumption   that
investment and government fiscal policies are the
key exogenous variables determining the level of
aggregate demand.   This tradition suffers from the
particular weakness that fluctuations in investment
are left unexplained.   An appeal to changes in the
state of long-run expectations and the resulting
shifts   in   the   marginal   efficiency   of   capital
(Keynes,   1936,   Chapter   12)   is   vague   and
unsatisfactory.   In   particular,   as   Coddington
(1976, pp.1262-3) points out, any notion of long-
run equilibrium is precluded by such an analysis.
However,   we   neglect   this   potentially   important
issue in order to concentrate our attention on the
labour   market   and   the   alternative   uses   of
employment fluctuations.

The use of this method also implies that the
analysis will be short-run in nature, with business
cycles being the key concern.   We do not discuss
the   conditions   required   for   sustained   long-run
growth in a capitalist economy, and in particular
whether the level or rate of growth of real wages
exerts a strong influence on the pattern and rate
of   accumulation.[12]   Thus   our   theme   on   'the
importance   of   being   unimportant'   has   only   the
limited   aim   of   enquiring   whether   real   wage
movements are relatively unimportant in the course
of business fluctuations.

Our analysis throughout the book is couched in
choice-theoretic terms.   This should not be taken
to suggest that this is the only way to understand
the   debates   concerning   the   movement   of   aggregate
variables.   Indeed, some commentators argue that
this is in fact a misleading way to consider these
issues.[13]   However,   the   monetarist   counter-
revolution   is   based   on   a   consideration   of

individual choice as derived in standard microeconomic analysis. Our re-examination of these issues in choice-theoretic terms is designed to show that Keynesian theory can be made compatible with such a method.

Finally, the arguments developed in the following pages consider effective demand failures and the Keynesian pessimism concerning self-regulation of capitalist economies. We do not enter into a discussion of the other dimension of Keynesianism: the optimism concerning the ability of macroeconomic stabilisation policy, or so-called Keynesian fine-tuning, to achieve a fast growth, high-employment capitalist economy.[14] Our presumption, and it is only that, is that such policies are necessary but not sufficient to achieve this goal.

NOTES

1. Laidler also includes in his list the monetary approach to the balance of payments as exemplified by Frenkel and Johnson (1976).

2. See Laidler's 'British Commentary' in the Appendix to Friedman (1975).

3. Although in Lucas (1972) these propositions are derived using self-employed producers, Alogoskoufis (1983) shows how the arguments can be made in a model which includes wage labourers.

4. Hoover (1984) describes important methodological differences between what he calls 'two types of monetarism'.

5. Lucas (1981) describes this perspective in the introduction to his collected essays.

6. Quoted in the Guardian, 11 November 1980.

7. Such arguments have also been made during the past year in the editorial columns of popular weeklys such as the Economist. Although we do not consider this issue in the following pages, it is an interesting puzzle to note that, while President Reagan has often been quoted as claiming that Americans have never experienced such high living standards as achieved during his first term in office, average real earnings in the US have reportedly fallen in the past ten years. One potential explanation for this puzzle may lie in that, although average real earnings for most of those in continuous employment may have in fact been rising, the establishment of new industries (particularly in the 'sun belt' southern states) based on low average wages may account for the recorded fall in real average earnings in the economy as a whole. Needless to say, this possible explanation must be regarded as only tentative.

8. We use the term 'business cycles' to describe movements in employment away from a full-employment position. Thus the term encompasses periodic and regular fluctuations in employment as well as prolonged periods of low and stagnant employment levels.

9. Marshall (1977) describes the four conditions under which a 'check to the supply' of a factor of production (he uses plasterers as an example) 'may cause a very great rise in its [relative] price' (p.319).

10. Our methodological approach to these debates is therefore based on Kuhn's (1980) notion of competing paradigms.

11. The only exception to this is in our discussion in Chapter Three of the potential effects of real wage changes on the level of aggregate demand.

12. The Marxist approach recently expressed by Gordon, Weisskopf and Bowles (1983) provides a link between short-run business cycles and 'long swing expansions' and 'crises' in the accumulation process. Their analysis stresses institutional restructuring, the so-called 'social structure of accumulation (SSA), which provides the economic stability and modernisation of political economic conflict essential for favourable profit expecations and therefore for rapid capital accumulation' (a 'reproductive cycle') (p.152). The differences between long swing expansions and crises are classified in terms of the 'ratio of the product [real] wage to output per [labour] hour', in other words the wage share in output (p.154). In terms of our analysis, this position is unhelpful. While Gordon et al. attempt to show that a reproductive cycle occurs when the wage share in output tends to fall, the key consideration here is not this alleged negative relationship between the wage share in output and rapid (and sustainable) capital accumulation, but rather what sets the process in motion. A monetarist would argue that it is the fall in the real wage rate that generates the fall in the wage share; the Keynesian would emphasise the increase in demand which stimulates output, thereby reducing the wage share in output by raising output per labour hour. That is, both monetarist and Keynesian analyses emphasise profitability in the accumulation process, but differ on the mechanism by which profitability is restored after a cyclical downswing.

13. See Coddington's (1976) review for a discussion of this perspective.

14. See Modigliani (1977) for a recent statement of the Keynesian faith on this issue.

Chapter Two

HISTORICAL ANTECEDENTS REVISITED: KEYNES, CLASSICAL THEORY AND THE SYNTHESIS MODEL

The optimism which characterised the Keynesian era was a two-sided affair. Keynesianism was premised on a pessimistic view of the capitalist economy - it was seen to be lacking strong self-regulating properties. Keynes (1936) argues that:

> In conditions of laissez faire the avoidance of wide fluctuations in employment may, therefore, prove impossible.... I conclude that the duty of ordering the current volume of investment cannot be left in private hands. (p.320)

Thus there was a need for government macroeconomic intervention. Keynesians were optimistic about the eventual success of such activism. A sufficiently large and competently managed state could help regulate the capitalist economy by counteracting the deficiencies of the market mechanism.[1]

Both aspects of the Keynesian vision have come under attack. Monetarists, most notably Friedman (1968), used the natural rate hypothesis to argue that capitalist economies have stronger equilibrating forces than presumed by Keynesians. However, Friedman admitted that on the 'examination of the historial evidence', the process of adjusting inflationary expectations could be sluggish, possibly lasting for 'a couple of decades' (1968, p.11). Friedman firmly denied, however, that the government could speed up this process using macroeconomic tools. Activist policies, if unanticipated, could have a short-run effect on output and employment, Friedman argued. But he denied their effectiveness over a longer time span. Even worse, Friedman claimed that such

12

policies could actually destabilise the economy.(2) Thus he argued that monetary policy should be set 'on a steady course' and 'make a major contribution to promoting economic stability' (Friedman, 1968, p.17).

The core of the monetarist critique of Keynesian policies, if Milton Friedman is accepted as an adequate representative of the monetarist perspective, centres on a negation of the Keynesian optimism concerning the ability of the state to control and modify business cycles in advanced capitalist economies. We argue in Chapter Three below that different views do arise within the monetarist camp concerning the Keynesian pessimism on the self-regulating properties of the market mechanism.

The establishment of new classical economics during the 1970s presented a new and perhaps more far-reaching critique of Keynesianism. New classical economic models develop the monetarist analysis in what Sargent (1973) claims is 'an alternative and less confining form' (p.431). The new classical restatement of monetarism derives from the introduction of rational expectations into natural rate models. The resulting theories imply that capitalist economies will almost always be observed at the natural rate of output and employment with markets everywhere and at all points in time clearing. The Keynesian pessimism on the efficacy of capitalist markets is totally denied in new classical theory, and thus the need for government macroeconomic intervention negated (Hahn, 1980).

Monetarist and new classical theory share much common ground. Their theories of long-run equilibrium are virtually identical, with the natural rate defining this position.(3) Both theories are in Coddington's (1976) term 'reductionist', since the natural rate is determined by the decisions of rational agents maximising objective functions subject to resource constraints. Further, the choice-theoretic structure of both theories leads to great stress being placed on relative prices. Relative prices play a major role in determining the decisions of agents. As was mentioned above, the natural rate and thus long-run equilibrium is defined in terms of relative prices.

The two theories differ, however, in their respective analyses of movements around the natural rate of output and unemployment - their version of the business cycle. The source of cycles is the same in both theories - imperfect information. These theories stress unanticipated developments which lead certain agents to draw incorrect inferences concerning key variables (relative prices).[4] Thus both theories define a short-run equilibrium position as one in which markets clear, but where expectations are not realised.[5] However, the similarities end here. The monetarist analysis of business cycles focuses on the sluggish adjustment of expectations. New classical economics, based on rational expectations, cannot rely on such an explanation of business cycles. Although the rational expectations hypothesis does not imply that agents' expectations are always correct, the suggestion is that such expectations will not be systematically wrong over time. The new classical economists, particularly Lucas, have 'been almost exclusively concerned with the attempt to discover a useful theoretical explanation of business cycles' (Lucas, 1981, p.2). To this date, this attempt has been unsuccessful, with new classical theories relying exclusively on an ad hoc appeal to adjustment costs to explain these cycles (Lucas, 1975; McCallum, 1979; Sargent, 1978).[6]

Another difference between monetarists and new classicals relates to their common heritage - what Keynes (1936) called 'classical' theory. Monetarist and new classical theory, in different ways, have provided answers to some of the criticisms of the classical theory made by Keynes in the General Theory. Indeed, the success of the monetarist and new classical counter-revolution stems, in part at least, from an ability to correct certain defects in the classical theory which had left it such an easy target for the Keynesian revolution. However, the monetarist and new classical elaborations of the classical theory have different strengths and weaknesses and, in fact, certain important conflicts between the theories have arisen. It is for this reason that as monetarists, Laidler (1982) and Stein (1982) advocate in their recent books that monetarist analysis can and should be distinguished from new classical theory, even though both schools derive their analyses from the same foundations. In this chapter we review the background leading to the successful monetarist and new classical counter-revolution in macroeconomics.

1. CLASSICAL THEORY

The roots of the contemporary debates in macroeconomics are found in the 'Keynes vs. the classics' debate of the 1930s (and 1940s), instigated during a period of world depression characterised by high unemployment. In a recent defence of Keynesianism, Tobin (1980) argues:

> The controversy of the 1930s is being replayed today. The issues are basically the same. The contestants are of course different. Just as the Keynesian revolution challenged the then prevailing orthodoxy of economic theory and policy, so the counter-revolution now challenges the Keynesian orthodoxies, both theory and policy. (p.20)

The current 'replay' of the debate of the 1930s has also led to a revival of interest in reinterpreting the contribution made by Keynes in the General Theory. Leijonhufvud (1969) re-examines the early debates from the modern Keynesian perspective described by Coddington as 'reconstituted reductionism' (1976, especially p.1268). A skirmish on 'reinterpreting Keynes' was recently published in the Journal of Economic Literature;[7] and Coddington's (1976) exploration into the methodological foundations of Keynesian economics is motivated by a reference to the 'threat' posed by Keynes' General Theory to the classical analysis (p.1258). In addition, the current debates appear to have stimulated Benjamin and Kochin's (1979) reinvestigation of the causes of unemployment in the UK during the 1920s and 1930s, and the ensuing debate, which appeared in a recent issue of the Journal of Political Economy.[8]

The body of analysis which Keynes called 'classical' essentially provided a theory of long-run full-employment equilibrium in a competitive, barter-type capitalist economy. 'Since classical economists ordinarily "pierced the veil of money" and discussed things in real terms, as if money did not exist' (Hagen, 1949, p.11), their analysis was not easily extended to a monetary economy.[9] This extension was achieved by assuming that money reduces the costs of exchange, and so is in some senses 'useful', but at the same time money does not influence the terms of exchange based on the relative prices of goods. However, the

15

introduction of money used only for exchange does mean that all goods must be priced in nominal terms; that is, at a price relative to the value of money and not directly in relation to other goods. This coincidentally provides the theory with a potential explanation for business cycles and prolonged slumps, later to be exploited by monetarists and new classicals. We discuss this issue below after first describing in broad terms the mechanisms by which the classical theory generates the full-employment position. Our review is based on the descriptions of the classical theory presented in Hagen (1949) and Hicks (1937).

Consider an aggregate model of the capitalist economy (with money) made up of numerous agents who trade simultaneously in three markets - a market for all goods, a labour market, and a market for borrowing and lending money. The model only considers the flow of exchange in any period. Production is assumed to take place instantaneously under given technical conditions, and thus the dynamics of the system are for the moment ignored. The markets describe the determination of the aggregate levels of output, employment, and savings and investment. Within each of these markets, there exist specialist producers and traders operating atomistically in a large set of small markets where all decisions taken are based on relative prices. Important issues concerning market structure and the question of who sets relative prices are ignored. Further, the distribution of output and trade within each market is assumed to be fixed and independent of aggregate movements.

The interaction between the three markets can be captured in the well-known equation of exchange:

$$MV = PY \qquad\qquad (2.1)$$

where M is the total quantity of the monetary unit ('high-powered' money) for a given period of time, determined outside the economic system by some monetary authority; V is the velocity of circulation of money - how many times the monetary unit is used to purchase goods within each time period; P is the average price of the goods produced and sold during the period; and Y is a unique index of the volume of goods produced and sold in the period.[10] Equation (2.1) defines an identity where the total flow of monetary expenditure on goods is equal to the flow of money

16

income received for selling the goods. To arrive at a theory of long-run equilibrium, certain postulates are required defining behaviour in each of the three markets.

The classical model of long-run equilibrium is derived by postulating that the velocity of circulation of money (V) and the volume of output (Y) are stable variables and, in particular, are independent of the aggregate money stock (M) and price level (P). These postulates are based on the presumption that relative prices determine V and Y in two separate and independent markets - the loanable funds and labour markets respectively. Once these variables are determined, the price level in any period is determined in the goods market for a given quantity of money. We consider each market in turn.

The first market to consider is the loanable funds market where an analysis of the first classical postulate concerning the velocity of circulation (V) can be conducted. Since all variables in the model are determined simultaneously, we can investigate behaviour in this market for an initial given value of output (PY) which is distributed to all agents in the economy as money income. This defines the maximum potential level of monetary expenditure during the period. The role of the loanable funds market in the model is to ensure that the actual level of monetary expenditure equals this potential level.

Income can be used to finance current expenditure or current savings (used to finance any future expenditure over and above future income). Current monetary expenditure itself is divided into two components - consumption and investment. Consumption expenditure provides for the immediate needs and desires of agents. Investment is undertaken in order to improve the technical conditions of production such that the volume of goods produced in future periods can be increased for a given supply of available resources.[11] A key feature of the model is the presumption that those agents who save some of their income are not necessarily those who undertake investment even though both actions involve current decisions with a view to increasing future consumption. Presumably the theory of comparative advantage provides a justification for why some agents merely save while others undertake investment. Thus these different savers and investors meet in the loanable funds market.[12]

17

Actual monetary expenditure will equal the potential level as long as all savings can be translated into investment expenditure. In such circumstances, the velocity of circulation of money (V) will be determined for a given quantity of money and value of output. Further, the velocity of circulation (V) will remain constant as long as changes in consumption or investment expenditure lead to equal and compensating changes in the other. This constancy of V is assured in the loanable funds market where the rate of interest takes on a prominent role.

The interest rate is the price of future purchasing power of money relative to purchasing power today. It provides the suppliers of funds (savers) with the inducement to postpone current consumption expenditures in return for increased expenditure at some future date.[13] The demanders of these funds (investors) pay a penalty for borrowing money by committing themselves to repaying in future years an amount of money greater than that originally borrowed. The rate of interest is the cost to borrowers and the return to lenders in this market. An equilibrium is attainable in the loanable funds market when the rate of interest adjusts to equalise saving and investment in the economy.

This model generates two key propositions. First, there is no reason for any agent to hold money except for purposes of financing expenditure during the period of analysis. Holding savings in the form of money involves sacrificing interest earnings for no apparent reason. Thus the classical theory presumed that all savings would be supplied to the loanable funds market. Second, as long as consumption and investment decisions are governed primarily by the interest rate, any changes in consumption or investment expenditure will induce, through changes in the interest rate, an equivalent compensating change in the other component of expenditure. The interest rate absorbs these changes ensuring that the velocity of circulation (V) remains constant. Thus V is determined by the spending patterns of agents within the period.[14] There is no reason in this model for monetary expenditure to be less than the given level of money income in any period. This proposition is what we can call the monetary version of Say's Law - that the value of aggregate supply creates an equal amount of monetary expenditure. Hagen (1949) claims that this proposition is 'the central pillar of the classical theory of employment' (p.4).

The second classical postulate is that the volume of output is independent of M, and P can be investigated by considering the second market in the model - the labour market. The volume of output in this theory is determined by the level of employment through a technologically determined 'production function'. The analysis is conducted by assuming that all factors of production other than labour (the 'capital stock') are fixed and that production is subject to the law of diminishing returns to any given factor.[15] These assumptions ensure, first of all, that any increase (decrease) in employment generates an increased (decreased) volume of output in any given period. Second, they generate the proposition that the marginal product of labour falls as more workers are employed. Thus if capitalists employ workers up to the point where the marginal product of labour equals the real wage rate, then the model predicts that in the aggregate there exists a demand for labour function which is inversely related to the real wage rate.

The classical postulate concerning the level of output (Y) therefore depends on the determinants of the level of employment in the labour market. This market consists of two sets of agents; capitalists who demand labour in the pursuit of producing and selling goods at a profit, and workers who supply labour with a view to receiving wages in order to purchase goods and thus obtain the highest level of material satisfaction possible. The real wage rate, the purchasing power (in terms of goods) of the money wage rate paid to workers, is the key relative price determining the equilibrium 'full employment' level of employment and output. The higher the real wage rate, the higher is the level of potential material satisfaction available to workers, and thus the larger the quantity of labour supplied to the markets as more workers are induced to trade leisure (itself considered an element of material satisfaction) for more goods.[16] In contrast, higher real wages reduce the total profits of capitalists. The maximum profit available to capitalists involves a level of employment which tends to fall as the real wage rate rises. Thus the real wage rate adjusts to equilibrate the competing desires of workers and capitalists. The level of employment considered to be 'full

employment' is that level where, at the going real
wage rate, all potential workers who wish to be
employed can find work and all capitalists employ
workers such that, for a given capital stock, they
obtain the maximum level of profits in each
period.[17]   Movement in the real wage rate
provides the mechanism by which this equilibrium
level of employment is attained. This in turn
determines the equilibrium level of output.

    There is however a problem at this stage, one
which received wide attention in subsequent
macroeconomic analysis. Since the classical model
describes a monetary economy, all prices must be
set in monetary units. In the labour market this
implies that the supply of, and demand for, labour
determine the _money_ wage rate. How is the
equilibrium real wage rate to be determined, and
how can it be assumed that the actual rate in any
given time period is equal to the equilibrium real
wage rate? This is achieved by what Leontief
(1937) called the zero homogeneity postulate; that
the quantities of labour demanded and supplied
depend on _relative_ prices only - the real wage rate
- and not on nominal variables. This zero
homogeneity postulate implies that in the event of
an increase (decrease) in the price of goods which
originates from sources outside the labour market,
the demand for labour will increase (decrease) and
the supply of labour will decrease (increase) in
equal amounts at all levels of money wages, such
that the equilibrium money wage rate achieved will
have risen (fallen) to a level that maintains the
original real wage rate. Prices and wages change
in equal proportions, thereby ensuring that the
equilibrium level of employment, and thus output
(Y), are independent of forces outside of the
labour market.

    The full-employment flow equilibrium in the
classical model becomes completely specified once
the price level is determined. This analysis is
conducted in the goods market where the price level
defines the price of goods relative to holding
money. Until now the model specifies a determinate
level of monetary demand for goods (MV) based on
the operation of the loanable funds market (and for
a given supply of money), and a determinate level
of output (Y) based on a given real wage rate and
capital stock. The equilibrium price level in this
model is therefore that level which reduces the
monetary demand for a _value_ of goods into a demand
for a _quantity_ of goods which is equal to the given

quantity of output. For a given money supply, velocity and level of output, the price level in this model is a free variable which moves to produce a level of demand for a _quantity_ of goods which is equal to the (given) quantity of goods supplied. This proposition captures what we can call the _real_ version of Say's Law, that the _volume_ of aggregate supply generates an equal volume of goods demanded. The real version of Say's Law is equivalent to arguing that capitalists are able to sell as much output as they desire. They are on both their supply curves of output and their demand curves for labour. In such circumstances movements in the aggregate price level ensure that if the _monetary_ version of Say's Law holds, the _real_ version will hold as well.

Finally, the classical model provides a theory of inflation in this capitalist economy. Taking time derivatives in equation (2.1) we have:

$$\dot{M} + \dot{V} = \dot{P} + \dot{Y} \qquad\qquad (2.2)$$

where dots above the variables represent instantaneous proportionate rates of change of those variables. With velocity and output at their long-run equilibrium levels, so that $\dot{V} = \dot{Y} = 0$, and with the supply of money determined by some outside monetary authority, this model leads to the proposition that price inflation is determined by the rate of growth of the money supply. Further, if the model is expanded to allow long-run growth in output (due to, say, continuous and sustained productivity growth) and a long-run rise in velocity (due to the expansion of financial intermediaries), then price inflation is determined by the combination of these trends with the rate of growth of the money supply. However, in this case _variations_ in inflation rates would then be attributed to variations in the rate of change of the money supply. Further, the theory implies that by appropriate control of the growth rate of the money supply, the monetary authorities could in such circumstances generate stable prices.

Business cycles - the unresolved problem in classical theory

The classical theory therefore provided a reasonably coherent perspective of long-run equilibrium in a capitalist economy. Competitive

forces in the economy would ensure that relative
prices would move in such a fashion as to maintain
full employment. In terms of equation (2.1), the
three-sector version of the classical theory can be
represented as follows:

$$MV(T) = PY(w) \qquad\qquad (2.3)$$

where T represents agents' preferences on their
spending patterns within a period of time (an
increase in T implies slower spending); w is the
real wage rate; and $V(T)$ and $Y(w)$ represent
continuous functions of the variables with negative
partial derivatives.   However, this presumption
that relative prices would always adjust to such
changes left classical theory with a weak basis to
explain business cycles.   Hicks argues using
quotations from the writings of Marshall and Pigou
(and others) that when the classical theory 'is
applied to industrial fluctuations, it gets into
difficulties in several ways' (p.140).   He goes on
to discuss three ways in which the classical theory
might explain the fact that 'total money income
experiences great variations in the course of the
trade cycle' (1937, p.140, emphasis mine), but
finds each of these unsatisfactory.   However,
Hicks' characterisation of the problem is
misleading; business cycles are characterised by
movements in real variables such as output and
employment, and not merely by movements in nominal
variables.   To have an explanation of business
cycles, the model must first explain the source of
such cycles and, second, explain the mechanism by
which the cycle is at first sustained and then
corrected.
     Hicks (1937) and Hagen (1949) argue that
shocks to monetary demand cause business cycles in
the classical theory.   Such shocks must arise due
to changes in either the velocity of circulation of
money (V) or in the available money stock (M).
Hagen, for example, suggests that the classical
economists appeal to unusual changes in velocity to
generate business cycles:

> When asked what, then, was the cause of
> such depressions, the classical
> economists could only reply that their
> onset was due to some unusual shock to
> the economic system - a banking crisis,
> bursting of a speculative bubble, or a

> major shift in demand, such as a sudden
> drop in the rate of investment.   (p.14)

However, an appeal to such shocks is
insufficient here, since we are still left with the
question of how such shocks are transmitted into
changes in output and employment. This can only
occur in a model where the real version of Say's
Law is maintained if such shocks somehow alter
relative prices, and in particular the real wage
rate, and thus the equilibrium levels of output and
employment. One possible explanation for such
cases is provided by classical theory by appealing
to the fact that, although exchange takes place on
the basis of relative prices, in a monetary economy
only nominal prices are set within each market.
Thus if a shock to monetary demand leads directly
to a change in the aggregate price level, then
unless money wages adjust instantaneously, the real
wage rate - and thus employment and output - will
have been moved from their initial equilibrium
positions. The transmission of monetary shocks to
the real sectors of the economy therefore relies on
money wage 'rigidity'. In addition, the classical
model explained how such shocks could become
prolonged slumps by an appeal to 'the stubborn
refusal of labourers to accept [money] wage cuts'
(Hagen, 1949, p.14).[18] Finally, the completion
of a full business cycle by the return to the full-
employment equilibrium position must be achieved in
this model by postulating some mechanism by which
money wages eventually adjust to the intital shock.
Thus the classical theory became associated with
deflationary policies designed, in some way or
another, to reduce money wage rates in order to
stimulate employment and output.

The strength of the classical model, its
characterisation of the long-run equilibrium
position, was the source of its weakness. If
relative prices play the crucial role in the
determination of long-run equilibrium then they
must be relied upon to explain business cycles.
The classical theorists did not provide an
explanation for nominal wage rigidity, nor did they
consider dynamic models to explain how the
capitalist economy would eventually return to the
full-employment position. Further, if the source
of such cycles are shocks to monetary demand, then
the foundation of the classical model - the long-
run equilibrium position - was also suspect. The
appeal to such shocks must imply the existence of

uncertainty in the economy. This suggests that a new set of variables - expectations - also play a role in determining both the long-run equilibrium position in a capitalist economy and the movements around that equilibrium.

The modern inheritors of the classical theory, the monetarists and new classicals, were therefore faced with three crucial and unanswered questions. The first is why money wages may be rigid, at least for short periods. The second question concerns business cycles: what transmission mechanisms can be found to explain the dynamics of fluctuations in output and employment and, in particular, what are the forces in a competitive capitalist economy which ensure a return to the long-run equilibrium position? And finally, does the classical theory of long-run equilibrium, based on the operation of the price mechanism in the small competitive markets making up this capitalist economy, survive the inclusion of expectational variables into the model?

These unanswered questions left the classical theory vulnerable to the critique mounted by Keynes in the <u>General Theory</u>. They are also the questions addressed by monetarists and new classicals more than thirty years later which paved the way for the successful rehabilitation of classical theory.

2. KEYNES' CRITIQUE AND THE KEYNESIAN REVOLUTION

Keynes' attack of the classical model in the <u>General Theory</u> was primarily a pessimistic one, but included optimistic elements as well. Keynes argued that the classical theory of long-run equilibrium was an empty concept. This theory, he claimed, provided only a 'limiting point of the possible positions of equilibrium' which 'happen not to be those of the economic society in which we actually live' (1936, p.3).[19] He argued further that the capitalist economy 'seems capable of remaining in a chronic condition of sub-normal activity for a considerable period without any marked tendency either towards recovery or towards complete collapse' (p.249). Thus he ridiculed the 'celebrated <u>optimism</u> of traditional economic theory' for teaching 'that all is for the best in the best of all worlds provided we will let well alone' (p.33, emphasis his). However, Keynes did seem to replace the classical optimism with an optimism of his own. In his concluding 'Notes on

social philosophy' Keynes argued that a 'mixed'
capitalist economy could solve the deficiencies of
the market mechanism:

> I conceive, therefore, that a somewhat
> comprehensive socialisation of investment
> will prove the only means of securing an
> approximation to full employment...
> beyond this no obvious case is made out
> for a system of state socialism.... But
> if our central controls succeed in
> establishing an aggregate volume of
> output corresponding to full
> employment... then there is no objection
> to be raised against the classical
> analysis of the manner in which private
> self-interest will determine what in
> particular is produced.   (pp.378-9)

Thus he concluded that 'it may be possible by a
right analysis of the problem [of unemployment] to
cure the disease whilst preserving efficiency and
freedom [i.e. capitalism]' (1936, p.381).
     Among the many arguments to be found in the
General Theory one particular theme prevails - the
level of output in a capitalist economy can be, and
in general is, determined by the level of aggregate
demand.   Once the existence of uncertainty in a
market economy is acknowledged, the classical
notion of a unique equilibrium position determined
by supply factors becomes untenable.   Thus Keynes
questioned the whole of the classical causal
mechanism running from the labour market to the
level of output.   He argued that the view that
supply creates its own demand 'underlies the whole
classical theory, which would collapse without it',
(p.19).   Keynes offered an alternative theory of
the determination of output and employment which
depends on the level of aggregate effective demand.
This in turn is influenced fundamentally by
expectational variables:

> It follows, therefore, that, given what
> we shall call the community's propensity
> to consume, the equilibrium level of
> employment, i.e. the level at which there
> is no inducement to employers as a whole
> either to expand or contract employment,
> will depend on the amount of current
> investment.   The amount of current
> investment will depend, in turn, on what

we shall call the inducement to invest; and the inducement to invest will be found to depend on the relation between the schedule of the marginal efficiency of capital and the complex of interest rates on loans of various maturities and risks.[20]   (pp.27-8)

Thus Keynes contended that the level of effective demand 'associated with full employment is a special case, only realised when... by design or accident, current investment provides an amount of demand just equal to the excess of the aggregate supply price of the output resulting from full employment over what the community will choose to spend on consumption when it is fully employed' (p.28).   In other words, it is the level of investment demand, itself determined fundamentally by the state of long-term expectations (the marginal efficiency of capital) which, when combined with a stable consumption function, determines the level of output and employment in capitalist economies.

A notable contribution of Keynes' theory of employment was in providing the basic ingredients needed for the development of both formal and informal theories of the determination of output and employment in the context of an uncertain environment.   However, the <u>nature</u> of his contribution has to this day remained clouded in controversy and debate.   There appear to be two related reasons for this confusion.   The first relates to the explanation Keynes provided for why and how a deficiency of aggregate effective demand arises; that is, why the monetary version of Say's Law may not necessarily be valid.   Keynes did not fully clarify whether this deficiency of demand arises because of a failure of the interest rate to influence the key components of demand, or whether it arises as a result of a failure of the interest rate to adjust sufficiently to changes in expectations.

The second reason for confusion arose from Keynes' emphasis on demand factors in the <u>General Theory</u> and the resulting neglect of the factors determining the aggregate supply of goods.[21]   The question here relates to the real version of Say's Law and the widely-discussed issue of whether Keynes' demand-determined theory of output and employment <u>depends</u> on the rigidity of the money prices of some variables (particularly labour)

26

entering into marginal costs.[22]   These two issues
therefore turn on the same question - did Keynes'
contribution depend on the (empirical) assertion
that certain prices in capitalist economies are
relatively rigid, or was his contribution based on
the (theoretical) proposition that the price
mechanism, however flexible, is at times incapable
of _directly_ influencing the level of output and
employment in capitalist economies? We discuss the
two issues in turn with the aim of showing that
Keynes used _both_ arguments to support his
contention that the classical model is based on a
'fundamental misunderstanding of how... the economy
in which we live actually works' (p.13).

Expectations, the loanable funds market and Say's Law

Keynes' attack on the monetary version of Say's Law
centred on the loanable funds market and, in
particular, on the determinants of the supply and
demand for finance.   The demand for finance is
based on the investment function.   The level of
investment, he argues, will be determined by the
point 'where the marginal efficiency of capital in
general is equal to the market rate of interest'
(p.137).   The marginal efficiency of capital is a
key expectational variable, defined as the rate of
discount which makes the present value of _expected_
returns to a productive asset equal to its supply
price:

> The most important confusion concerning
> the meaning and significance of the
> marginal efficiency of capital has ensued
> on the failure to see that it depends on
> the _prospective_ yields of capital, and
> not merely on its current yield.
> (p.141, emphasis his)

The marginal efficiency of capital, upon which the
level of investment depends, is a precarious
creature which depends fundamentally on the state
of confidence because 'our knowledge of the factors
which will govern the yield of an investment some
years hence is usually very slight and often
negligible' (1936, p.149).[23]   Changes in the
state of confidence generate shifts in investment
and thus demand in the loanable funds market.   This
is the source of business cycles in Keynes'

Theory.[24] How, then are such (exogenous) shocks
to investment transmitted into a deficiency of
aggregate demand? The answer lies in the theory of
liquidity preference which determines <u>actual</u> rather
than <u>potential</u> supply in the loanable funds
market.[25] The potential supply of funds is equal
to or less than the level of savings.

Keynes distinguishes between the actual and
potential supply of funds by introducing the theory
of liquidity preference.[26] This theory suggests,
in contrast to classical theory, that savers may
wish to hold (or hoard) some of their savings in
the form of money balances. The key to this
proposition lies in two concepts - the fact that
the rate of interest is a reward for parting with
current liquidity (lending funds), and that future
circumstances are by definition uncertain. The
optimising individuals will provide funds to the
loanable funds market when the interest returns are
sufficient to compensate for the risks involved in
parting with liquidity. These risks are manifold:
they arise from potential capital losses resulting
from changes in the future rate of interest, from
the possibility of bankruptcy of those who borrowed
the funds, and from the possible future need for
liquid funds by the lender which may conceivably
arise before a fixed-term loan has matured.[27]
All these reasons provide an explanation why all
savings will not necessarily find their way into
the loanable funds market and thus why the velocity
of circulation of money will depend not merely on
spending patterns, but also on the state of
confidence in the economy.[28] Thus in Keynes'
model the velocity of circulation can be written
as:

$$V = V(T,R) \qquad\qquad (2.4)$$

whre R is a positive index of risk and uncertainty.
Equation (2.4) states that a <u>ceteris paribus</u>
increase in risk reduces the velocity of
circulation of money.[29]

These considerations provide the grounds for
arguing that a deficiency of aggregate demand can
arise in a capitalist economy. A fall in the state
of confidence reduces investment expenditure,
shifting the demand for funds schedule backwards.
In the classical model, such an occurrence would
lead to a fall in the interest rate, a fall in
savings, and thus a compensating rise in
consumption expenditure. In contrast, Keynes'

theory of liquidity preference leads to the
proposition that such an occurrence might well
induce increased money holdings and thus a
backwards shift in the supply of funds schedule.
The new equilibrium position between demand and
supply in the loanable funds market (savings and
investment) will be associated with a lower level
of monetary expenditure since more of income is
being held in the form of money balances. The
velocity of circulation has therefore fallen. The
monetary version of Say's Law, that a given value
of output will generate an equal amount of monetary
demand, has now been denied.
But here is where the first confusion
concerning the nature of Keynes' contribution
arises. If it is assumed that investment and
savings (and thus consumption) depend on the rate
of interest, then when investment falls, a
sufficient fall in the interest rate should be
capable of re-establishing the former level of
aggregate expenditure and thus maintain the
original velocity of circulation of money. One
view of Keynes' contribution on this issue,
therefore, concerns the possibility that the
interest rate may be sticky in a downwards
direction in the event of a fall in investment.
This is the view adopted by Hicks (1937), for
example, in his celebrated paper 'Mr Keynes and the
"classics"'.
Two explanations for this 'rigidity' can be
offered. The first is that shocks to the demand
for funds (investment) arising from a change in the
state of confidence will generally be accompanied
by a similar shock to the supply of funds. As
already suggested above, the original shock to the
state of confidence may itself raise money holdings
and thus reduce the available supply of funds at
every rate of interest. Another reason why demand
shocks will be accompanied by supply shocks in the
loanable funds market is that the reduction in
interest rates which follows a fall in the demand
for funds leads to a decreased reward (relative to
the risks) for parting with liquidity, thus
generating a reduction in the actual supply of
funds.(30) In either case, the new equilibrium
position in the loanable funds market will be
characterised by a rate of interest which is higher
than that presumed by the classicals. The fall in
the rate of interest has been hindered if not
completely forestalled (if the shift in the supply
for funds function is of equal magnitude to the

shift in the demand for funds function) by the increased propensity to hold some savings in the form of increased money.[31]

The second reason for interest rate 'rigidity' lies in the so-called 'liquidity trap' position, where the interest rate has reached some minimum level equal to the amount of risk associated with lending money. Keynes notes that in such circumstances 'liquidity preference may become virtually absolute in the sense that almost everyone prefers cash to holding a debt which yields so low a rate of interest' (p.207). It is precisely this case, which Keynes himself claimed to 'know of no example of it hitherto' (p.207), that Hicks (1937) used to demonstrate that Keynes' 'General Theory of Employment is the economics of depression' (p.143).

Thus Keynes' demonstration that aggregate monetary demand can be insufficient to absorb the value of output focuses on uncertainty as the potential source of such a situation (the fall in investment expenditure). Furthermore, uncertainty can be appealed to in explaining why this position can be sustained (increased money holdings). However, while interest-rate 'rigidity' is sufficient to explain situations of deficient demand, and Keynes surely provided an explanation as to why interest rates will be rigid,[32] this is not necessary to argue that monetary demand can be deficient.

An alternative (and sufficient) argument can lie in suggesting that both savings and investment do not depend fundamentally on the interest rate. This argument was also advanced by Keynes in the General Theory. He argues that the 'short-period influence of the rate of interest on individual spending out of a given level of income is secondary and relatively unimportant' (p.94). Keynes replaced the classical view that the interest rate is the key determinant of the consumption to savings ratio with his fundamental psychological law embodied in the consumption function:[33]

> ... because the behaviour of the public is, in general, of such a character that they are only willing to widen (or narrow) the gap between their income and their consumption if their income is being increased (or diminished). (p.248)

The consumption function is a key __stable__ relationship in the __General Theory__.[34]

Keynes advanced similar arguments regarding the influence of the rate of interest on the level of investment. This is particularly important, in his view, when the fall in the marginal efficiency of capital is substantial. This is a point Keynes makes over and over again. In his Chapter 12 on the 'State of long-term expectation', he concludes that changes in the rate of interest exercise 'a great, though not decisive, influence on the rate of investment' (p.164). He goes on in this section to argue that the state should take 'an even greater responsibility for directly organising investment' since most movements in the marginal efficiency of capital 'will be too great to be offset by any practicable changes in the rate of interest' (p.164). The same argument is found in Chapter 22 of the __General Theory__. Here Keynes suggests that although a reduction in the rate of interest will be 'a great aid to recovery and, probably, a necessary condition of it' (p.316), he still believes that:

> ... with markets organised and influenced as they are at present, the market estimation of the marginal efficiency of capital may suffer such enormously wide fluctuations that it cannot be sufficiently offset by corresponding fluctuations in the rate of interest. (p.320)

Thus Keynes advanced two complementary, but dramatically different, arguments to pursue his claim that monetary demand may be deficient. One argument is that the interest rate is relatively rigid, thereby inducing variations in the velocity of circulation of money. The second argument is that in the event of dramatic shifts in the (investment) demand for funds schedule, the free movement of the interest rate would be insufficient to correct and counteract the fall in aggregate expenditure. The basis for both arguments lies in emphasising uncertainty, and the role this uncertainty plays in generating __shifts__ in the schedules making up the loanable funds market. That is, Keynes' dispute with the classicals did not centre on the slopes of these functions at the full equilibrium position and for given states of confidence. Rather his dispute centres on the nature and effects of the combined shifts in these functions. The theory of liquidity preference and the concept of the marginal efficiency of capital together imply that the <u>equilibrium</u> rate of interest depends on the extent of uncertainty in the economy. And, since uncertainty is at least in part a psychological variable subject to sharp swings, the concept of a natural (or long-run equilibrium) interest rate is untenable according to Keynes (pp.183-4). There exists, in Keynes' view, a continuum of equilibrium interest rates, only one of which (what he calls the 'neutral interest rate', p.183) is associated with a level of real expenditure consistent with full employment. Thus Keynes offered an alternative to the classical linkage between volatile prices (the rate of interest) and quantities (consumption and investment expenditure) in the loanable funds market by postulating a stable linkage between two <u>quantities</u> - consumption and income. This is a key role for the consumption function in Keynes' theory.

The consumption function also provides a coherent transmission mechanism by which impulses to investment, first felt in the loanable funds market, would lead to further reverberations which magnify the initial disturbance. As long as the initial fall in expenditure becomes translated into a fall in real income, then the consumption function plays the role of further amplifying the initial fall in demand and output.(35) As emphasised by Leijonhufvud (1969), the consumption function and the associated concept of the multiplier plays the role of a 'deviation-amplifier' in Keynes' system (p.29).

The introduction of the multiplier into the analysis implies that the impact of the initial disturbance to monetary demand falls, at least in part, on the volume of output and not solely on the aggregate price level. This raises the second question surrounding the nature of Keynes' contribution. What mechanisms did Keynes advance to explain how changes in monetary demand feed through to changes in the volume of output? In particular, does Keynes' theory rely fundamentally on a denial of the zero homogeneity postulate as suggested in Leontief's (1937) review of the <u>General Theory</u> and later modelled in terms of the ⌐igid money wage hypothesis in Modigliani (1944)? Or is Leijonhufvud (1969) correct in suggesting that wage rigidity plays no role in the analysis of the <u>General Theory</u>? This question turns on an analysis of the determinants of the aggregate supply of output.[36]

Wage rigidity and the synthesis Keynesian model: a critique

There is, first of all, little doubt that in parts of the General Theory money wages are indeed assumed to be rigid. In providing a 'brief summary of the theory of employment', Keynes assumes 'that the money-wage and other factor costs are constant per unit of labour employed' (p.27). He goes on to suggest that the 'essential character of the argument is precisely the same whether or not money-wages etc. are liable to change' (p.27). Thus Keynes introduced rigid money wages as a simplifying assumption to facilitate his exposition. This assumption allowed him to follow Pigou in using the money wage rate as the deflator in his schema. The question that remains is whether this assumption is purely a simplifying analytical device or whether it plays a fundamental role in the analysis itself.

Keynes exploits the rigid money wage assumption to such an extent in the General Theory that it in fact often appears as a central feature of the analysis. Early on in the General Theory he contests the zero homogeneity hypothesis of the classicals by arguing that 'within a certain range the demand of labour is for a minimum money-wage and not for a minimum real wage' (p.8). Keynes argues that workers base their money wage demands on relative rather than absolute real wage rates – a type of demonstration effect – and that this is a 'sufficient justification' for workers to resist a reduction in money wages (p.14).[37] This relative wage hypothesis implies that money wages will tend to be stable relative to real wages over the business cycle.[38] Finally, once Keynes accepts the (classical) proposition that real wages are equal to the (diminishing) marginal product of labour, then 'an increase in employment can only occur to the accompaniment of a decline in the rate of real wages' (p.17). At this point an (apparently) complete picture of the determinants of the aggregate supply of output in Keynes' General Theory can be seen which provides a mechanism whereby a change in aggregate demand is transmitted into change in output and employment.

This is the mechanism summarised by Keynes in

Chapter 3 of the General Theory (in particular pp.28-30). For a given money wage rate, the level of output and employment are determined by the level of effective demand made up of consumption and investment expenditure. Once these variables are set, then the marginal productivity of the amount of labour employed 'determines the real wage rate' (p.29). Thus Keynes argues that:

> The propensity to consume and the rate of new investment determine between them the volume of employment, and the volume of employment is uniquely related to a given level of real wages - not the other way around. (p.30)

These sets of propositions imply the breakdown of the classical analysis of the economy in terms of three separate and independent markets. The volume of output (Y) now depends on the level of monetary demand (MV). The level of employment, far from being determined independently in the labour market as in the classical model, can be and usually is influenced by developments in the other two markets. The causal chain of analysis of the classical model has been turned upside down. With money wages rigid, the real wage rate is determined not in the labour market but in the goods market through movements in the aggregate price level. The key aspect of this interpretation of the General Theory is the flexibility of prices relative to money wages.[39] Completely rigid money wages are not essential to the theory. This version of the theory requires that real wages vary more than money wages over the business cycle.
        The Keynesian revolution became enshrined in the income-expenditure system as expressed in Hicks' (1937) IS-LM apparatus. Modigliani (1944) appended to this system a theory of the determinants of aggregate supply in which the marginal productivity theory of the demand for labour is combined with the assumption of a rigid money wage rate to form what became known as the Keynesian-neoclassical synthesis model.[40] This model still allows for fluctuations in investment expenditure to be the source of fluctuations in output and employment, as emphasised by Keynes. However, the mechanism by which such fluctuations are transmitted into business cycles relies on counter-cyclical real wage movements resulting from the rigidity of money wages relative to prices.

There does exist, therefore, a good deal of evidence to support this particular interpretation of the General Theory. However, some contraditions do arise here. Three particular difficulties with this interpretation are relevant for our purposes. First, the synthesis view implies that reductions in money wages would in fact lead to increases in employment by reducing the real wage rate.[41] Keynes disputed this proposition:

> But the other fundamental objection, which we shall develop in the ensuing chapters, flows from our disputing the assumption that the general level of real wages is determined by the character of the wage bargain.... There may exist no expedient by which labour as a whole can reduce its real wage to a given figure by making revised money wage bargains.[42]
> (1936, p.13)

Furthermore, Keynes advertised rigid money wages as an 'advisable policy' to produce a 'fair degree of stability in the price level' (p.270). Keynes expressed opposition to policies designed to cut money wages for a variety of reasons. One of his arguments emphasises the theoretical similarity between flexible monetary policies and flexible wage policies, the former being preferred to the latter because of the social difficulties associated with attempting to secure 'uniform wage reductions for every class of labour' within the context of a democratic and non-authoritarian society (p.267). However, Keynes firmly denied that either policy, flexible wages or flexible monetary policies, are 'capable of maintaining a state of continuous full employment' (p.267).

Thus the 'fundamental' argument advanced by Keynes in opposition to wage cutting policies is that they could not be expected to work. Rather than stabilising employment at the full-employment level, a flexible wage would destabilise the price level, which could in turn have damaging consequences on the determinants of the level of aggregate effective demand.[43] Two reasons are advanced for this in Chapter 19 of the General Theory. First, a fall in wages and prices would be accompanied by a redistribution of real income between groups with different propensities to consume, which 'is more likely to be adverse than favourable' to the aggregate level of consumption expenditure (p.262). Second, a fall in wages and prices could destabilise capitalists' expectations, thereby potentially reducing investment expenditure. Both effects have been noted in Keynesian contributions concerning the effectiveness of deflationary policies. Tobin (1980), for example, emphasises the distribution effects that accompany a generalised deflation. Patinkin (1951), on the other hand, concentrates on the expectations effect. In both cases the main concern of the authors is to counter the argument first advanced by Pigou (1943) that a fall in the price level would raise the real value of individual money holdings and thereby stimulate consumption expenditure. Their arguments suggest that the analysis of the General Theory is based on a denial of the existence, or relevance in the short run, of this real balance effect.[44] Aggregate consumption expenditure may indeed be stimulated by a fall in the price level which raises the real value of individual money holdings but, at the same time, the distribution and expectations effects may generate countervailing forces which leave total expenditure largely unchanged. The importance of these arguments in the discussion here lies in the fact that the rigid money wage interpretation of the General Theory fails to capture what Keynes himself called a fundamental aspect of his dispute with the classical theory.

Even more striking, perhaps, is that the picture of the labour market provided by the synthesis model is consistent with classical theory. The view that rigid money wages constitute the fundamental assumption in Keynes' model could be interpreted as implying that the fundamental contribution of the General Theory lies in providing a firm foundation for rejecting the hypothesis that the labour supply function is homogeneous of degree zero in money terms. Indeed, it is this particular interpretation of the General Theory which provided the foundations for a revival of an amended version of the classical theory, as we discuss in Chapter Three below.

This view raises the second difficulty with the synthesis model – the explanations advanced to explain this phenomenon are not entirely convincing. It must be remembered that the key to this theory lies in the rigidity of money wages relative to other nominal variables (the aggregate price level in the one variable factor model). Tobin (1951) reviews a number of potential

explanations which can explain the phenomenon of
what he calls 'money illusion' in the supply of
labour function, concluding that 'the support for
Keynes' assumption in regard to the supply of
labour is convincing' (p.221). However, each
argument can be equally attributed to capitalists
and their enterprises (and other factors of
production) and thus the relative rigidity of money
wages argument cannot be sustained.

Consider, for example, three explanations for
wage rigidity examined by Tobin (pp.220-1). These
are: (1) the relative wage hypothesis mentioned
earlier; (2) the fact that 'wage-earners have
obligations fixed in money terms' (p.221); and (3)
that labour may have formed what Hicks (1939)
called 'inelastic expectations'. The last two of
the arguments can easily be transferred to
capitalists.[45] The flaw in the first argument
results from a more subtle issue concerning certain
asymmetries in the margins of choice available to
workers and capitalists. The relative wage
hypothesis relies on the presumption that money
wage bargaining on the part of unions, say, is
based on a desire to protect the real incomes of
their members relative to other groups of
workers.[46] Even if workers within a union accept
that a failure to adjust wages downwards will
result in some of them losing their jobs, as long
as each worker attaches a low probability to the
job loss falling on themselves, they may be
perfectly 'rational' in resisting a reduction in
their wage rates. An individual capitalist, on the
other hand, is presumed to work on a margin
trading-off unit prices for total sales. As long
as capitalists maximise current profits, they will
adjust prices downwards in the event of a fall in
(aggregate) demand. The margin available to
capitalists is somehow not available to
workers.[47] This argument is, however, based on a
lacuna in the theory of labour supply. The
traditional method used to derive the supply curve
of labour is based on an income-leisure trade-off
derived in terms of hours of labour services
offered at each real wage rate. This analysis is
often translated without question into a schedule
relating numbers of workers supplying labour at
different real wage rates. It is the translation
of the analysis from hours to quantities which
removes the margin by which workers would indeed
protect their relative incomes by trading-off lower
wages for more hours of work. Thus the case for

'money illusion' arising only in the supply of labour function is not as convincing as Tobin believes. Of course, this does not negate the almost too obvious fact that 'money illusion' as a general behavioural phenomenon is 'a belated theoretical recognition of the facts of economic life' (p.221). Rather, the implication here is that the case for relative 'money illusion' on the part of workers cannot be sustained on a priori grounds.

The third difficulty with the synthesis model relates to the problem of inflation. How can the model, based on the assumption of relatively rigid money wages, be adjusted to incorporate inflationary pressure, and how is this inflationary pressure explained by the model? The classical theory explained inflation by appealing to an increasing money supply in the context of a full-employment equilibrium position. Excess demand for goods generates inflation in this theory. Keynesian theory faces the particular problem of explaining inflation within the context of an unemployment equilibrium where some excess capacity exists. The version of the synthesis model where relative wage rigidity is generated by assuming a strictly rigid money wage rate in all positions of less than full employment implies that any inflation will be associated with a falling real wage rate and thus increasing employment levels. A constant inflation rate with stable employment levels is only admitted in the model when full employment has been achieved. However, the relative wage rigidity hypothesis does permit money wages and prices to rise continuously as long as with constant employment levels they rise at the same rate, and with falling (rising) employment levels money wages are rising at a faster (slower) rate, than the aggregate price level. This requires a theory of wage adjustment and a corresponding theory of price adjustment. The former was provided by the seminal empirical research reported by Phillips (1958) and Lipsey (1960). A theory of price adjustment was, however, never fully clarified in the context of the Phillips relation. In particular, it is not clear whether the movement from one point on a given Phillips curve to another is characterised by wage and price inflation proceeding at the same identical rate or at different rates. The emphasis placed on the movements of money wages in Phillips' analysis led to a corresponding neglect of associated movements in real wages. This neglect was also exploited by Friedman (1968) to explain the Phillips curve in the context of a reconstituted classical model.

Phillips provided the Keynesian model with a theory of wage adjustment which allowed for inflationary pressure at different employment levels. He discovered with annual UK data an inverse and non-linear relation between unemployment rates and money wage inflation. The key proposition in Phillips' analysis is that a fall in the' unemployment rate generates a relatively larger increase in the rate of growth of money wages than the fall in the rate of growth in money wages which follows an equivalent rise in the unemployment rate. Thus Phillips transferred the synthesis assumption of downwardly rigid money wage rates to a theory of asymmetric wage adjustments.

But the Phillips curve describing asymmetric money wage adjustments is notably silent on the issue of corresponding price adjustments. This issue consists of two elements. First, the position of the Phillips curve should depend on price inflation. As is now widely accepted, it is virtually inconceivable that, for any given unemployment rate, money wage increases remain the same regardless of whether price inflation is, say, close to zero or equal to 100 per cent. Second, the effects of wage inflation feeding back to the rate of price inflation need to be considered.[48] A typical approach to this latter issue is provided by Samuelson and Solow (1960) in deriving a 'price Phillips curve'. This is obtained by subtracting from a given rate of wage inflation read off the original (wage) Phillips curve an exogenously given rate of productivity growth to determine the rate of price inflation. This approach is inconsistent with the synthesis model since it defines a constant growth rate of real wages equal to the exogenously given rate of productivity growth.

The Phillips curve therefore generalised aspects of the synthesis model to incorporate inflationary pressures by replacing the rigid wage assumption with a theory of asymmetric money wage adjustment. However, Phillips (1958) and others neglected the issue of price adjustment, adopting instead a rough and ready type of mark-up model of pricing to derive an explanation for price inflation. Real wages, so critical in the synthesis model, were relegated to a position of relative unimportance. The Phillips curve analysis

can be reconciled with the synthesis model if an
appropriate theory of price adjustment is
postulated. Indeed, we argue in the next chapter
that one aspect of the theoretical perspective
adopted by Friedman (1968, 1975) in his
expectations-augmented Phillips curve provides such
a reconciliation. But in doing so Friedman
successfully rehabilitated classical rather than
Keynesian theory.

An alternative interpretation of Keynes' analysis

The synthesis interpretation of the General Theory
provides a transmission mechanism between aggregate
demand and output and employment by substituting
the zero homogeneity hypothesis in the behaviour of
labour supply with the theory of relative money
wage 'rigidity'. In this interpretation changes in
the level of aggregate effective demand generate
changes in output and employment indirectly through
its effects on the aggregate price level and thus
on the real wage rate. However, such a view rests
uneasily with Keynes' fundamental dispute with
classical theory and, furthermore, appears to be
consistent with at least some aspects of the
classical view, particularly with respect to
prolonged stagnation.[49]
    An alternative perspective (at least) implicit
in some of Keynes' arguments relies on a direct
influence of aggregate demand on the level of
output and employment. In Chapter 20 of the
General Theory Keynes replaces the aggregate supply
function with its inverse, the employment function.
He derives (mathematically) the 'elasticity of
employment' which measures the percentage change in
aggregate employment which follows a given
percentage change in aggregate effective demand
(pp.282-3). Keynes' stated reason for replacing
the aggregate supply curve with the employment
function is that it 'is consonant with the methods
and objects of the book' (p.281). Expressing the
relation between demand and employment in this way
is preferable because it 'expresses the relevant
facts in terms of units to which we have decided to
restrict ourselves' and because it 'lends itself to
the problems of industry and output as a whole'
(p.281). Thus Keynes argues that for given levels
of consumption and investment expenditure in real
terms, 'there will be a corresponding [level of]
aggregate employment' (p.281).[50]

In Chapter 19 of the General Theory Keynes contrasts this direct demand-employment relationship with the direct wage-employment relationship emphasised in classical theory. He first asks whether wages and employment are directly linked in the aggregate. Keynes answers this question with an emphatic 'no':

> The volume of employment is uniquely correlated with the volume of effective demand measured in wage units, and that effective demand, being the sum of expected consumption and the expected investment, cannot change, if the marginal propensity to consume, the schedule of the marginal efficiency of capital and the rate of interest are all unchanged. If, without any change in these factors, the entrepreneurs were to increase employment as a whole [in response to a money wage reduction], their proceeds will necessarily fall short of their supply-price... and employment will fall back to its previous figure.
> (p.261)

These arguments suggest that in contrast to the rigid wage view, an alternative perspective presented by Keynes in the General Theory implies that wage rates (real or nominal) are relatively unimportant in the determination of the level of employment (away from the full-employment level).

These arguments are analogous to those made by Keynes concerning the classical view of the linkages in the loanable funds market. Interest-rate movements are of secondary importance in determining levels of savings (and consumption) expenditure. Keynes suggested that a stable relation exists between two quantities - consumption (and savings) expenditure and the level of real income. However, as noted above, this analysis implies that interest rates will appear to be relatively rigid. The same is true of Keynes' arguments concerning the labour market. A reduction in aggregate effective demand reduces the level of employment. As a result, Keynes suggested that this might induce a coincidental rise in real wage rates.

Further evidence in support of this alternative interpretation is provided by Keynes (1939) himself where he reviews his arguments concerning the labour market, in response to empirical investigations reported by Dunlop (1938) and Tarshis (1939). Keynes argues that although he did in the General Theory accept the 'traditional conclusion' that 'in the short period real wages tend to move in the opposite direction to the level of output', this 'conclusion was inconvenient, since it had a tendency to offset the influence of the main forces which I was discussing' (1939, p.400, emphasis mine). Keynes goes on to clarify the differences between the 'main forces' in his analytical system and that of classical theorists such as Pigou:

> In particular, the traditional conclusion played an important part, it will be remembered, in the discussions, some ten years ago, as to the effect of expansionist policies on employment, at a time when I had not developed my own argument in a complete form as I did subsequently. I was already arguing at that time that the good effect of an expansionist investment policy on employment... was due to the stimulant which it gave to effective demand. Prof. Pigou, on the other hand, and many economists explained the observed result by the reduction in real wages covertly effected by the rise in prices which ensued on the increase in effective demand. It was held that public investment policies... produced their effect by deceiving, so to speak, the working classes into accepting a lower real wage. (pp.400-1)

Keynes then concludes that if the 'traditional conclusion' is not valid, then 'it would be possible to simplify considerably the more complicated version of my fundamental explanation which I have expounded in the General Theory' (1939, p.401, emphasis mine). Keynes' own reinterpretation of the 'fundamental arguments' in the General Theory emphasises a direct aggregate demand to output and employment relationship rather than the classicals' direct real wage-employment relationship. The movements in real wages are incidental or, to borrow Keynes' term, 'secondary' to the main linkages he emphasised.

Thus we have two alternative interpretations

of the key elements of Keynes' critique of the
classical view of the workings of the market
mechanism in a capitalist economy. The first and
most popular interpretation (captured in the
synthesis model) emphasises the failure of certain
prices (in relation to the value of money) to
adjust fully to changes in investment expenditure.
The fundamental cause of business cycles and
prolonged slumps is price stickiness resulting from
a failure of the homogeneity postulate to hold. We
use the term 'cause' to imply that in the absence
of such alleged stickiness, the classical optimism
surrounding the self-adjusting properties of the
market mechanism would be realised. The real
version of Say's Law is confirmed in this theory
since, as in classical theory, the real wage rate
determines the levels of employment and output for
a given monetary value of expenditure.

The second alternative interpretation centres
on replacing the direct linkage between prices and
quantities in all markets as emphasised in
classical theory with a theory of direct
interaction between quantities in different
markets. In terms of the classical model, this
interpretation of the General Theory is based on
considering the effects of price changes on the
different components of aggregate effective demand.
The distribution and expectations effects discussed
above indicate that the classical assumption that
decisions in particular markets are independent of
aggregate developments may be invalid. By
redistributing income and influencing that state of
long-term expectations, movements of relative
prices and the general price level may fail to
perform their allocative role. Indeed, dramatic
changes in prices may have such a haphazard effect
on the operation of markets that instability might
ensue. Thus in this interpretation of the General
Theory a fall in demand in the loanable funds
market resulting from a fall in the marginal
efficiency of capital leads directly to a reduction
in the level of aggregate effective demand in the
goods market. But the fall in aggregate demand in
turn directly generates a fall in output and
employment. The levels of output and employment
can be constrained by the level of aggregate demand
in the goods market. Now the real version of Say's
Law is denied. Output and employment are not
determined by constraints imposed by the relative
prices but are determined directly by constraints
imposed by the level of aggregate demand. Price

movements are incidental, or secondary, to the 'main forces' operating in the aggregate in capitalist economies. But even worse, fully flexible prices would in fact generate instability rather than stability in a capitalist economy.[51]

We have endeavoured to show how both interpretations of Keynes' critique of classical theory can be derived from a reading of the General Theory. This explains why debates on 'interpreting and reinterpreting the General Theory' can rage on even today. In an attempt to sway the economics profession away from the traditional methods in favour of his own method of analysis, Keynes marshalled as many arguments as possible to support his contention on the theoretical inadequacies and erroneous policy conclusions associated with classical economic analysis.[52] Furthermore, the first interpretation of the General Theory, emphasising the inadequacy of the homogeneity postulate, laid the groundwork for the successful rehabilitation of the classical theory in the form of the monetarist and new classical counter-revolution based on the natural rate hypothesis. As we shall argue in the next chapter, the second interpretation of Keynes' General Theory has been mostly ignored, leaving a basis for a further elaboration of Keynesian analysis which, although incomplete particularly as regards the theory of inflation, is not susceptible to monetarist critique.

NOTES

1. In his famous textbook Samuelson (1970) argues that 'by means of appropriately reinforcing monetary and fiscal policies, a mixed economy can avoid the excesses of boom and slump and can look forward to healthy progressive growth' (p.348).
2. This view is expressed in many of Friedman's writings. A simplified version is provided in Friedman (1962), Chapter 3.
3. The 'long run' in these models is perhaps best described in terms of the Marshallian short run. That is, most of the debates in this literature centre on models in which the capital stock is ignored and, therefore, implicitly assumed to be fixed (or non-existent). Lucas (1975) is an exception to this in that the long-run position is defined for an optimal level of the capital stock (determined by relative prices).
4. Further, the monetarist and new classical literature

emphasises government monetary policy as the source of these shocks.

5. We note below, however, that differences within the monetarist school do arise on the issue of whether markets clear in the short run.

6. The adjustment cost explanation of business cycles implies the existence of a family of short-run natural rates where markets are clearing, the expectations are realised, but with the economy moving towards what might be called a long-run natural rate of output and unemployment. See the discussion of Sargent's demand for labour model in Chapter Five below. Notice as well that the monetarist theory of business cycles as described by Friedman (1968) defines only one 'long-run' natural rate.

7. Meltzer (1981, 1983); Patinkin (1983); Davidson (1983). See Chapter Four below for a discussion.

8. Benjamin and Kochin (1979, 1982); Collins (1982); Cross (1982); Metcalf, Nickel and Floros (1982); Ormerod and Worswick (1982).

9. Hagen (1949, p.11) provides a number of quotations by so-called classical economists on this issue.

10. Equation (2.1) is most readily understood in terms of a model which includes only one good, thus avoiding the index number problems regarding the appropriate definitions of the aggregate price level (P) and volume of output (Y) when the distribution of aggregate output changes. It should also be recognised that the velocity of circulation (V) must be defined in terms of expenditure in the goods market only. The borrowing and lending of money, which constitutes exchanging money in the current period with a promise to exchange in a later period, does not enter into the measurement of velocity.

11. An important lag has been introduced into the analysis here. Almost all of macroeconomic analysis treats investment as a component of expenditure and ignores the consequences of investment expenditure on the potential volume of output in the current period. Lucas (1975) is an exception.

12. These sets of definitions could be stated without reference to investment by relying solely on the notion of time preference. Savers can be defined as those agents who are willing to postpone current consumption in order to supplement consumption expenditure in the future. Investors could be defined as those agents who wish to increase their current levels of consumption expenditure over and above their current income levels at the cost of reducing consumption expenditure in the future. However, given the important role attributed to investment in Keynes' General Theory, it is best to identify lenders and borrowers in terms of savers and investors.

13. As noted by Hicks (1939), the positive correlation

between prices (interest rates) and supplies of any commodity (loanable funds) is derived by assuming that substitution effects dominate income effects (pp.72-3).

14. It is implicitly assumed here that the spending patterns of investors and savers within each period are identical.

15. We again reiterate the point made in note 11 above that any net investment in the current period is assumed in most macroeconomic models to exert no influence on the size of the effective 'capital stock' in that period.

16. An important lacuna in the analysis arises here. The typical analysis used to generate an aggregate labour supply function is derived in terms of <u>hours</u> of labour power supplied to the market. This analysis is usually transferred to encompass the <u>quantity</u> of workers supplied to the market without question. This issue plays a particularly relevant role in our discussion of Keynesian theory below.

17. This long-run position could alternatively be defined in terms of an 'optimal' capital stock where the relative price of these capital goods determines this position as well. However, introducing this notion requires the addition of a further market, the capital goods market, thereby complicating the analysis. Further complications would arise when the link between investment decisions, the size of the capital stock and the resulting demand for labour function at each real wage rate are taken into account. It is perhaps for this reason that most of macroeconomic analysis concerns an equilibrium position, and fluctuations around this equilibrium, in terms of a fixed capital stock.

18. Keynes (1936) attributed such arguments to A.C. Pigou. See p.42 below.

19. All undated references to Keynes relate to the 1973 edition of the <u>General Theory</u>.

20. See also Chapter 5 of the <u>General Theory</u>, which is aptly titled: 'Expectations as determining output and employment'.

21. See Keynes' comments in his introduction to Books III and IV, which are devoted to the determinants of 'the aggregate demand function' (p.89).

22. See, for example, Leijonhufvud's (1969) review of this issue.

23. Keynes (1937) develops this argument. The emphasis given to this aspect of the arguments in the <u>General Theory</u> by various authors leads Coddington (1976) to call them 'fundamentalist Keynesians'.

24. See Keynes (1936, pp.313-20).

25. Our discussion in this section focuses on the loanable funds market rather than, as is typical in the macroeconomic literature, translating the analysis to the money market. This is done in order to compare Keynes' analysis with that of the classicals. See also Hicks (1937)

for a discussion.

26. Keynes (1936, Chapters 13 and 15).

27. All these arguments can be found in the General Theory, Chapters 13 and 15. See also Hicks (1937) for a discussion.

28. It can be noted in passing that Leijonhufvud (1968) is correct in claiming that Keynes linked the marginal efficiency of capital and the state of liquidity preference to similar determinants. Keynes argues: 'Just as we found that the marginal efficiency of capital is fixed, not by the best opinion, but by the market valuation as determined by mass psychology, so also expectations as to the future of the rate of interest as fixed by mass psychology have their reactions on liquidity preference' (1936, p.170). Keynes adds to this in Chapter 22 on 'Notes on the trade cycle', suggesting that 'the dismay and uncertainty as to the future which accompany a collapse in the marginal efficiency of capital naturally precipitates a sharp increase in liquidity preference' (p.316).

29. Notice that the interest rate does not enter into (2.4) since the supply of and demand for funds schedules are assumed to be subject to sharp shifts. Thus there is no particular relation assumed in Keynes' analysis between V and the rate of interest. See below for a further discussion.

30. This latter argument could be interpreted in terms of the interest elasticity of supply in the loanable funds market. The classical theory implies the following supply curve of funds: $S = S(r)$, where S is the quantity of money supplied to the market in any given period, and $S(r)$ defines savings as a positive function of the interest rate. This argument suggests, 'in contrast, an alternative supply curve: $S = S(r) - \Delta M(r/R)$, where $\Delta M(r/R)$ defines an inverse relation between the flow of savings held as additional money balances and the interest rate (relative to the risks of parting with liquidity (R)). It is obvious that for given risks (R), the alternative supply curve of funds is more interest elastic than the first.

31. Indeed, on p.316 of the General Theory Keynes suggests that the rise in liquidity preference 'which accompanies a collapse in the marginal efficiency of capital' may lead to a rise in the rate of interest.

32. Keynes summarises these arguments in pp.232-4 of the General Theory.

33. Notice that an income inelastic savings function can be derived by postulating that the income effects produced by interest-rate changes counteract the substitution effects (Hicks, 1939). This argument does not appear implicitly or explicitly in the General Theory.

34. Keynes discusses the stability of this relationship in pp.89-98 of the General Theory.

35. This multiplier effect provides a further

explanation for why the supply schedule in the loanable funds market shifts backwards in the event of a fall in investment expenditure. The fall in investment which leads to a fall in income will, through the consumption function, lead to a further fall in the supply of funds. See pp.180 and 181 of the General Theory for an exposition on this point.

36. Our discussion of this issue ignores the importance of time lags in the analysis. Leijonhufvud (1969), for example, argues that Keynes' theory depends on quantities (output and employment) adjusting before prices (p.29). However, Keynes himself does not appear to use such an argument in the General Theory. See, for example, the discussion of certain time lags involved in the multiplier process presented on pp.122-5 of the General Theory.

37. See pp.13-15 and 252-3 of the General Theory.

38. Some evidence to this effect is provided on p.276 of the General Theory. This relative stability argument is repeated on pp.291-301 of the General Theory.

39. It is interesting to note that throughout the General Theory Keynes neglects to mention the importance of movements in the aggregate price level in generating an unemployment 'equilibrium'. Even in Chapter 21 on 'The theory of prices', Keynes only discusses the determinants of prices in the context of increases in the level of demand.

40. This is the model presented as the Keynesian model in most popular textbooks. See for example Branson (1972); Parkin and Bade (1982); or Sargent (1979).

41. Since the model under discussion only admits labour as a variable factor of production, substitution between variable factors cannot be used to explain the (alleged) positive effects on employment of a money wage reduction. See Tobin (1951) for a discussion of this point.

42. Notice, as well, that Keynes argues that his observations on the nature of the labour supply curve are 'not theoretically fundamental' (p.8).

43. See the General Theory, pp.232, 239, 253 and 303-4 for a discussion of this point. See Chapter Four below for a formal analysis of these issues.

44. I would like to thank Maurice Peston for bringing this to my attention.

45. Indeed, the argument concerning obligations fixed in monetary terms is perhaps more relevant to capitalists than workers.

46. It could be argued alternatively that the relative wage hypothesis relates to actual wage rates rather than income levels. Such an argument could then be easily applied to capitalists and the prices of their products.

47. It is sometimes argued that money wage rigidity arises from the fact that unemployed workers have no mechanism by which they can influence the money wage rate in order to 'price themselves into jobs' (see, for example,

Solow, 1980). A similar argument could be made with regard
to potential firms, and thus used to explain price rather
than wage rigidity.

48. A further difficulty that must be considered here is
the effect of wage and price inflation on the level of
aggregate demand in real terms. In the context of the simple
IS-LM model, steady increases in the price level must be
matched by corresponding increases in either the money supply
(the LM curve) or in its velocity of circulation (the IS
curve) if the level of aggregate demand is independent of
wage and price inflation. The Keynesian literature has only
treated this problem in rough terms. A particularly British
view on this subject - the Radcliffe view - emphasises the
endogeneity of the 'effective' money supply by appealing to
the existence and ready availability of close money
substitutes (see, for example, Ritter, 1963). This view
proposes that, for policy purposes, the relevant monetary
target is total liquidity - notes and coins in circulation
plus all close money substitutes - rather than 'high powered'
money itself. Kaldor (1970) goes further to argue that total
liquidity is a fully endogenous variable supposing, it seems,
that close money substitutes are in infinitely elastic
supply. No matter how this phenomenon is explained, it is
clear that total liquidity must be increasing at a rate
similar to the rate of price inflation if the feedback from
wage and price inflation to the level of aggregate demand can
safely be ignored.

49. We argue in Chapter Four below that some of the
arguments advanced by Keynes in Chapter 19 of the General
Theory are inconsistent with his earlier synthesis-type
arguments presented in Chapters 2 and 3 of his book. We
argue there that Keynes in fact presented two competing
theories of the determination of employment in the General
Theory.

50. For completeness, Keynes also needs to assume that
'corresponding to a given level of aggregate effective demand
there is a unique distribution of it between different
industries' (p.282).

51. Keynes' views on flexible prices were perhaps formed
on the basis of his experiences in the stock market. His
discussion of the stock market in the General Theory (see
pp.149-64) reveals his distrust of flexible prices. Writing
in the aftermath of the stock market crash on Wall Street in
the US in 1929, Keynes argues that prices on the stock
exchange are governed by, and they themselves govern, the
state of expectations in the future. Prices of shares will
therefore be 'subject to waves of optimistic and pessimistic
sentiment' (p.154) which leads specialist agents in this
market to speculative activities in attempts 'to outwit the
crowd and to pass the bad, or depreciating, half-crown to the
other fellow' (p.155). The operation of such a flexible

price market 'cannot be claimed as one of the outstanding triumphs of <u>laissez faire</u> capitalism' (p.159).

52. This suggests that Frazer and Boland's (1983) description of Friedman's methodology as <u>instrumentalist</u> might be equally applicable to Keynes.

Chapter Three

VARIATIONS ON A THEME - THE REHABILITATION OF CLASSICAL THEORY[1]

The publication of the General Theory ushered in an era in the economic analysis of aggregate variables - macroeconomic theory - in which Keynes' method of analysis stood supreme. Fiscal policy became the dominant instrument for direct control by the authorities of the aggregate levels of output and employment in capitalist economies, particularly in the immediate post-World War II period. Keynesian economics became associated with an optimistic view on the ability of the state to control through fiscal policy, the level of aggregate demand and thus output and employment in capitalist economies (Beveridge, 1944). Monetary policy, in contrast, played the role of accommodating fiscal policy by attempting to avoid so-called crowding-out problems by stabilising nominal interest rates at pre-designed levels.

The early vintage of monetarist theory was concerned with countering the Keynesian optimism on the efficacy of fiscal policy.[2] This was manifested in Friedman's two-pronged attack on the reliability of the Keynesian multiplier effect. Friedman's (1956) restatement of the classicals' quantity theory of money in terms of the theory of the demand for money as a durable good was designed to show that 'there is an extraordinary empirical stability and regularity to such magnitudes as income velocity' (the velocity of circulation of money) (1956, p.159).[3] This proposition led to the 'characteristic monetarist belief in a stable demand for money function' (Laidler, 1981, p.4). However, Laidler (1982, Chapter 2) points out that this stable demand for money function was established empirically only with the introduction of a lagged dependent variable in the regression equation.[4] Monetarist theory must therefore

account for short-run cyclical movements in the
velocity of circulation of money around its long-
run position. Friedman has offered two
explanations for this phenomenon; one based on the
permanent income hypothesis (Friedman, 1959), the
other on adaptive expectations (Friedman, 1968).
We return to this issue in our review of Friedman's
(1968) statement of the natural rate hypothesis.

The second prong of the monetarist attack on
the reliability of the income multiplier comes from
Friedman's elaboration of the theory of the
consumption function. Friedman's (1957) permanent
income hypothesis, while providing the basis for
further theoretical and empirical research into the
choice-theoretic foundations of the consumption
function, implies that the income multiplier in
Keynesian theory is less stable (particularly when
fiscal policy measures are temporary in nature)
than presumed by Keynesians. Friedman's definition
of permanent income as the stock value of
discounted lifetime income flows (plus initial
endowments) also implies that changes in interest
rates, particularly when perceived to be permanent,
might exert a strong influence on levels of
consumption expenditure in real terms.[5] The
permanent income hypothesis can therefore be
characterised as a 'restatement in modern terms of
the classical theory of consumption and savings
behaviour'. When taken together, Friedman's
restatements of the quantity theory of money and
the classical theory of savings behaviour lead
directly to the monetarist proposition that it is
variations in the quantity of money, and not those
in the velocity of circulation, that are in the
main responsible for fluctuations in money income -
Laidler's (1981) first 'key characteristic of
monetarism'.[6] Thus monetarists replace the
stable multiplier with the theory of a stable
demand for money function.

The early versions of the monetarist critique
accepted a crucial premise articulated by Keynes
(1936) and (apparently) by his classical
predecessors; that the source of business cycles
lies in movements in aggregate demand.[7] In
addition, Keynes' emphasis on expectations and
uncertainty in generating these cycles is also
present in monetarist theory. However, while
Keynes (and Keynesians) emphasise fluctuations in
the marginal efficiency of capital and thus
investment expenditure, monetarists focus on
unanticipated movements in the quantity of the

money stock in circulation.[8]   Friedman (1968)
argues that _every_ 'major contraction in this
country [the US] has been either produced by
monetary disorder or greatly exacerbated by
monetary disorder' (p.12).   Thus he concludes that
monetary policy should be designed primarily to
'avoid major mistakes' and to 'provide a stable
background for the economy' (pp.12-13).   But here
lies Friedman's and most monetarists' fundamental
antipathy to stabilisation policy of either the
monetary or fiscal variety.   Even when cycles are
generated not by government monetary policies but
within the private sector itself, the government is
too ignorant to counter such fluctuations
successfully.[9]

The monetarist opposition to Keynesian demand
management policies is therefore based on one of
two arguments.   Either such policies are fairly
ineffective due to the instability of the income
multiplier, or such policies can themselves be the
source of economic instability due to our ignorance
of the 'structure of the economies we live in'
(Laidler, 1981, p.19).   However, monetarists do
seem to differ on the implications they draw from
the analysis, particularly with reference to fiscal
rather than monetary policy. For example, Friedman
(1968) argues that practical considerations
relating to long implementation lags limit the
potential efficacy of discretionary changes in
government expenditure.   Discretionary tax changes,
on the other hand, suffer from problems of
'political feasibility' (p.3).   Thus Friedman
believes that, as with monetary policy, fiscal
policy should follow a stable rule.   In addition,
he has often argued that governments should pursue
balanced budgetary policies.[10]   Further,
Friedman's long-standing commitment to traditional
19th century liberalism leads him to the view that
the size of the public sector should be greatly
reduced 'now that government has become so
overgrown' (1962, p.32).

Laidler (1981, 1982) on the other hand argues
that the question of fiscal fine-tuning and related
issues concerning the desirability of balanced
budgets and the overall size of the public sector
are 'peripheral' to the monetarist position and
'are fundamentally microeconomic in nature' (1981,
p.20).   The key monetarist position as regards
aggregate demand policies is, according to Laidler,
'that there are severe limits to the extent to
which public sector borrowing can be financed by

money creation (1981, p.20). This rather weaker
proposition still requires a theory of supply side
determination if the 'limits' to monetary creation
arise, as they must do in monetarist theory, from
the inflationary pressures that result from such
policies. This theory is provided by the natural
rate hypothesis.

1. MONETARIST SUPPLY SIDE THEORY

We have argued above that the determinants of
aggregate supply play a crucial role in <u>both</u> the
monetarist theory of inflation and the associated
theory of business cycles. Friedman (1968) and
Phelps (1968) provided this analysis in terms of
the expectations-augmented Phillips curve, which
forms Laidler's (1981) second key characteristic of
monetarism.
    Friedman (1968) provided an integrated
analysis of both aspects of the monetarist
perspective, albeit in rough form, which fits
neatly into the original classical model described
in the previous chapter.[11] The model can be
understood in terms of the equation of exchange,
equation (2.1) above. The main difference between
Friedman's model and that of the classicals is that
inflationary expectations are explicitly introduced
into the analysis. In particular, Friedman keys on
the difference between anticipated and
unanticipated inflation. His model can be
summarised using the following version of the
equation of exchange (equation (2.1) in the
previous chapter):

$$MV(T, \dot{P}^e - \dot{P}) = PY(\dot{P}^e - \dot{P}) \qquad (3.1)$$

where all variables are defined as in the previous
chapter; the superscript e represents the value of
the variable expected to hold in the relevant
period; and the functions V( ) and Y( ) have
negative partial derivatives. Monetarist theory as
captured by (3.1) implies that the <u>source</u> of
deviations of V and Y from this equilibrium or
natural level arises from divergences between
actual and expected inflation ($\dot{P}^e - \dot{P} \neq 0$).
According to (3.1), unanticipated and expected
inflation (i.e. $\dot{P}^e - \dot{P} < 0$) leads to increases in
both V and Y.[12]
    To make use of (3.1) we must first specify the
determinants of the equilibrium levels of V and Y

in the model. These are virtually identical to those in the classical model as expressed in equation (2.3) of the previous chapter except for the important difference that Friedman (1956, 1968) accepts the Keynesian proposition that average money holdings are not fixed in real terms by spending patterns alone (T), but are presumed to depend inversely on the rate of interest. Thus monetarists believe that the velocity of circulation is positively related to the real interest rate, with increases (decreases) in real interest rates leading to decreased (increased) money holdings and therefore a rise (fall) in the velocity of circulation of money. Thus Friedman argues that 'the monetary authority can make the market [interest] rate less than the natural rate [where the velocity of circulation is at the long-run equilibrium level] only by inflation' (1968, pp.7-8). This impact effect arises, however, only because inflationary expectations are 'slow to develop and also slow to disappear'. Friedman goes on to suggest that it may take several decades for a full adjustment 'of inflationary expectations to the actual rate' (p.6).

Friedman's analysis therefore adds three new elements to the classical analysis of the velocity of circulation in order to explain cyclical variations in aggregate expenditure. First he introduces into the model a choice-theoretic basis for why the demand for real money balances, and thus the velocity of circulation of money, depends on the real interest rate. Second he explicitly introduces uncertainty into the analysis by emphasising the distinction between anticipated and unanticipated inflation. This allows for variations in the level of aggregate expenditure. Third he suggests that inflationary expectations will adjust to the higher level of inflation that results from unanticipated increases in the growth rate of the money stock, albeit in a fairly gradual manner. Thus over time lenders will demand, and borrowers will be willing to pay, higher nominal interest rates to compensate for the higher expected inflation rate. The adaptive expectations schema, where expectations adjust partially but continuously to recent forecast errors, ensures that (asymptotically) expectations will eventually become realised. At this point the velocity of circulation will have returned to its initial level associated with the natural (real) rate of interest. Nominal interest rates will have risen to compensate fully for the higher inflation rate. It is for this reason that Friedman argues that monetary policy cannot be used to 'peg interest rates for more than limited periods' (1968, p.5). We have now described a complete cycle in aggregate expenditure.

Friedman (1968) applies 'essentially the same theoretical analysis' to explain deviations in output and employment from their long-run equilibrium positions (p.5). The natural rate of output and unemployment is determined, as in classical theory, by the real wage rate (for a given capital stock). Deviations from this position arise from movements in real wages resulting from unanticipated price inflation. Friedman's analysis is derived on the presumption that suppliers of labour (workers) face an inference problem concerning prices which the demanders (capitalists) do not. The demand for labour depends on the money wage deflated by the price of the firm's product. The supply of labour, on the other hand, depends on the nominal wage deflated by an aggregate price index. Thus Friedman argues that 'employers may have the same anticipations as workers about the general price level, but they are more directly concerned about the price of products they are producing and far better informed about that' (1975, pp.20-1). An unanticipated increase in the money supply therefore generates price increases, which produce an increased demand for labour at prevailing money wages. This induces a rise in money wages (as long as the quantity of labour supplied is somewhat elastic with respect to perceived real wages). Since workers do not anticipate the increase in prices, the higher money wage offer is perceived as a rise in the real wage rate and thus more labour is supplied at this higher money wage rate. This occurs despite the fact that real wages have actually fallen. Thus Friedman's explanation for the observation that expansionary monetary policies generate increased output and employment levels relies on the proposition that such a policy, when unanticipated, leads to a 'simultaneous fall ex post in real wages to employers and rise ex ante in real wages to employees', and thus to levels of employment and output that are higher than their equilibrium levels (1968, p.10). Unanticipated changes in the money supply therefore influence both the price level and the level of output. However, just as in his analysis of the velocity of circulation, Friedman argues that over time the 'decline ex post in real wages will soon come to affect anticipations', creating additional upward pressure on the money wage rate and 'so real wages will tend to rise toward their initial level' (1968, p.10). The unanticipated expansion in the money supply leads to a temporary growth in output and employment through the resulting fall in actual real wages, but over time the adjustment of inflationary expectations leads to a return of the real wage rate to its initial level and thus a reduction in output and employment back to their initial values. In the long run, defined in terms of the full adjustment of expectations, all nominal variables will have increased by the same percentage amount as the money supply, leaving velocity and output at their initial long-run positions. How long does the adjustment period last? Friedman ventures that 'a full adjustment to the new rate of inflation takes about as long as for interest rates; say, a couple of decades' (1968, p.11).

Friedman's model provides a complete theory of the business cycle based, almost self-consciously, on the original classical analysis. The model captures his long-held views that imprudent financial policies on the part of the state are the main source of cycles in output and employment. It also provides him with a fairly complete explanation of the Great Depression based on the unexpectedly severe deflationary monetary policies pursued by the United States government after the stock market crash of 1929 (Friedman and Schwartz, 1963). His analysis in particular reveals how the monetarist analysis of the workings of modern capitalist economies represents a major advance over the rather vague analysis of business cycles provided by classical theory.

As was stressed in Section 1 of Chapter Two, classical theory left a legacy of three important but unanswered questions. Monetarists, and particularly Milton Friedman, provide answers to two of these. His model explains first of all why money wages may indeed be rigid relative to prices in the short run by explicitly introducing expectations formation into the determination of supply behaviour in the labour market. Friedman's expectations-augmented Phillips curve explains why the short-run labour supply function is not homogeneous of degree zero in all nominal variables within the context of an equilibrium model in which the homogeneity postulate is satisfied in the long run. Workers in this model always satisfy the homogeneity postulate in terms of <u>perceived</u> real wages. Thus short-run non-homogeneity arises due to expectational errors. In the long run, defined as a situation when expectations are realised, homogeneity is then assured. Second, Friedman's model provides the mechanism, missing in classical theory, whereby competitive forces ensure a return to long-run equilibrium - the theory of the sluggish adjustment of expectations as captured in the adaptive expectations mechanism.

Finally, the monetarist model of the labour market also provided what Laidler called 'a crucial correction' to the orthodox Keynesian view as captured in the synthesis model based on relative wage rigidity (1981, p.10).[13] It is virtually inconceivable, Friedman argues, that workers in an economy experiencing inflation rates of over 75 per cent - he uses Brazil during the 1960s as an example - will not incorporate inflationary expectations into their demands for money wage increases (1968, pp.8-9). In such a highly inflationary environment, inflationary expectations <u>must</u> exert a dominant influence on money wage growth since, if other factors such as comparability considerations dominate, it would be easy to imagine how real wages could be lowered both dramatically and within a very short space of time. Keynesians working within the synthesis tradition could not ignore this argument.

A new analysis derived from the synthesis model has emerged in recent years, where the assumption of relatively rigid money wage rates is replaced by the assumption of a rigid <u>real</u> wage rate.[14] Unemployment in this amended synthesis model is then explained on the basis of aggregate supply shocks (e.g. the oil price rises of 1973-4 and 1979-80) which reduced the demand for labour at the going (fixed) real wage rate. The theoretical basis to explain rigid <u>real</u> wages is not however addressed in this literature. But perhaps even more damaging is the fact that this new synthesis view leaves little room for Keynesian demand management policies. In the original synthesis model based on relative rigid money wages, demand management policies produced their desired effects on the level of output and employment by altering the aggregate price level and thus inducing a change in the real wage rate. If <u>real</u> wages are relatively rigid, the effectiveness of such policies is at least seriously weakened, if not totally eliminated. Friedman's arguments, therefore, left Keynesians working within the synthesis model little room to persuasively argue their case for demand management policies. The monetarist counter-revolution was now a success.

2. RATIONAL EXPECTATIONS AND NEW CLASSICAL ECONOMICS

The strength of the monetarist model lies in providing a coherent and fairly simple theory of the <u>dynamics</u> of business cycles based on the interaction between expectations formation and relative price movements. Unanticipated changes in the money supply lead to deviations in output and employment from the natural rate because workers (and capitalists) hold incorrect price expectations. Over time, expectations adjust as past forecasting errors are observed, generating adjustment paths of output and employment back towards their long-run equilibrium position.

This model is in some senses curiously deterministic. Once a particular adjustment of expectations mechanism is added to the model, the paths of wages and prices and thus of output and employment are pinned down (in the absence of subsequent monetary shocks). The treatment of uncertainty in the model is therefore extremely limited, relating only to the possibility that government monetary policies may be unanticipated.

New classical theory is motivated by a further consideration of the notion of uncertainty captured by the anticipated-unanticipated distinction in monetarist theory. To be able to correctly anticipate some future event (e.g. inflation rates) agents must obtain and use information other than merely past forecasting errors. This information can be provided by the model itself. If, as in Friedman's model, fully anticipated increases in the money supply lead to equiproportionate increases in all nominal prices leaving real variables unchanged, then workers must have information on the future evolution of the money stock itself if they are to update their expectations and correctly forecast increases in the future price level. Thus, if Friedman's model captures the notion of anticipated inflation, all agents in the economic system must behave as if they know how the model itself works or, at least, they must know that the money supply is an excellent predictor of aggregate prices. Further, this additional information must be used by the agents.(15)

Rational expectations formalise this proposition.(16) As suggested by the architect of the theory, John Muth (1961), rational expectations are defined as 'informed predictions of future events, [they] are essentially the same as the predictions of the relevant economic theory' (p.316). If, as in classical and monetarist theory, the natural rate is a position of long-run equilibrium determined by the voluntary decisions of agents, then any temporary deviations from this position must be suboptimal for at least some agents. Thus they have a material incentive to obtain information on relevant aggregate variables in order to avoid such deviations from their preferred position. However, agents will not necessarily predict the values of these variables perfectly if the market economy is subject to random disturbances. Agents will at best only be able to form probability distributions of future variables and therefore form point estimates of these variables based on their expected values. As derived in Sargent (1973), rational expectations imply that agents' forecasts will be correct subject to random errors. Notice that this proposition is clearly valid when it is assumed that the mean values of the probability distributions are known with certainty.(17) As described by Sheffrin, the rational expectations hypothesis as originally used in macroeconomic models is therefore predicated by what he calls a 'stable stochastic system' (1983, p.15). The extent of uncertainty in the model is therefore limited to a consideration of deviations of variables from their mean values. Problems of error-learning, relating to the difficulty agents may have in uncovering the expected values of any given variable, have been recently explored but such problems are mostly ignored in new classical models.(18) The mean values of all endogenous variables in such models must be anchored by some exogenous variables with expected values that are known with certainty in any given period. The rational expectations hypothesis therefore implies that the mean values of the subjective probability distributions, those formed by rational agents, will equal the expected values of the model-determined, objective probability distributions.

This proposition suggests that rational expectations are perhaps best considered as <u>model consistent expectations</u>,[19] so that point expectations are correct subject to a random error term.[20] Indeed, evidence of the importance of viewing rational expectations as model consistent expectations is provided by a recent vintage of fixed price Keynesian-type models which, under rational expectations, still produce Keynesian results (e.g. policy effectiveness).[21] New classical theory is derived, therefore, by embedding the rational expectations hypothesis in a particularly classical model.

As elaborated by Sargent (1973) in a conventional macroeconomic setting and by Lucas (1972) in a general equilibrium framework, new classical theory is derived by introducing model consistent expectations into Friedman's natural rate hypothesis (as captured in equation (3.1) above).[22] In such a setting, agents form their expectations of inflation on the basis of the reduced form price equation derived from the natural rate model. Apart from random disturbance terms, the key exogenous variable in this equation is the aggregate money stock. Now inflation can become fully anticipated when the government announces (and is believed) a projected increase in the rate of growth of the money supply (assuming no other random shocks hit the system in that period). Unanticipated inflation can arise because the money supply increases without such an announcement; because such announcements are discounted if the government lacks credibility; or if other random (unpredictable) shocks hit the system (say, to productivity). Even if such forecast errors do arise, a key insight provided by rational expectations is that agents in the following period will use the <u>new</u> reduced form price equation to update their forecasts. These new reduced form equations will contain any new information obtained in the previous period. Unlike Friedman's (1968) model based on a sluggish adjustment of expectations, the forecast errors generated in this model will be serially uncorrelated. Thus we arive at an important proposition produced by the natural rate-rational expectations model as derived by new classicals - the economy will always be observed at the natural rate of unemployment, subject only to a random error.

At first sight, new classical and monetarist

analyses are very similar, lending credence to Tobin's (1980) view that they are merely two different versions of monetarist (and classical) theory. The two theories are based on the natural rate hypothesis and therefore single out relative prices (and in particular the real wage rate) as the key variables determining the aggregate levels of output and employment. Both theories explain deviations from the natural rate in terms of imperfect information; forecast errors on the part of agents generate movements in relative prices away from their full equilibrium level. This induces deviations in output and employment as expressed in the so-called 'Lucas supply function'.

There are, however, two important differences in their respective analyses. The first centres on the microeconomic foundations of the natural rate hypothesis and the anticipated-unanticipated distinction emphasised in both theories. New classical theory, particularly the analysis of Lucas (1972, 1973, 1981), provides such a foundation based on considering signal extraction problems in a stochastic multi-market setting. The monetarist model, as expressed in Friedman (1968, 1975) is seriously lacking in this respect. Although Friedman's analysis is derived from the choice-theoretic framework provided by traditional microeconomic theory, his analyses have virtually always been couched in aggregate terms. This perhaps reflects Friedman's <u>instrumentalist</u> methodology, where his analysis is geared not towards formal completeness but rather to urge the adoption of particular policy measures (Frazer and Boland, 1983).[23]   Second, the two theories present radically different explanations for the existence of business cycles in capitalist economies. We discuss each point in turn.[24]

Consider once again Friedman's expectations-augmented Phillips curve. His model of the labour market focuses on a distinction between the real wage rate that influences workers' and firms' decisions respectively. Workers and firms may be surprised by unanticipated increases in the aggregate price level, but firms are informed about the price of their own product, and this is the relevant wage deflator in their demand for labour. Workers, although they have the same information set as firms, are interested in the purchasing power of their wages; i.e. the money wage deflated by the perceived aggregate price level. Output and unemployment deviate from their natural levels in the event of an unanticipated aggregate price change because the ex post real wage rate (that which interests firms) falls while the ex ante real wage rate (observed by workers) rises. Workers are fooled, albeit for temporary (though prolonged) periods.

But now consider rational expectations, and in particular the idea that in the aggregate agents form expectations as if they know the underlying model of the economy. In such circumstances, workers need to find the best predictor of the aggregate price level. In Friedman's model the price of the firm's product can perform this role, since it appears as a perfect index of aggregate prices. This occurs because Friedman fails to consider, or at least emphasise, any market-specific variations in prices.[25] If market-specific prices are a perfect index of aggregate prices, then workers only need to have the same information as firms to avoid any deviations from their preferred initial positions. Even if firms have an informational advantage as to the price of the products they sell, it is in the interest of workers to pay their employers a small sum in return for this information. In such circumstances, the ex ante and ex post real wages would again be equalised, thereby denying the precise mechanism by which Friedman generates deviations in output and employment.[26]

Lucas (1972, 1973) provides a major advance in this analysis. His model can be describes in terms of an economy comprising specialist producers on each of many 'islands' of the economy. Islands are separated by informational barriers (water) such that current island-specific prices are known with certainty by all agents on the island, but where information on other prices (aggregate prices) is obtained after a one-period lag (when the daily boat arrives at the island with goods from the other islands). Here workers and firms on each island are treated as a single unit with similar interests.[27] The island assumption captures the problem of incomplete information. Each island represents a particular industry in the economy. The specialist producers on each island also have specialist knowledge. They know the prices of their own products better than inhabitants on other islands, but rely on the market place (the boat) to obtain information on aggregate prices. A critical feature of the model lies in postulating that island-specific prices are not perfect indices for

Classical theory rehabilitated

the aggregate price level, since market- (or
island-) specific prices are also assumed to be
subject to stochastic demand shocks which are
normally distributed with zero means and known
constant variances.[28] Producers on each island
therefore face an inference problem. They are
aware of current changes to their own prices, but
need to draw an inference as to whether such
changes represent an improvement in their terms of
trade (their relative price), or whether they
reflect the fact that all prices have changed in
similar proportions. In other words, producers on
the island have to disentangle aggregate from
market-specific shocks in order to decide their
production levels. We are again firmly in a
classical world where relative prices determine
production (and employment) levels. Uncertainty is
captured by this analysis as a micro-macro, or
general-specific, inference problem.

Assume that in the economy made up of
specialist island producers there exists a
government whose only role is to provide money to
facilitate exchange.[29] This money stock is
stationary - there are no inflationary pressures -
but is subject to independent random shocks in any
period which are distributed normally with a zero
mean and constant variance which is known with
certainty by all agents. Suppose that in a
particular period the money supply increases
unexpectedly and that this increase is distributed
equiproportionately across the islands. Prices of
all goods are presumed, as in classical theory,
always to move such that demand and supply is
equalised in all markets. The price of the good
produced on any particular island is observed by
all agents on the island, but remains unobserved in
the current period on all the other islands. This
island-specific price reflects both the general
increase in prices resulting from the unpredicted
increase in the aggregate money stock, and any
temporary changes in the demand for the island's
product relative to other goods. The agents on
each island now face an inference problem - how
much of the change in price is the result of a
relative price change, and how much can be
attributed to any potential but unobserved
aggregate price change? As long as agents attach
non-zero probabilities to both cases occurring
simultaneously, some proportion of the price change
will be attributed to a relative price change. The
island producers, seeking to take advantage of any

64

perceived temporary improvement to their terms of trade and thus any windfall gains thay can accrue in the current period, will adjust their production levels in a direction presumed by classical theory (substitution effects dominate income effects).[30] Perceived increases in relative prices produce increased output levels in this model.

Signal extraction techniques analysed by Lucas (1972, 1973) provide the optimal solution to the agents' inference problem in the above setting. In particular, the optimal proportion of the price change attributed to a relative price change is given by the ratio of the variance of the market-specific shock to the total variance in the price of the product (the sum of the variances of the market-specific and aggregate shocks, assuming the two shocks are independent). As long as both variances are non-zero, agents on each island will presume that a given proportion of the change in the price of their product represents a change in their terms of trade and will adjust their output levels accordingly. Thus although the prices of some products fall and others rise as a result of market-specific shocks in the current period, the increase in the aggregate money supply ensures that the average price of products has increased; thus output on average will increase. Although each agent in the economy makes random errors in predicting the aggregate price level, these random errors are correlated across the agents in the economy because random shocks to the aggregate money supply 'simultaneously impinge on each agent and therefore upon the economy as a whole' (Laidler, 1982, p.81). Unanticipated increases in the aggregate money stock have generated an increased level of aggregate output. We can further impose on this analysis a permanent inflationary effect resulting from known steady increases in the money supply, and obtain the same results. Agents in this case would be concerned with inflation rates, where the extent of the increase in prices in any period is uncertain due to market-specific (and unanticipated) changes in the growth rate of the aggregate money stock.

We have now arrived at a complete general equilibrium view of a market economy which will be observed at the full equilibrium position in all periods subject to random aggregate and market-specific shocks. Unlike Friedman's (1968) analysis, which provided only a vague and incomplete picture of the long-run equilibrium

Classical theory rehabilitated

position, the new classical analysis provides what a celebrated general equilibrium theorist, who is in fact a critic of this analysis, called 'a well-worked theory of competitive equilibrium' (Hahn, 1982, p.106). The new classicals have added to the classical model of competitive equilibrium an element of uncertainty, arising in the form of random shocks.[31] The model explains how on average the zero homogeneity postulate holds, while in any particular period one would observe behaviour which violates this postulate. Expectational errors explain this phenomenon.

The second major difference between monetarist and new classical theory concerns business cycles. The monetarist theory of cycles is derived by considering the sluggish adjustment of expectations in the aftermath of an unanticipated shock to the economy. Indeed, one of the main arguments advanced by monetarists against government fiscal and monetary activism concerns the destabilising influence such policies can exert on capitalist economies. New classical theory implicitly denies these arguments. Rational expectations imply that agents will update forecasts on the basis of each period's reduced form price equation, which incorporates any new information arising, such that forecast errors will be serially uncorrelated. Thus the 'destabilising' influence of such policies can only last for one period. Prolonged slumps or business cycles - 'persistence effects' - cannot therefore be explained by serially correlated forecast errors when the rational expectations hypothesis is invoked. In addition, since rational expectations are optimal (linear) predictors,[32] agents in an equilibrium model would be behaving sub-optimally if they did not adopt such optimal forecasting techniques. Thus Lucas (1977) notes that pre-Keynesian economists (Hayek in particular) were correct in worrying that there exists an 'apparent contradiction' between 'cyclical phenomena' and 'economic equilibrium' (p.220). In contrast to the sub-optimality of behaviour apparently underlying the monetarist theory of business cycles, new classical theorists have sought to explain such cycles within a complete equilibrium model with imperfect information - that is, in terms of agents choosing such patterns in the context of constraints imposed by natural or technical conditions. The new classical analysis of business cycles is therefore derived by

considering serially correlated movements in the
natural rate itself.

Lucas (1975) for example introduces a semi
putty-clay analysis of capital accumulation which,
when combined with imperfect information and an
accelerator effect, shows how unanticipated
monetary growth yields serially correlated
movements in the capital stock around an
equilibrium (optimal) level. An unanticipated
aggregate demand shock leads to over-accumulation
of capital which adjusts sluggishly back to its
initial equilibrium level. This model yields
cycles in the natural rate of output which Lucas
himself admits 'does not quite work: there are too
many compromises of convenience granted per unit of
convenience received' (1981, p.15).

An alternative explanation for business cycles
as observed in the labour market in particular is
based on Sargent's (1978) ad hoc appeal to
differential costs of adjustment in the stock of
labour employed by firms relative to the amount of
overtime hours offered. This model, which has been
quoted widely in subsequent empirical research,[33]
provides an explanation of cycles in employment,
though cycles in both unemployment rates and in
output levels are not necessarily explained by the
model.[34] Notice that by appealing to technical
(or natural) adjustment cost factors in explaining
such cycles, the Lucas (1975) and Sargent (1978)
models implicitly imply that such cycles would
arise in centralised or planned economies as well,
since they also must suffer from at least some
random shocks. This seems to be misleading since,
at least at first sight, it appears that cycles in
employment levels and unemployment rates are
primarily a problem in capitalist rather than
centrally planned economies.

The notable contribution of new classical
theory as regards business cycles has therefore
been essentially a negative one. The natural rate-
rational expectations model suggests that the
monetarist theory of business cycles, so appealing
at first sight, lacks a strong choice-theoretic
foundation. Rational expectations therefore pose a
serious threat to one of the major contributions
provided by monetarists to the classical theory.
It is not surprising therefore that some
monetarists have recently reassessed the theory of
expectations formation. Laidler (1982) argues, for
example, that even if one assumes that agents
behave rationally and will therefore update their

forecasts of particular variables (e.g. the future
inflation rate), 'there is no reason to believe
that they will do so quickly' (p.177). He argues
that the 'planning period over which expectations
are formed is itself something that must be chosen'
(p.176). This argument is based on an implied
discreteness of decision-making which is not
dissimilar to the generation of natural rate-
rational expectations models with binding contracts
introduced into the analysis (Phelps and Taylor,
1977; Taylor, 1979). In such models, behaviour is
locked during the planning (or contract) period
such that unanticipated changes in exogenous
variables within each period can produce serially
correlated movements in output and employment
during that period. Laidler also appeals to
problems agents may have in inferring whether
changes in, say, the rate of growth of the money
supply are viewed by agents as permanent or
temporary. Stein (1982) advances a similar
argument in proposing that monetarism, which is
'intermediate between the poles of Keynesian and
new classical economics' in macroeconomic theory
(p.13), is 'a synthesis of the two poles' and is
'closer to the truth' (p.218). Stein's argument is
based on considering 'asymptotically rational
expectations'. These are expectations which
converge asymptotically to those described by Muth
(which Stein calls 'Muth rational expectations'),
but adjust sluggishly in the face of both
anticipated and unanticipated developments because
agents face an inference problem of whether to
regard any shock to the economic system as
temporary or permanent. Stein argues that agents
in such circumstances need to acquire more
information over time to increase the sample size
on which to derive optimal predictors of the
relevant variables. As with most predictors used
in statistical theory, the predictors used by
agents are consistent but may be biased in small
samples.

Stein's analysis is motivated in particular by
considering the credibility problem of a government
announcement (pp.87-91). Suppose the government
announces that it intends to pursue a less
expansionary monetary policy than previously
undertaken. In such circumstances, agents must
decide whether the government will indeed
accomplish this task. 'In view of past experience,
the public is sceptical', and may therefore take a
long time to come to believe the original

announcement (p.88). Stein argues that agents will therefore require further information in the form of a larger sample before the confidence intervals of the predicted values of relevant variables are sufficiently small 'to induce the public to alter its evaluation of monetary policy' (p.90). This will create a lag between a 'currently announced change in policy and the public's acceptance of the change' (p.89). Agents need to obtain a sufficiently large sample before they believe, and therefore act upon, the government's announcement.[35] Expectational errors will, according to Stein, be serially correlated as a result of the lags that arise between government announcements of policies and the decisions of agents to act on these announcements.[36]

The analyses presented by Laidler and Stein are designed to advance the view that monetarist analysis can and should be distinguished from new classical theory even though both schools of thought are predicated on the same foundations - the natural rate hypothesis. The main policy rule derived from new classical theory is low variance - as macroeconomic policy becomes more predictable, the forecast errors of agents will in general be smaller. Thus the economy will experience smaller variations around the full employment equilibrium position. Particular monetary growth rules as advocated by monetarists are rendered irrelevant by this analysis.

Furthermore, the inheritors of the classical model therefore arrive at starkly different views concerning business cycles in capitalist economies. Monetarists hold to the view that expectations adjust sluggishly and therefore business cycles arise from serially correlated expectational errors. The particularly dramatic and sustained fall in output and employment witnessed in the UK following the election of the Thatcher government in 1979 was the result, according to monetarist theory, of the sluggish adjustment of inflationary expectations when deflationary policies were pursued. According to this view, the adjustment of such expectations will ensure a return, albeit sluggishly, to a full-employment equilibrium position. New classical theory suggests, in contrast, that some change in the underlying structural characteristics of the UK economy are responsible for such developments. In both cases, however, there is a unifying theme. The source of high unemployment rates in the UK today is a rise

in real wages which limits the amount of labour
demanded by firms (and potential firms). The
classical policy prescription for such slumps or
depressions was based on finding some mechanism to
reduce real wages. Monetarism and new classical
theory are in total agreement on this particular
issue. However, while confirming the classical
position on this issue, monetarist and new
classical theory in different ways advanced the
original classical model to incorporate certain
specific elements of uncertainty into the analysis.
Their respective explanations of why the zero
homogeneity postulate will not hold in the short
run left the synthesis Keynesians in a relatively
weak position from which to argue for expansionary
demand management policies. As Hahn (1980) points
out, both theories suggest that there is no need
for macroeconomic intervention. Keynes'
pessimistic view of capitalist economies has now
been rejected, with the original classical optimism
on the self-correcting properties of such economies
regaining prominence in macroeconomic analysis.

3. THE RECONSTRUCTION OF THE KEYNESIAN PESSIMISM: SUPPLY SIDE CONSIDERATIONS

The preceding analysis has led to the question:
following the monetarist counter-revolution, what
remains of the Keynesian pessimism concerning the
self-regulating properties of the capitalist
economy? This question can be addressed by
considering the main determinants of the aggregate
supply of goods in capitalist economies. We argued
in the earlier sections of this chapter and in the
previous chapter that the synthesis Keynesian,
monetarist and new classical theories share the
view that the main constraint on the levels of
aggregate output and employment is the level of the
aggregate real wage rate. Each of these theories
implicitly accepts the real version of Say's Law,
which predicts that a reduction in aggregate real
wages would generate increases in aggregate
employment. The models present different views,
however, on how such real wage reductions could be
engineered. The synthesis model, for example,
suggests that an expansion in aggregate expenditure
would generate increased employment levels for a
substantial period of time because the price level
would rise by more than money wage rates.
Monetarist and new classical models deny this

possibility by invoking the zero homogeneity postulate in the long run. Increases in aggregate expenditure, by increasing the general level of prices, might temporarily reduce real wages, but over time these effects would be eclipsed by workers' wage demands designed to compensate for these price rises. Both monetarist and new classical analysis suggests that such developments will merely lead to a temporary increase in employment levels which will be matched by an equal reduction in employment levels in future periods.

All three theories disagree, however, that a permanent stimulus to aggregate employment could be generated through changes in the structural characteristics of labour markets designed to permanently reduce real wage levels. This also underlies the Thatcher government's supply side policies (Lawson, 1984). Such a view also provides the basis for Minford's (1983, 1984) widely-debated explanation of the currently high levels of unemployment in the UK, which emphasises the combined effects on real wage rates of an alleged increase in the power and militancy of trade unions and increasing levels of unemployment benefits (relative to net wage income) provided by the UK government during the 1970s and 1980s. Minford's proposals, designed to reduced both union power and unemployment benefits, are based on the view that such policies would permanently reduce real wages and therefore stimulate aggregate employment.

Key critics of the Minford policy package have been almost exclusively concerned with arguing that such policies would not lead to significant reductions in aggregate real wages. Nickell and Andrews (1983) present empirical evidence suggesting that the effects of trade unions and unemployment benefits on aggregate real wages are very much smaller than those supposed by Minford. Nickell (1984) explains these results by arguing that the real wage equation adopted by Minford in forming his policy proposals is misspecified on theoretical grounds. He argues further that, when the misspecification is corrected, the estimated effects on real wages of adopting Minford's policies appear to be very much reduced. However, Nickell does not dispute Minford's view that if such policies succeeded in substantially reducing real wages, a rise in employment levels would ensue. Thus Minford (1984) responds to Nickell by arguing that, regardless of their differing opinions on the desirability of cuts in unemployment benefits, Nickell 'must in principle be committed to a <u>similar family</u> of policies' (p.958, emphasis his); i.e. policies designed to reduce real wage rates.

The alternative output to employment model which we ascribed in Chapter Two to Keynes himself suggests that real wage reductions, however engineered, would <u>not on their own</u> be expected to provide a major stimulus to employment. This view is predicated on a distrust of flexible prices and the corresponding position that, in the aggregate, employment and output levels are constrained by the level of aggregate effective demand. This perspective suggests that increases in aggregate expenditure are a necessary but perhaps not a sufficient (see below) component of any policies designed to increase employment levels and reduce unemployment rates. The Keynesian pessimism concerning the self-adjusting properties of capitalist economies is resurrected by such a perspective as a pessimism concerning the effectiveness of relative price movements in generating adjustments in real quantities such as output and employment.

This alternative perspective can be motivated by a reconsideration of the determinants of the aggregate demand for labour schedule. The synthesis Keynesian, monetarist and new classical models all include the classical labour demand schedule based on a <u>direct</u> inverse real wage-employment relationship. On what basis can this view be challenged? There appear to be four main avenues by which this challenge has been mounted.

The first issue concerns technology. The classical labour demand schedule is based on the assumption of diminishing marginal productivity of labour. In a recent paper Weitzman (1982) argues that if, in the relevant range, production is subject to increasing returns to labour, then the <u>real</u> version of Say's Law will not hold and the level of aggregate demand will directly determine the level of employment. He also shows how real wage reductions will not cure mass unemployment under these technological conditions.[37] Another consideration relating to technology is derived by an analysis closely related to Leibenstein's (1966) notion of 'X-efficiency', known as the efficient wage hypothesis (Stiglitz, 1976; Solow, 1979; Akerlof, 1982). This hypothesis suggests that the marginal product of labour depends not only on the level of employment and on the capital stock (and technology) as emphasised in classical theory, but also on the effort of workers. These models assume that workers' effort depends at least in part on the real wage rate they receive. This implies that a reduction in money and real wage rates may not yield increases in employment since effort, and thus labour productivity, will fall in such circumstances. As explained by Yellen (1984), these considerations lead to the proposition that the firm's 'profit function relating wages to profits is flat' (p.204).

A second strand of argument is based on market structure and, in particular, on the question of who sets prices. In monetarist and new classical theory, wage and price setting is essentially ignored, with these variables always determined at their (short-run) equilibrium levels. The synthesis Keynesian model is derived on the presumption of some asymmetry in market power and price-setting behaviour. Workers or their unions are able to exert some monopoly power in order to resist wage reductions in the slump. Capitalists, on the other hand, are motivated by competitive forces to reduce prices in such circumstances. McDonald and Solow (1981) show, on the other hand, how in one particular model of bilateral monopoly, where real wages and employment are determined on the basis of firm and union bargaining, changes in the demand for the firm's products will in the main fall on employment and not on real wage rates. In such a model, the classical labour demand schedule will not even be properly determined.[38]

A third argument is based on dynamic considerations and the possibility of multiple equilibrium in the classical macroeconomic model.[39] Tobin (1975) demonstrates how, even if wages and prices are fully flexible, 'the adjustment mechanism of the economy will be too weak to eliminate persistent unemployment' (pp.201-2). This analysis is derived by considering the effects of real wage movements on the distribution of income and wealth and thus on the level of aggregate effective demand. Such considerations imply that the adjustment process in a flexible price model of the capitalist economy will be chaotic. In a similar vein, Leijonhufvud (1969) suggests that Keynes' arguments rely on time lags and in particular on the proposition that quantities such as output and employment adjust before prices in response to changes in aggregate demand (p.29). Although we argued in Section 2 of

Chapter Two above that this dynamic argument was not advanced by Keynes, it does provide the basis for rejecting the classical emphasis on a direct real wage-employment relationship. Hahn (1982) advances a similar set of arguments in a dynamic rational expectations context to show how the adjustment in capitalist economies will 'be a pretty messy affair' (p.58). He argues that unless strict Gorman-type (1953) assumptions are imposed on the model, changes in real wages and the money stock will alter the distribution of wealth and thus the eventual full-employment equilibrium positions.[40] Thus introducing distribution effects into a classical-type model will yield multiple equilibria (Hahn, 1982, pp.37-40). In such circumstances the inverse real wage-employment relationship will not necessarily hold.

The fourth set of arguments is derived by considering disequilibrium or non-Walrasian macroeconomic theory set in a static framework (Clower, 1965; Leijonhufvud, 1968, 1969; Hahn, 1978, 1980; Grandmont, 1977; Barro and Grossman, 1971).[41] This analysis is based on a distinction, originally due to Clower (1965), between notional and effective demand. Notional demand is the demand for any commodity which is constrained only by relative prices and endowments. These are the demands considered in barter-type microeconomic theory and are the only demand functions considered in classical (or Walrasian) economic theory. Effective demand, on the other hand, is the demand for commodities backed by purchasing power (money). These demands are derived by considering how the potential existence of quantity constraints (or rationing) in any one market will 'spill over' and restrict the level of effective demand in another market. This analysis leads to a view of business cycles as arising from the interaction of a mutually reinforcing circle of events. As derived in Clower (1965), the existence of unemployment acts as a quantity constraint in determining the aggregate level of consumption. The unemployed workers' demand for goods is constrained by their inability to obtain employment and thus to exert effective purchasing power over commodities. Patinkin (1965, Chapter 13) shows how firms, when faced with such a sales constraint, will demand less labour than when such a constraint does not arise for any given real wage rate. Barro and Grossman (1971) combine both sets of analyses in developing a general disequilibrium model of employment fluctuations where these mutually reinforcing quantity constraints interact to produce an unemployment <u>equilibrium</u> position. In such circumstances, the demand for labour is determined directly by the level of effective demand for goods in the product market. A further implication of this analysis is that changes in real wages would not necessarily lead to increased employment levels unless they act to remove or reduce the extent of these constraints.

Although this disequilibrium analysis implies a breakdown of the classical direct real wage-employment relationship, there remains a problem of interpreting the spirit of such models. This is the result of the invariable use of fixed-price models by the theorists working within this analytical framework, which raises doubts about how such models would operate when a flexible price assumption is adopted. These doubts are, however, misconceived. In addressing this particular question, Clower argues that he adopts fixed prices only in order to express 'a logical point, not a question of mechanics' (1965, p.303). Thus these fixed price disequilibrium models can be interpreted as expressing the <u>spirit</u> of Keynes' pessimism in terms of quantity constraints and spillover effects, therefore providing the basis for the claim that 'the causes of short-period fluctuations are to be found in the demand for labour, and not in changes in its real-supply price' (Keynes, 1939, p.411). In addition, the introduction of the distribution and expectation effects produced by real wage changes into the disequilibrium models provides an avenue by which these models can be made to accommodate flexible prices.

All four approaches provide a basis for Keynes' pessimism and in particular his view that 'there is, therefore, no grounds for the belief that a flexible wage policy is capable of maintaining a state of continuous full employment' (1936, p.237). Further, this alternative Keynesian perspective, based on a distrust of flexible prices, is not subject to the monetarist critique based on the strict adherence to the zero homogeneity postulate. This approach suggests that even if money wages do eventually adjust to changes in the price level, this will not necessarily influence aggregate employment levels. A key issue according to this perspective is whether there exists a direct linkage between real wages and employment at the aggregate level. This issue will form the basis of the theoretical and empirical questions addressed in Part Two below.

Before proceeding to this analysis, we conclude this chapter by briefly considering how this alternative Keynesian perspective can accommodate perhaps the most important technical development in modern macroeconomics - rational expectations. We suggested in Section 2 above that rational expectations are best considered as model consistent expectations. However, in Chapter Two we argued that at the source of business cycles in Keynes' analysis are fluctuations in investment expenditure generated by waves of optimism and pessimism on the part of capitalists. These waves in expectations are treated as essentially exogenous by Keynes because 'judgements about the future... [do not rest] on an adequate or secure foundation' (Keynes, 1937, p.221). Thus Keynes' analysis appears to deny even the possiblity of deriving model consistent expectations with regard to investment decisions. There is simply no model to base such expectations on! However, his analysis is consistent with the proposition derived from considering rational expectations; that expectations are on average correct. In Keynes' analysis, waves of pessimistic sentiment generate economic downturns through the multiplier process. The very fact that capitalists are pessimistic leads to their pessimism being confirmed. That is, Keynes' analysis is based on self-fulfilling prophesies. Thus we suggest that his analysis of business cycles is best interpreted in terms of an expectations consistent model. Expectations are on average correct, but the results of the model are themselves determined by exogenous waves of pessimistic and optimistic sentiment.

NOTES

1. Some of the themes developed in this chapter are taken from Drobny (1983).

2. This review of monetarist theory is based extensively on the writings of its foremost advocate, Milton Friedman (1956, 1957, 1962, 1968, 1975). See also Desai (1981) for a critical review.

3. Friedman's model of the demand for money does include an important Keynesian element; namely that money holdings are interest sensitive. This element of his theory does constitute a substantial change from the classical view.

4. See, for example, the empirical study by Goldfeld (1973).

5. The extent of the interest-rate effect on consumption, and its direction, will depend on whether the private sector as a whole is a net borrower or saver.

6. Friedman (1959) combines both restatements to form his first explanation for observed short-run variations in velocity. He introduces into his demand for money function the distinction between permanent and transitory changes in income, originally expressed in his (1957) permanent income hypothesis of consumption.

7. See Laidler (1981, p.5) for a discussion of this point.

8. Indeed, Friedman has throughout his career been notably silent on the issue of the uncertainty which characterises investment decisions.

9. See Friedman (1953, 1962, 1968) and Laidler (1981, 1982). Note that Friedman does accept that a discretionary monetary policy might be desirable when 'major disturbances' arise in the private sector (1968, p.14). However, he emphasises that the effectiveness of such policies 'is far more limited than commonly believed' (p.14).

10. See, for example, Friedman (1962, Chapter V). Friedman also expresses here the same view concerning the destabilising influence of activist fiscal policy that he ascribed to monetary policy: 'Far from being a balance wheel offsetting other forces making for fluctuations, the federal budget has if anything been itself a major source of disturbance and instability' (1962, p.77).

11. Friedman (1968, 1975) does not provide a formal model to describe his theory, but such a model can be derived directly from his analysis. See Drobny and Wriglesworth (1984) for an elaboration.

12. Notice that equation (3.1) is merely a restatement of the 'Lucas supply function'.

13. Hoover (1984) also makes this point (p.62).

14. See Sachs (1982) for a review of this argument.

15. See the introduction to Lucas (1981) for a discussion of the evolution of new classical theory.

16. See the excellent review of this issue in Sheffrin (1983).

17. An alternative explanation is derived by assuming that agents form divergent expectations of the mean value of the distribution, but that these expectations are distributed normally around the true value (see Sheffrin, 1983, pp.9-11).

18. See Sheffrin (1983, pp.12-16) for a discussion of this point.

19. This is noted by Currie (1985) for example.

20. Thus the adaptive expectations scheme is, in certain special cases, consistent with the definition of rational expectations in terms of model consistent expectations. This

is the force of Muth's (1960) article which showed how exponentially weighted forecast schemes such as in the adaptive model will in certain models satisfy this model consistency criterion.   In particular, if the variable that is forecast follows an independently determined random walk with a (first-order) moving average error, the adaptive mechanism is precisely the forecasting model by which agents' expectations would be realised subject to a random error term.

21. See Sheffrin (1983, pp.66-70) for a review.

22. Sargent's (1973) classical-type macromodel, though set in a standard IS-LM context, is exactly of the form expressed by equation (3.1).   Lucas (1972), on the other hand, ignores the loanable funds market.

23. Lucas, in contrast, seems to be primarily concerned with 'high theory'.   Indeed, he points out that his original dissatisfaction with Friedman and Schwartz (1963), for example, arose because the book 'was made unduly difficult by its failure to use any explicit, general equilibrium framework to give structure to the complicated history of US economic time series' (1981, p.16).

24. A third but perhaps minor difference between these schools concerns their respective analyses of the velocity of circulation.   Monetarists have traditionally concentrated much attention to this issue in terms of the stable demand for money function.   New classicals, on the other hand, have only given very slight attention to this issue.

25. In defining the natural rate of unemployment, Friedman (1968) does mention 'actual structural characteristics of labour and commodity markets', including 'stochastic variability in demands and supplies', as playing a role in determining this long-run equilibrium position (p.8).   However, he totally ignores these factors in the discussion of unanticipated monetary growth.

26. Note that Friedman (1968) does suggest that output and employment may rise before prices rise (see Friedman, 1968, p.10).   This is not compatible with a competitive model of markets.   His model requires that either unanticipated increases in the money supply lead to some increase in prices (and thus a fall in real wages) or that in long-run equilibrium firms produce at a point where some excess capacity exists.   Our analysis is therefore premised on an interpretation of Friedman which rules out the possible existence of excess capacity in long-run equilibrium.

27. Alogoskoufis (1983) extends this model to incorporate a labour market.

28. This knowledge is justified by an appeal to history. Agents in this economy have in the past observed both general and market-specific shocks to their prices and have obtained (unbiased) estimates of the variances of these random shocks. It is further assumed that the market-specific and general

(aggregate) shocks to prices are mutually independent. This can be justified by assuming that general shocks to prices are distributed equiproportionately across all markets. See Lucas (1973, pp.327-8) for a simple discussion.

29. Lucas (1972) introduces two generations into the analysis in order to justify the existence of a demand for money balances. The young work and receive an income in terms of money balances. Some of this money is spent to purchase current (non-durable) goods, the rest is hoarded (saved) to finance expenditure for the retirement period. Money therefore acts as a store of value in this model.

30. This rather neglected point is as crucial for this theory as it is for classical analysis. If income effects dominate substitution effects on the supply side of the model, then unanticipated increases in the money supply will reduce output and lead to price increases that are proportionately greater than the increase in the money supply. The model in such cases may become unstable. In addition, it should be noted that since in Lucas' model producers behave essentially as spectators substituting leisure for work when their perceived terms of trade are disadvantageous, short-run supply elasticities should exceed long-run ones.

31. Lucas himself notes that his 1972 paper 'renewed my interest in pre-Keynesian literature on business-cycle theory' (1981, p.9).

32. See, for example, the discussion of optimal predictors in the introduction to Lucas and Sargent (1981).

33. See Chapter Six below for a review of this literature.

34. This type of model is analysed formally in Chapter Four below.

35. The length of the lag in this circumstance depends on previously observed variances in monetary growth and the level of confidence required by agents. See also the analysis of Backus and Driffill (1985).

36. Stein introduces further lags in behaviour arising from sources other than the credibility problem. See Stein (1982, pp.87-91).

37. Kalecki (1969) presents a similar argument based on the assumption of constant marginal costs of production. Keynes (1939) also uses this argument to explain pro-cyclical movements in real wages observed with UK data by Dunlop (1938). See Chapter Six below for a discussion.

38. Kahn (1980) argues further that bargaining models will often imply a positive relation between real wages and employment.

39. Coddington's (1976) 'fundamentalist Keynesians' are characterised by their questioning the framework of classical-type economic theorising. A particular target of these critics is the static equilibrium framework generally

adopted in this theory, which is based on a presumption of dynamic stability. Thus authors such as Robinson (1971), Kaldor (1972) and Shackle (1972) question the usefulness of such an approach in the analysis of historical episodes in capitalist economies.

40. Gorman (1953) shows how aggregate relationships are independent of the distribution of income and wealth if all agents possess identical and homothetic preference schedules.

41. See also Patinkin (1965, Chapter 13).

Part Two

ALTERNATIVE VIEWS OF THE AGGREGATE DEMAND FOR

LABOUR SCHEDULE

Meanwhile, I am comforted by the fact
that their conclusions tend to confirm
the idea that the causes of short-period
fluctuations are to be found in changes
in the demand for labour and not in
changes in its real-supply price.
Keynes (1939, p.411)

Chapter Four

THE DEMAND FOR LABOUR SCHEDULE: STATIC ANALYSIS

A unifying characteristic of Keynesian theory is the emphasis placed on aggregate demand movements in generating fluctuations in output, employment and unemployment. In the General Theory, Keynes gave prominance to changes in business confidence which can alter the level of aggregate demand for goods, thereby providing a stimulus for changes in output and employment at the aggregate level. Keynes clearly interpreted his analysis as providing an alternative to the then dominant supply-constraint theories of the determination of output and employment levels in the short run.[1] In particular, Keynes attempted to discredit classical theory which attributed much, if not all, of the unemployment observed during the 1920s and 1930s to relatively rigid money and real wage rates. Early on in the General Theory he criticises classical theory for suggesting that:

> ... apparent unemployment... must be due at bottom to a refusal by the unemployed factors to accept a reward which corresponds to their marginal productivity. (1936, p.16)

Furthermore, Keynes denied that, in the presence of mass unemployment, money and real wage reductions could in fact secure an eventual return to a full employment position:

> There is, therefore, no ground for the belief that a flexible wage policy is capable of maintaining a state of continuous full employment.... The economic system cannot be made self-adjusting along these lines. (1936, p.267)

It is surprising, therefore, that Keynesian economics has traditionally been associated with the synthesis model as elaborated by Modigliani (1944), which is based on the rigid money wage hypothesis.[2] This analysis is consistent with the classical view that a general (aggregate) reduction in money wage rates would be expected to lead to increased employment levels in the aggregate. On the other hand, the synthesis model fails to reflect Keynes' own doubts concerning the likely effects on aggregate employment levels of an all-round reduction in money (and real) wage rates. These issues turn on the determinants of the aggregate supply of goods schedule which in turn depends on behaviour in the labour market.

In this chapter we investigate the determinants of the supply-side of Keynesian analysis, based on what we called in Chapters One to Three the alternative post-Keynesian perspective. This analysis emphasises the relative unimportance of real wage movements over the course of business cycles and focuses instead on the direct output-employment relationship. Rather than focusing on labour supply behaviour in explaining business cycles as in classical, neoclassical and synthesis Keynesian models, our analysis considers further the determinants of the demand for labour schedule in uncovering an alternative to the monetarist explanation of employment fluctuations.

This chapter is organised as follows. Section 1 provides a brief analysis of static models, emphasising the inverse real wages-employment relationship. Because this analysis is unified by its classical roots and the corresponding attention given to relative prices, we adopt the term neoclassical in the discussion. In Section 2 we review the range of arguments presented by Keynes himself. Our analysis leads to the conclusion that in Chapters 2 and 19 of the General Theory Keynes presented two competing and contradictory theories of the determinants of the demand for labour schedule. The arguments in Chapter 19 of the General Theory provide the basis from which an alternative model of the demand for labour schedule can be derived using a choice-theoretic framework. Our discussion in this section also provides an explanation as to why competing interpretations of Keynes' views of the labour market can all find support for their views by a careful, though selective, reading of Keynes' writings.[3]

In Section 3 we consider a static version of the alternative Keynesian model of the demand for labour, based on the disequilibrium analysis of Clower (1965) and Barro and Grossman (1971). Emphasis is given to the output and substitution effects of real wage changes on employment. This analysis yields two versions of the alternative Keynesian model of the demand for labour. The 'strong' version of the theory denies any direct role for real wages in the determination of aggregate employment levels; the 'weak' version admits some direct real wage effect operating through substitution of factors of production. This section ends with a brief comparison of the alternative demand for labour schedules considered in this chapter.

1. THE DEMAND FOR LABOUR SCHEDULE - THE BASIC MODEL

The neoclassical models of employment fluctuations are derived by investigating the behaviour of representative agents on the demand and supply sides of the market. Aggregation across individuals is therefore ignored (or Gorman, 1953, assumptions are implicitly applied). The agents are all price takers with prices either set exogenously (when a partial analysis of one side of the market is conducted) or fixed by an auctioneer at an equilibrium position when both the demand and supply schedules are considered. Fluctuations in this equilibrium position are therefore generated by movements or shifts in these schedules. The problem set in these models is to uncover plausible explanations of these movements based on optimising behaviour by the representative agents within an equilibrium framework. Following the analysis of Friedman (1968), these models explain such movements on the supply side of the labour market as arising from imperfect information concerning relative prices. In this section we describe the foundations of the demand side of the market in these models.

We start with a representative price-taking competitive firm maximising profits within a full-information static framework. The quantity of labour employed is assumed to be the only variable of production; hours worked are therefore assumed to be fixed. Under these assumptions the firm maximises current profits by choosing an optimal level of employment in the current period. The

solution to this problem yields a derived demand
for labour schedule. The firm therefore solves the
following problem:

$$\text{Max } \pi = PQ - WN - X \tag{4.1}$$

subject to

$$Q = f(N,K) \tag{4.2}$$

where π is the money profits earned by the firm; P
is the price of the product; Q is the level of the
firm's output; W is the money wage rate; N the
level of employment; X represents all other (fixed)
costs incurred by the firm; and K represents the
(fixed) quantities of all other factors of
production ('capital stock').[4] The production
relation in equation (4.2) is standard, exhibiting
diminishing marginal productivity of labour (N) for
a given capital stock, and either diminishing or
constant returns to scale when both labour and the
capital stock are permitted to vary. The solution
to this problem yields a derived demand for labour
schedule (N*) of the form:

$$N^* = F(W/P, K) \qquad F_W < 0, \quad F_K > 0 \tag{4.3}$$

where N* is the desired demand for labour. In the
simple static model we assume that the desired
demand for labour (N*) equals the actual employment
level (N) - there are no costs involved in
adjusting the level of employment. The critical
element of equation (4.3) is that the desired
employment level in a neoclassical model depends
only on relative prices and on the (given) levels
of all other inputs. No other variables enter as
arguments in the demand for labour schedule.[5]
        This exceedingly simple equation on its own
generates a number of features which are
fundamental in neoclassical models of employment
fluctuations. First, the level of demand for the
firm's product, which in the static macroeconomic
model represents aggregate demand, does not enter
directly into the labour demand schedule. Changes
in aggregate demand can exert an influence on
employment levels only indirectly, if at all, by
somehow generating changes in relative prices.
Thus the position of the demand for labour schedule
is independent of aggregate demand. Shocks to
aggregate demand influence employment levels by
altering the particular point obtained along a

given demand for labour schedule. Secondly, what are commonly referred to as 'supply shocks' in macroeconomic analysis[6] - exogenous changes in labour productivity or relative factor prices - influence employment levels by altering the position of the labour demand schedule. Thus if business cycles are in the main generated by aggregate demand shocks, as emphasised in virtually all of macroeconomic analysis, then these shocks will exert an influence on employment levels by generating movements in the supply schedule of labour. Thus the attention given to the supply side of the labour market in neoclassical macroeconomic models is not an accident but reflects the proposition that, on choice-theoretic grounds, the real demand for labour function should be stable over the business cycle. This explains why issues concerning the zero homogeneity hypothesis have dominated macroeconomic debates. This is not to say that this labour demand schedule does not shift periodically. Indeed, recent theoretical and empirical analysis has stressed the role of the oil price rises in 1973-4 and 1979-80 in generating a backwards shift in the labour demand schedule which, when combined with the synthesis Keynesian presumption of sluggish downwards adjustment in the rate of change of money wages, can be appealed to to explain the high unemployment rates observed in advanced capitalist countries since the late 1970s (Sachs, 1979, 1982; Grubb, Jackman and Layard, 1981; Symons and Layard, 1984). But in the process of the 'normal' business cycle generated by aggregate demand shocks, the neoclassical model maintains that fluctuations in employment result from inverse movements in the real wage rate.

The third point to notice about equation (4.3) concerns technology and corresponding propositions relating to the real wage elasticity of the demand for labour schedule. The presumption in this analysis is that the demand for labour schedule will be elastic; i.e. the elasticity is greater than one (in absolute values). This presumption is based on two considerations. The first is what might be called a 'stylised fact' of business cycles - namely, that observed variations in either output or employment over the cycle exceed those of relative prices. If this observation is accurate, then neoclassical models which depict such cycles as movements along the stable demand for labour function require that this function exhibit a large real wage elasticity. Second, the actual specification adopted for the production function (equation (4.2)) in neoclassical models often presumes this to be the case. Consider for example the widely-used Cobb-Douglas specification of equation (4.2).[7]

$$Q = AN^{\alpha}K^{\beta} \qquad (4.2a)$$

where Q, N, and K are defined as above; and A, α and β are given parameters. The solution to the firm's profit maximisiation problem using (4.1) and (4.2a) for a fixed capital stock can be expressed as the following log-linear relation:

$$n* = -[1/(\alpha-1)]Y - [\beta/(\alpha-1)]k + [1/(\alpha-1)]w \qquad (4.3a)$$

where lower case variables represent the logs of the variables, and $Y = \ln(\alpha A)$. Since by assumption α is a fraction, the real wage elasticity of the demand for labour (ε_w^D) exceeds unity:

$$\varepsilon_w^D = \delta n*/\delta w = 1/(\alpha-1) < -1. \qquad (4.4)$$

The traditional (microeconomic) theory of the firm decomposes this elasticity into two components: a substitution and an output effect. The substitution effect is generally ignored in macroeconomic models since labour is usually assumed to be the only variable factor of production. Thus the elasticity of the labour demand function in the basic model corresponds to the output effect on employment of a real wage change. The introduction of additional variable factors would in general lead to an increased real wage elasticity of the demand for labour.[8]

An alternative and somewhat more general specification of equation (4.2) is derived by considering technology based on the constant elasticity of substitution (CES) production function:[9]

$$Q = [\delta K^{-\rho} + (1-\delta)N^{-\rho}]^{(-v/\rho)} \qquad (4.2b)$$

where Q, K and N are defined as above; δ is a 'distribution' parameter ($0<\delta<1$); $1/(1+\rho)$ is the elasticity of substitution (σ) ($0<\sigma<\infty$); and v is a return to scale parameter ($v>0$). If we restrict the analysis to the case of constant returns to scale ($v=1$), we show in Appendix 1 of this chapter that the real wage elasticity of the labour demand curve is defined as:

$$\varepsilon_w^D = -\sigma\{1/[1-(1-\delta)(Q/N)^\rho]\} \qquad (4.5)$$

For the price-taking competitive firm, the elasticity of the labour demand curve cannot be positive if the model is to yield a unique maximum. Further, σ is defined over a range from zero to infinity. These two factors together imply that the term in square brackets must be positive. In addition it must be a fraction, since Q, N and $(1-\delta)$ are all positive. Thus J is multiplied by a number exceeding unity.

With these restrictions in mind, we can now investigate the admissible range of ε_w^D in the model based on a CES production function by considering the extreme values of σ. Consider the case where $\sigma=\infty$ ($\rho=-1$); i.e. there is perfect substitutability of factors of production. In such circumstances ε_w^D equals minus infinity - the labour demand curve is perfectly elastic with respect to the real wage rate (the 'law of one price' operates in the labour market). At the other extreme, where $\sigma=0$ ($\rho=\infty$), the production function is of a fixed proportions form. In this case $\varepsilon_w^D=0$; the labour demand curve is perfectly inelastic. Finally notice that in the special case of a Cobb-Douglas production function where $\sigma=1$ ($\rho=0$), the elasticity of the labour demand curve will exceed minus one (as shown by equation (4.4) above).[10]

The preceding analysis shows how this model implies in general that the labour demand curve will be elastic with respect to the real wage rate. It is only in the range where the elasticity of substitution lies between zero and one that there exists the possibility that the labour demand curve will be inelastic.[11] Notice, however, that even if $\sigma<1$, ε_w^D will in some circumstances still exceed minus unity since, as was noted above, the factor on σ in (4.5) must be greater than unity. It is for this reason that we suggest that there is a presumption in neoclassical macroeconomic models that the real wage elasticity of the labour demand curve exceeds unity. This presumption is further strengthened when the 'stylised fact' concerning the relative variations of employment and real wages over the business cycle is taken into account.

The simple static analysis based on a demand for labour schedule as expressed in equation (4.3) generates two clear empirical propositions. First, real wage movements are the dominant <u>cause</u> of fluctuations in employment over the business cycle. In the absence of such movements we would not observe systematic fluctuations in employment. Second, employment levels will be inversely associated with real wages. Thus the static version of the model predicts a counter-cyclical movement in real wages. We show in the next chapter that the first proposition survives an extension of the model to incorporate elements of uncertainty and sluggish adjustment of employment levels. However, the second proposition is modified by this extension. In particular, although no clear prediction emerges concerning the association between movements in <u>current</u> real wages and employment levels, the more elaborate models do confirm the proposition that the peaks and troughs in employment will be associated with a lower than average or higher than average real wage rate respectively.

The model does not, however, generate any clear propositions concerning cyclical movements in real wages relative to labour productivity; in other words, cyclical movements in real unit labour costs (or equivalently, labour's share in output).[12] It can be noted first of all that the first order conditions for profit maximisation require that labour productivity at the margin always equals the real wage rate. However, the more typical analysis of this issue concerns <u>average</u> real unit labour costs (U).[13] This variable is defined as:

$$U = (WN)/(PQ) \qquad (4.6)$$

The restrictions embodied in a particular specification of equation (4.2) will in general produce conflicting predictions on the cyclical movement of this variable. Consider for example the Cobb-Douglas specification as in equation (4.2a). Profit maximisation, subject to (4.2a), yields the following first-order condition:

$$W/P = (\alpha Q)/N. \qquad (4.7)$$

Combining (4.7) and (4.6) we see directly that in the Cobb-Douglas specification, average real unit labour costs are constant:

$$U = \alpha \qquad (4.8)$$

90

Consider next the more general CES specification as expressed in (4.2b). The investigation of the cyclical movements in U in this case is most easily carried out by adopting a log-linear version of (4.6):

$$u = (w - p) + n + q \qquad (4.6a)$$

Since the simple static model requires counter-cyclical real wage movements, we can investigate the cyclical movement in u by examining the sign of the derivative $(\delta u/\delta w)(u_w)$. This defines the real wage elasticity of real unit labour costs. Real unit labour costs will move pro-cyclically if u_w is negative, and counter-cyclically if it is positive. It is shown in Appendix 1 that under constant returns to scale this variable depends only on the elasticity of substitution (σ). The specific relation between these variables is:

$$u_w = 1 - \sigma \qquad (4.9)$$

The benchmark case in the analysis of the sign of u_w arises when $\sigma = 1$; i.e. when a Cobb-Douglas specification is adopted. If σ exceeds unity, then u_w is negative and real unit labour costs will move pro-cyclically. When σ is less than unity, u_w is positive and real unit labour costs move counter-cyclically. Notice in addition that these conflicting predictions remain even when the neoclassical presumption of an elastic labour demand schedule is considered. This is most easily seen in our benchmark case where $\sigma = 1$. Under this specification, equation (4.4) reveals that the labour demand curve is elastic. Thus for a certain range of σ less than unity, the labour demand curve will still be elastic but real unit labour costs will move pro-cyclically. When σ exceeds unity, the labour demand curve is clearly elastic and real unit labour costs move counter-cyclically. The simple static neoclassical model does not therefore generate any predictions concerning the cyclical movement of this variable.[14] Our analysis in what follows therefore abstracts from exogenous movements in productivity.

With the neoclassical analysis firmly in mind, we proceed in the following sections to consider departures from this model. We begin in the next section by examining Keynes' own views of the neoclassical demand for labour schedule.

2. KEYNES AND THE DEMAND FOR LABOUR SCHEDULE

In a recent issue of the Journal of Economic Literature, Davidson (1983) and Meltzer (1983) debate the derivation of the demand for labour schedule as found in the General Theory. In an earlier paper, Meltzer (1981) presented yet another reinterpretation of the General Theory in which the aggregate supply of goods function is derived using the static neoclassical demand for labour equation as described in Section 1 above.[15] Davidson criticises Meltzer's use of this demand schedule in describing Keynes' analysis, since 'Keynes rejected the notion of a marginal product curve as this demand for labour function' (1983, p.53). As evidence of his position, Davidson cites Keynes' argument that the analysis in the General Theory is valid even 'if we treat real wages as substantially constant in the short period' (Keynes, 1939, p.403).[16] Davidson then notes that the neoclassical labour demand function adopted by Meltzer is 'not consistent with the stable real wage argument in Keynes' (p.52).[17] In response to Davidson, Meltzer (1983) quotes Keynes on the role of diminishing returns to labour to argue that:

> Keynes' demand for labor [sic] is obtained from the first-order condition of the neoclassical production function. I have found nothing in the General Theory that denies my proposition and, as noted here, some statements to support it. (p.74, emphasis mine)

In the remainder of this section we review Keynes' arguments in the General Theory and in Keynes (1939) concerning the labour market in an attempt to document how both Meltzer's and Davidson's competing views receive some support from Keynes' writings. The reason why these apparent inconsistencies arise is provided by Keynes (1939), where he implies that the real wage-employment relationship is incidental to 'the main forces I was discussing' (1939, p.400).

Keynes, classical theory and the labour market

In Chapter 2 of the General Theory Keynes sets out his main departures from the classical theory as regards the specification of labour market behaviour. He also discusses 'an important point of agreement' between his analysis and that of classical theorists (p.17).[18] We review these issues in turn.

Keynes' departure from the classical model of the labour market concerns two issues. First, he argues that the supply of labour function is not homogeneous of degree zero with respect to money wages and prices. He claims that:

> It may be the case that within a certain range the demand of labour is for a minimum money-wage and not for a minimum real wage. The classical school have tacitly assumed that this would involve no significant change in their theory. But this is not so. For if the supply of labour is not a function of real wages <u>as its sole variable</u>, their argument breaks down entirely. (p.8, emphasis mine)

What variables other than the real wage influence the supply of labour? Keynes suggests that:

> Whilst workers usually resist a reduction of money-wages, it is not their practice to withdraw their labour whenever there is a rise in the price of wage goods. (p.9)

Thus Keynes' analysis implies that, while the labour supply function may in part depend on the real wage rate, over certain ranges the elasticity of labour supply (in the short run) with respect to the money wage rate will far exceed that with respect to the price level.[19] Thus unlike the theories of labour supply behaviour presented in Pigou (1933) and by Hicks (1932), Keynes' analysis implies that the supply of labour may actually fall in the event of a real wage rise if this is accompanied by a fall in money wage rates. His supply of labour schedule can therefore be expressed in the following general form as:

$$N^S = g(W,P,w) \qquad (4.10)$$

where W is the money wage rate; P is the aggregate price level;[20] and w is the real wage rate. The quotation reprinted above implies that, of the partial derivatives in (4.10), g_W is far greater than g_p. To support this contention, Keynes appeals to the 'relative wage hypothesis', where those 'who consent to a reduction in money-wages relatively to others, will suffer a <u>relative</u> reduction in real wages, which is a sufficient justification for them to resist it' (p.14, emphasis his).[21]

Keynes' second point of departure from the classical system concerns the determination of the real wage rate. He disputes the assumption underlying classical theory 'that the general level of real wages is directly determined by the character of the wage bargain' negotiated by employers and workers (p.13). This argument, which he claims is the 'more fundamental' of his two objections to classical theory, implies that real wages may be determined outside the labour market. Keynes argues:

> There may exist no expedient by which labour as a whole can reduce its <u>real</u> wage to a given figure by making revised <u>money</u> bargains with entrepreneurs.... We shall endeavour to show that primarily it is other forces which determine the general level of real wages. (p.13)

Keynes cements these arguments in Chapter 3 (see pp.27-30) of the <u>General Theory</u> where he summarises his theory of employment. He introduces into the analysis the assumption of a constant money wage rate as a substitute for the more complicated labour supply equation such as (4.10). This 'simplification', he claims, 'is introduced solely to facilitate the exposition' and the 'essential character of the argument is precisely the same whether or not money-wages, etc., are liable to change' (p.27). This simplification captures in a rather subtle way <u>both</u> elements of Keynes' departure from classical theory. The fixed money wage rate implies that, as a first approximation, labour supply is infinitely elastic with respect to the money wage and does not depend on the price level ($g_W = \infty$ and $g_p = 0$ in (4.10)). Second, under the fixed money wage assumption, the real wage is determined by the setting of the aggregate price level. Thus Keynes in his summary of his theory implies that the level of employment is determined in the goods market at the point of equilibrium between the supply and demand for goods, and that 'for every value of N [employment] there is a corresponding marginal productivity of

labour... which determines the real wage' (p.29).
Keynes considers this argument to reverse the
causation of the classical model. In his analysis:

> The propensity to consume and the rate of
> new investment determine between them the
> volume of employment, and the volume of
> employment is uniquely related to a given
> level of real wages - not the other way
> around.   (p.30, emphasis mine)

Davidson argues that these passages support his
contention that Keynes' demand for labour schedule
does not depend on the real wage rate as in
Meltzer's (1981) model, but rather that the real
wage is determined by the level of employment
(1983, p.53). However, the interpretation of
causation in terms of static analysis, as in
Meltzer's model, is not at all clear. The
determination of two endogenous and 'uniquely
correlated' variables, which employment and real
wages are in both Keynes' analysis and Meltzer's
interpretation, is independent of whether the
equation linking these variables is written with
employment on the left-hand or right-hand side of
the equation. The behaviour described by the
system of equations may change according to how the
real wage-employment relation is specified, but the
equilibrium of the model for given exogenous
variables remains unchanged by these alterations.
It is only in a dynamic analysis which allows for
lagged relationships that the issue of causation
between endogenous variables takes on any
relevance.(22)
     The specific elements of Davidson's critique
of Meltzer become even more questionable when the
'important point of agreement' between Keynes and
classical theory is considered. In Chapter 2 of
the General Theory Keynes makes it abundantly clear
that he accepts the classical linkage between the
marginal product of labour and the level of real
wages:

> ... with a given organisation, equipment
> and technique, real wages and the volume
> of output (and hence of employment) are
> uniquely correlated, so that, in general,
> an increase in employment can only occur
> to the accompaniment of a decline in the
> rate of real wages. Thus I am not

disputing this <u>vital fact</u> which classical
economists have (rightly) asserted as
indefeasible.   (p.17, emphasis mine)

Thus in Chapter 2 of the <u>General Theory</u>,
Keynes describes a view of the labour market in
which real wages and employment are directly
linked. As noted by Davidson, Keynes' view of the
causal relationship between these two variables
runs from employment to real wages only. But as we
noted above such a view has no bearing on a static
model. There is little doubt in these passages
that Keynes accepted the classical linkage between
marginal productivity and real wages. The picture
of the labour market we observe in Chapter 2 of the
<u>General Theory</u> is therefore one in which
unemployment results from a real wage rate which is
too high to encourage employers to hire an amount
of labour equal to the quantity of labour available
at this real wage rate. However, this unemployment
equilibrium arises not as a result of the behaviour
of workers, who may not be able to influence the
real wage rate, but is the result of developments
in the goods market. Thus Davidson's
interpretation of Keynes' theory of employment does
not receive support from Chapter 2 of the <u>General
Theory</u>. However, a very different picture emerges
in Chapter 19.

Keynes' direct output-employment relationship

Keynes' alternative view of the labour market is
best described by a passage in his 1939 paper which
concerns the views he expressed in Chapter 2 of the
<u>General Theory</u>. He argues that the 'traditional
conclusion' that, over the business cycle, real
wages and employment are inversely related 'had a
tendency to offset the influence of the main forces
which I was discussing...'. He continues:

In particular, the traditional conclusion
played an important part, it will be
remembered, in the discussions, some ten
years ago, as to the effect of
expansionary policies on employment....
I was already arguing at that time that
the good effect of an expansionist
investment policy on employment, the fact
of which no one denied, was due to the
stimulant which it gave to effective

demand. Prof. Pigou, on the other hand, and many other economists explained the observed result by the reduction in real wages covertly effected by the rise in prices which ensued on the increase in effective demand. It was held that public investment policies... produced their effect by deceiving, so to speak, the working classes into accepting a lower real wage, effecting by this means the same favourable influence on employment which, according to these economists, would have resulted from a more direct attack on real wages (e.g. by reducing money wages whilst enforcing a credit policy calculated to leave prices unchanged). If the falling tendency of real wages in periods of rising demand is denied, this alternative explanation must, of course, fall to the ground.... If, however, it proves right to adopt the contrary generalisation, it would be possible to simplify considerably the more complicated version of my fundamental explanation which I have expounded in my General Theory. My practical conclusions would have, in that case, a fortiori force.

(Keynes, 1939, pp.400-1)

Thus Keynes is suggesting that real wage movements are incidental to 'the main forces' which generate employment fluctuations.[23]

This unimportance of real wages argument surfaces in Chapter 19 of the General Theory where Keynes considers the effects of changes in money and real wages on employment levels. In this chapter, Keynes applies what he calls his 'own method of analysis' in answering the question: what determines the actual volume of employment as a whole? His argument contains two elements: an analysis of (1) whether money wages and employment are directly linked in the aggregate; and (2) whether a fall in money wages could 'have a certain or probable tendency to affect employment in a particular direction' (p.260).

The answer Keynes gives to the first question is an emphatic 'no':

The first question we have already answered in the negative.... For we have

> shown that the volume of employment is
> uniquely correlated with the volume of
> effective demand measured in wage units,
> and that effective demand, being the sums
> of expected consumption and the expected
> investment, cannot change, if the
> propensity to consume, the schedule of
> the marginal efficiency of capital and
> the rate of interest are all unchanged.
> (pp.260-1)

If money and real wages are to affect employment,
then the transmission of these effects must work by
altering at least one of these components of
aggregate effective demand. In addition, Keynes
makes it clear that the direct effect of changes of
money wages on costs of production, and thus output
and employment, will in fact not operate as
suggested in classical theory. Although he accepts
that such a mechanism does operate for 'any given
industry', it is not valid to 'transfer the
argument to industry as a whole' (pp.258-9). The
reason for this concerns the income effects
generated by changes in money wages in the
aggregate:

> ... the precise question at issue is
> whether the reduction in money-wages will
> or will not be accompanied by the same
> aggregate effective demand as before
> measured in money, or, at any rate, by an
> aggregate effective demand which is not
> reduced in full proportion to the
> reduction in money-wages. (pp.259-60)

Keynes also makes it clear in this section that he
is not arguing that his denial of any direct effect
of money wages on employment works through
equiproportionate changes in the price level,
thereby leaving real wages unchanged, since 'prices
do not change in exact proportion to changes in
money-wages' (p.259). Indeed, throughout this
chapter Keynes is vague about the effects of money
wage changes on the level of real wages. At one
point he claims that 'prices certainly do not
change in exact proportion to changes in money-
wages' (p.259), whereas elsewhere he implies that
wage reductions 'would not, as a rule, have the
effect of reducing real wages and might even have
the effect of increasing them' (p.269). Here he
implies that prices may fall by a larger percentage

than money wages. Thus, Keynes is agnostic about
real wage movements arising from money wage cuts,
implying that they play at most a secondary role in
his analysis.

Keynes supplements these criticisms of the
direct money wage to employment relationship in the
Appendix to Chapter 19, where he confronts directly
Pigou's (1933) Theory of Unemployment. Keynes
discusses the technically determined demand curve
for labour as used in neoclassical theory. He
distinguishes between the 'State of Demand for
Labour', which he says can fluctuate dramatically
in the short run, and the (neoclassical) 'Real
Demand Function for Labour', which expresses
employment as an inverse function of the real wage
rate. This latter function is extremely stable
over the cycle. 'There is nothing in the world
less likely to be subjected to sharp short-period
swings than this factor' (p.179). Thus, Keynes
argues, fluctuations in aggregate employment are
not in any way related to the 'Real Demand Function
for Labour'.

It is the 'State of Demand for Labour' which
determines the actual level of employment in
Keynes' theory, and this is uniquely related to the
level of effective demand through what he calls the
'employment function' in Chapter 20 of the General
Theory. Keynes introduces this function as a
substitute for the ordinary (neoclassical) supply
curve of an industry (pp.280-1). This function
translates the amount of effective demand for
commodities into an amount of demand for labour.
Of course, the elasticity of employment with
respect to the level of aggregate effective demand
will be particularly sensitive to the actual
allocation of that demand among different sectors
of industry characterised by varying degrees of
labour intensity. Keynes pays considerable
attention in Chapter 20 to the various effects that
increases in the level of aggregate demand for,
say, consumer goods as opposed to investment goods,
can exert on the aggregate level of employment.

The second element of Keynes' argument
consists of an in-depth analysis of the effects
that an aggregate money and real wage reduction can
have on the level of employment working through the
'State of Demand for Labour'. Keynes assesses a
variety of possible effects a fall in money and
real wage might have on effective demand in Chapter
19. Here he shows how such changes will be
expected to generate changes in the components of

aggregate effective demand which are counteracting.[24] The first effect Keynes discusses is what we will call the 'distribution effect'. A fall in money wages would tend to reduce prices 'somewhat' (p.262). This results in a redistribution of real income from workers to capitalists as a result of the real wage reduction, and from capitalists to rentiers as a result of the fall in prices. Both effects tend to lower the aggregate marginal propensity to consume, thereby reducing the level of aggregate effective demand.[25] In addition, the ensuing fall in prices would redistribute income from debtors to lenders by increasing the real value of outstanding debts (the so-called Fisher effect). This would also lead to a fall in the aggregate propensity to consume since debtors, because they borrow to finance a level of expenditure over and above their income, are expected to have a higher propensity to consume than lenders, whose incomes often exceed their expenditure levels. Thus consumption demand would in general be expected to fall in the event of a fall in real and money wages (and prices); this would be unfavourable to employment in the short run. Keynes is therefore led to conclude that 'we must base any hopes of favourable results to employment... mainly on an improvement in investment due either to an increased marginal efficiency of capital [if current wages are below future expected wages]... or due to a decreased rate of interest' (p.265).

Keynes also expresses doubts about the potential beneficial employment effects of reductions in money wages, prices and real wages working through an improved marginal efficiency of capital (what we will call the 'expectations effect'). A fall in money wages relative to prices will indeed raise unit profits and this would, ceteris paribus, raise the marginal efficiency of capital (MEC). It may therefore 'produce an optimistic tone in the minds of entrepreneurs' (p.264). But counteracting this effect is the fall in prices which, if expected to continue, will reduce future expected profits and thus the MEC. It is only when wages and prices have hit a floor that the MEC will rise unambiguously. In addition, though unit profits increase, the demand for output may fall due to the fall in the aggregate marginal propensity to consume, and thus total profits may fall. Additional investment expenditure by firms would be constrained by the lack of availability of liquid funds in such circumstances. The net effects of the MEC are therefore ambiguous, according to Keynes.

The other variable which influences the level of investment is the rate of interest. A fall in money wages and prices would be expected to lower the rate of interest if the demand for money falls when prices are reduced (the Keynes effect). This would have a positive employment effect if investment demand is reasonably interest-elastic. However, Keynes points out that a flexible monetary policy would in theory produce the same result and is probably much more susceptible to government control. However, he questions whether such a 'monetary policy [is] capable, unaided, of achieving this result' (p.267, emphasis mine).

Thus Keynes argues that in a closed economy the effects on employment of a reduction in money wages will depend on the relative strengths of these countervailing effects. Real wages have little or nothing to do with these arguments. Since the level of aggregate consumption would be expected to fall when money (and real) wages are reduced, the main problem lies in finding some mechanism able to push investment back to a rate high enough to establish a level of effective demand compatible with full employment. A flexible wage policy cannot be expected to work unless capitalists' expectations are sufficiently elastic with respect to a change in money (and real) wages that investment responds favourably to diminished costs of production. Similarly, a flexible monetary policy may not stimulate enough investment if expectations (as captured by the MEC and liquidity preference schedules) are not very interest-elastic. The key point of this analysis lies in the volatile investment function which is dominated by the expectations and conjectures of capitalists. The effect on the level of employment of a fall in money wages depends crucially on how they influence these expectations and the resulting level of investment. The famous liquidity trap, the interest-inelastic investment function, and the 'day of judgement' case in which returns to investment are so low that capitalists are not willing to undertake the risks involved in increasing their production levels, are all simple textbook examples of the importance of capitalists' expectations in determining the level of effective demand, income and hence employment and unemployment in the short run.

This interpretation of the General Theory, which pays particular attention to the labour market, places the classical and neoclassical theories of employment fluctuations as special cases of the Keynesian one. The supposed positive employment effects of wage reductions arise if expectations are sufficiently elastic with respect to money and real wage changes to generate a substantial increase in investment (over and above the countervailing movements in aggregate consumption expenditure). The focal point of Keynes' analysis is the direct relationship between aggregate effective demand, output and employment working through the 'State of Demand for Labour'. Money and real wages influence employment levels only indirectly through their potential effects on aggregate effective demand. Further, Keynes is totally ambiguous about the direction of real wage movements over the business cycle in Chapter 19 of the General Theory.

Keynes returns to the question of the cyclical movement of real wages in his 1939 paper. This paper was written in response to papers by Dunlop (1938) and Tarshis (1939) which criticised the Chapter 2 theory of the labour market and, in particular, the suggestion that real wages tend to move inversely with both employment and money wages, particularly in periods characterised by low levels of employment.

Keynes offers two modifications to the analysis in Chapter 19 of the General Theory which would generate a pro-cyclical movement in real wages as suggested by Dunlop (1938) and Tarshis (1939). First, Keynes questions the reliability of the assumption of diminishing marginal productivity of labour when 'we start from a level of output very greatly below capacity' (1939, p.405).[26] If, in such a position, the marginal cost curve is falling as output increases, then as output and employment rise, real wages might rise since costs, and thus prices, would fall. Such a situation would, according to Keynes, reinforce the case for expansionist policies:

> In particular, the warnings given, quite rightly, by Mr D.H. Robertson of the dangers which may arise when we encourage or allow activity of the system to advance too rapidly along the upward slopes of the marginal-cost curve towards the goal of full employment, can be more

> often neglected... when the assumption
> (of increasing marginal costs) which I
> have previously admitted as normal and
> reasonable is abandoned.   (1939, p.406)

The second modification suggested by Keynes is to abandon the theory of perfect competition and the associated assumption that marginal cost equals price and to replace it with a theory of imperfect competition:

> For it may be the case that the practical
> workings of the laws of imperfect
> competition... are such that when output
> increases and money wages rise, prices
> rise less than in proportion to the
> increase in marginal money cost.... It
> is, beyond doubt, the practical
> assumption of the producer that his price
> policy ought to be influenced by the fact
> that he is normally operating subject to
> decreasing average costs, even if in the
> short period his marginal cost is rising.
> His effort is to maintain prices when
> output falls and, when output increases,
> he may raise them by less than the full
> amount required to offset higher costs
> including higher wages.   (1939, pp.406-7)

Both of the modifications considered by Keynes may lead to a pro-cyclical movement in money and real wages. Such changes do not alter the general working of his output-employment model, however, and are in fact quite consistent with it. The modifications are also consistent with our interpretation of Keynes' theory of the labour market which suggests that the marginal productivity theory and the associated real demand function for labour are irrelevant in the analysis of fluctuations in employment over the business cycle. In addition, the supply side theories of the classicals which, as we have argued, are incorporated in the neoclassical synthesis, appear to be totally rejected by Keynes. As he concludes in his 1939 paper:

> Meanwhile I am comforted by the fact that
> their [Dunlop and Tarshis] conclusions
> tend to confirm the idea that the causes
> of short-period fluctuations are to be
> found in changes in the demand for labour

and not in changes in its real-supply
price...   (p.411)

3. AGGREGATE DEMAND CONSTRAINTS AND THE KEYNESIAN DEMAND FOR LABOUR SCHEDULE

What is the basis for the alternative Keynesian
view that real wages are unimportant in the
determination of the level of employment in the
short run? This is the question we address in this
section by taking the static neoclassical model of
a profit-maximising, price-taking firm and
superimposing on the analysis demand-induced
quantity constraints in the product market. Our
analysis develops the arguments in Patinkin (1965,
Chapter 13) and Barro and Grossman (1971), yielding
two types of Keynesian models.

The 'strong' version of the Keynesian model is
derived by considering the case, typical of
macroeconomic analysis, where labour is the only
variable factor of production. This eliminates any
potential substitution effects between factors of
production. The 'weak' version of the model, which
considers additional variable factors of
production, admits the existence of substitution
possibilities between factors, thus allowing for
some direct influence of real wages on employment
levels. Both models share the common feature that
the level of the firm's output becomes a variable
which enters directly into its demand for labour
schedule.

The models capture the distinction made by
Keynes between the 'State of Demand for Labour' and
the 'Real Demand Function for Labour' in terms of
Clower's (1965) distinction between effective and
notional demand. In the labour market we define
the notional demand for labour as the level of
demand which is not constrained by the level of
aggregate effective demand. The effective demand
for labour, on the other hand, takes into account
product market constraints. We take as given
throughout our analysis the arguments reviewed in
Chapter Two above that demand constraints can arise
in the product market without operating through the
medium of relative prices. This can be interpreted
as implying that the price level is itself
(somewhat) sticky or, following Patinkin (1951) and
Tobin (1960), that the level of aggregate demand is
not responsive to changes in the aggregate price
level.(27)

Labour as the only variable factor of production

We consider first the case of a representative price-taking firm in which labour is the only variable factor of production. The firms chooses its desired employment level taking into consideration possible demand constraints on its level of output. Thus the firm may find itself in a disequilibrium position in the labour market. This formulation of the firm's optimisation problem immediately raises the problem noted by Arrow (1959) that a firm which is unable to sell all its output at going prices must behave as a monopolist and therefore may reduce its prices in such circumstances. We avoid this difficulty by assuming that wages and prices are set before the period under consideration, and that these prices are fixed throughout the period. Thus the period is defined as the length of time in which prices and wages remain unchanged. Wages and prices are allowed to change between periods.

Formally the firm's problem is to maximise profits by choosing its desired level of employment. The firm solves the following lagrangian:

$$\text{Max } Z = Y - WN + \lambda(Y^0 - Y) \qquad (4.11)$$

subject to

$$Y = F(N, \overline{K}) \qquad F_N > 0; \quad F_{NN} < 0 \qquad (4.12)$$

where N is employment; $\overline{K}$ is the given capital stock; Y is the level of the firm's output; Y^0 is the given level of demand for the firm's output; W is the real wage rate; λ is a lagrangian multiplier ($\lambda \geq 0$); F_N and F_{NN} represent, respectively, the marginal product of labour and the change in the marginal product of labour as more labour is used in the production of Y; and the production function (4.12) exhibits diminishing marginal productivity of labour ($F_{NN} < 0$). λ represents the cost to the firm in terms of foregone profits arising from a quantity constraint in the goods market. When $\lambda = 0$, the demand constraint does not restrict the firm's desired employment level. On the other hand, when λ is positive the demand constraint restricts the firm's demand for labour. In such circumstances the problem set out in (4.11) and (4.12) would include inequality constraints, so Kuhn-Tucker conditions will have to be satisfied.

The usual marginal conditions and the associated complementary slackness conditions for this optimisation exercise are:

$$\delta Z/\delta N = F_N - W - \lambda F_N \leq 0 \qquad (\delta Z/\delta N)N=0 \quad (4.13)$$

$$\delta Z/\delta \lambda = Y^O - Y \geq 0 \qquad (\delta Z/\delta \lambda)\lambda = 0 \quad (4.14)$$

If we restrict our analysis to cases where some output is produced, such that $Y^*, N^* > 0$ (where the * superscript represents the optimum values of a variable) then the complementary slackness condition in (4.13) implies that the associated marginal condition must be expressed as a strict equality. (4.13) then becomes:

$$F_N = W/(1-\lambda^*) \qquad (4.13')$$

where F_N is measured at the optimum employment level, N^*.

Consider the case when the firm's demand for labour is not constrained by the demand for its output. In this circumstance $\lambda^* = 0$ and by (4.13') the marginal product of labour (F_N) equals the real wage rate (W). In this case employment is determined by the notional demand for labour schedule where the level of employment is chosen such that the marginal product of labour equals the real wage rate. This notional demand for labour is the only labour demand schedule considered in the neoclassical models discussed in Section 1 above. Notice, in addition, that when $\lambda^* = 0$, the complementary slackness condition in (4.14) does not place any restrictions on whether the marginal condition in (4.14) is an equality or inequality. The optimum level of output (Y^*) may equal or be less than the level of demand for the firm's product ($Y^* \leq Y^O$).[28]

Consider next the case where $\lambda^* > 0$. The complementary slackness condition in (4.14) implies that the corresponding marginal conditions must be expressed as an equality. (4.14) thus becomes:

$$Y^* = Y^O = F(N^*, \overline{K}) \qquad (4.14')$$

The effective demand for labour schedule is derived in this circumstance using equations (4.13') and (4.14') which solve for the values of N^* and λ^*. This problem can be solved recursively as follows. Optimal output is determined by the level of effective demand in the goods market and, with all other factors of production fixed during the period, this in turn determines the level of employment to satisfy (4.14):

$$N^* = F^{-1}(Y^0) \qquad (4.15)$$

where F^{-1} is the inverse of the production function in (4.12). With employment set by conditions in the goods market, the marginal product of labour (F_N) is therefore pinned down and (4.13) can be used to solve for λ^*:

$$\lambda^* = 1 - (W/F_N). \qquad (4.16)$$

(4.16) states that λ^* is the difference between marginal revenues (expressed in real terms as the increase in output of one unit of the good) and the marginal costs associated with the increase of one unit of output.[29] It measures the amount of (marginal) real profits foregone by the firm as a result of being demand-constrained in the goods market. In other words, λ^* measures the unit profits of the firm at the margin. Notice that as a result of diminishing marginal productivity of labour, any relaxation of the demand constraint at the margin would not lead to a unit change in the firm's profits. Some profits are lost as a result of lower labour productivity (unit profits fall). Thus λ^* must be a fraction.[30] This result will be used in our analysis below.

Consider what happens if real wages adjust between periods. This can be analysed by investigating the slope of the effective demand for labour schedule. Is it necessarily vertical in the model? The answer is found by differentiating equations (4.13') and (4.14') with respect to the real wage rate. This yields the following two equations:

$$F_{NN} N^*_W - 1 - \lambda^*_W F_N - \lambda^* F_{NN} N^*_W = 0 \qquad (4.17)$$

$$-F_N N^*_W = 0 \qquad (4.18)$$

where the partial derivatives N^*_W and λ^*_W represent, respectively, the effects of changes in the real wage rate on the optimal level of employment and on the profits foregone by the firm at this optimal level. (4.18) implies that as long as Y^0, the level of aggregate effective demand, is fixed independently of the real wage rate ($Y^0_W = 0$), the effective demand for labour schedule will be

independent of the real wage rate. Since we assume
that some quantity of labour is always employed
such that $F_N \neq 0$, (4.18) requires that $N^*_W = 0$. This is
the case considered by Barro and Grossman (1971).
In this one variable factor model with a given
level of aggregate effective demand, the level of
employment is independent of the real wage rate.

Changes in the real wage rate do have an
effect on profits, however. First, total profits
of the firm are inversely related to the real wage
rate. This can be shown by taking the derivative
of the firm's profit function associated (4.11)
with respect to changes in the real wage rate. The
firm's profits (in real terms) at the optimum (π^*)
are defined as:

$$\pi^* = Y^* - WN^* \qquad (4.19)$$

Differentiating (4.19) with respect to the real
wage rate yields:

$$\pi^*_W = (F_N - W)N^*_W - N^* \qquad (4.20)$$

where π^*_W is the derivative of the firm's profits at
the optimum position with respect to the real wage
rate. By (4.18), $N^*_W = 0$, thus π^*_W is unambiguously
negative. Second, the amount of profits foregone
by the firm as a result of the demand constraint
(λ^*) is also inversely related to the real wage
rate. This can be shown formally by rearranging
(4.17) to solve for λ^*_W:

$$\lambda^*_W = [(1-\lambda^*)F_{NN} \; N^*_W - 1]/F_N \qquad (4.21)$$

Since by (4.18), N^*_W equals zero, (4.21) can be
rewritten as:

$$\lambda^*_W - -1/F_N \qquad (4.22)$$

The profits foregone by the firm are inversely
related to the real wage rate because the
difference between the marginal product of labour
and the new lower real wage rate has increased.

The prediction derived from this 'strong'
Keynesian model, that employment is independent of
the real wage rate, is fairly intuitive. The
introduction of an aggregate demand constraint on
employment rules out any output effect of real
wages on employment. Combined with this is the
assumption that labour is the only variable factor
of production. This rules out any potential

substitution effect. We return to the question of
substitution effects in the next section.

Although this analysis denies any direct real
wage effect on employment, it can be generalised to
incorporate indirect effects working through the
level of aggregate effective demand as suggested by
Keynes. This additional consideration can be
analysed by allowing the derivative Y_W^O to take a
non-zero value. Our discussion in Section 2 above
implied that this derivative can be considered in
terms of two components - the distribution effect
which is expected to be negative (a real wage
reduction leads to a fall in consumption
expenditure), and the expectations effect which may
be positive (if a real wage reduction leads to an
increase in investment expenditure). Thus the sign
of Y_W^O is ambiguous, with the case above where $Y_W^O=0$
considered a benchmark case.

The case where Y_W^O is non-zero can be analysed
using (4.17) and the following revised version of
(4.18):

$$Y_W^O - F_N \, N_W^* = 0 \qquad\qquad (4.23)$$

The model made up of (4.17) and (4.23) is again
recursive with (4.23) solving for N_W^* and the
resulting solution introduced into (4.17) to solve
for λ_W^*. From (4.23) we can solve for N_W^* as:

$$N_W^* = Y_W^O/F_N \qquad\qquad (4.24)$$

Substituting (4.24) into (4.17) and rearranging
yields, the corresponding solution for λ_W is:

$$\lambda_W^* = [1/F_N][(1-\lambda^*)(\{F_{NN} \, Y_W^O\}/F_N) - 1] \qquad (4.25)$$

Finally we can also solve for π_W^* when Y_W^O is non-
zero by substituting the expression in (4.24) for
N_W^* in (4.20) yielding:

$$\pi_W^* = (F_N - W)(Y_W^O/F_N) - N^* \qquad\qquad (4.26)$$

We are now in a position to consider the
indirect effects of real wage changes on the
effective demand for labour. What happens if Y_W^O is
negative; i.e. a fall (rise) in real wages
generates an increase (decrease) in the level of
aggregate effective demand? This implies that the
expectations effect of real wage changes on
investment expenditure outweighs the countervailing
distribution effect on consumption expenditure. In

this case, N_W^* in (4.24) is negative - a fall (rise) in the real wage rate tends to increase aggregate employment. The profits of the firm also move inversely with the real wage rate when Y_W^0 is negative. This is evident from (4.26) since the first term on the right hand side of the expression is unambiguously negative. A real wage fall, for example, leads to an increase in profits in two ways. First, unit profits on the output of Y^0 units of the good increase. Second, the firm's output also rises, thereby further increasing total profits.[31] The reverse holds for the case of a rise in real wages.[32]

Equations (4.24), (4.25) and (4.26) can also be applied to the case where the level of aggregate effective demand is positively associated with real wages; i.e. when $Y_W^0 > 0$. This case corresponds to what might be called the 'underconsumption case'.[33] By (4.24) we see that in this case employment is positively related to the real wage rate, while (4.25) shows that most profits at the margin become negatively associated with the real wage rate. A fall (rise) in real wages reduces (increases) aggregate demand and thus output and employment, thereby raising (reducing) the marginal product of labour, and thus leading to a rise (fall) in λ^*. Finally, the effects on the total profits of the firm when Y_W^0 is positive are ambiguous. A fall in real wages raises unit profits but reduces output. The reverse is true for a rise in real wages. The effect of real wage changes on total profits therefore depends on the relative strengths of these countervailing effects.

Thus the 'strong' version of the alternative Keynesian model of the effective demand for labour schedule denies any <u>direct</u> effect of real wages on employment. Unlike the static neoclassical model of employment fluctuations, the static model does not admit an output effect of real wage changes on employment since output, and thus employment, is constrained by the level of aggregate effective demand. The profit maximising firm in this analysis adjusts its output levels to the level of aggregate effective demand. Furthermore, potential substitution effects of real wages on employment are denied by the model simply because, as in most of macroeconomic analysis, labour is considered the only variable factor of production. This alternative Keynesian model can, however, be somewhat generalised to allow for substitution effects while denying the direct output effect of real wages on employment.
110

Substitution effects and an example

The above analysis can be easily extended to the case of two variable factors of production, labour (N) and other inputs (X). The firm maximises profits for a given real wage rate (W); the real price of the other input (M); and a given level of demand (Y^O). The firm therefore solves the following lagrangian equation:

$$\text{Max } Z = Y - WN - MX + \lambda(Y^O - Y) \qquad (4.27)$$

subject to

$$Y = F(N, X, \overline{K}) \qquad (4.28)$$

where $F_X > 0$; $F_{XX} < 0$. The marginal conditions and complementary slackness conditions for this problem are:

$$\delta Z / \delta N = F_N - W - \lambda F_N \leq 0 \qquad (\delta Z / \delta N) N = 0 \quad (4.29)$$

$$\delta Z / \delta X = F_X - M - \lambda F_X \leq 0 \qquad (\delta Z / \delta X) X = 0 \quad (4.30)$$

$$\delta Z / \delta \lambda = Y^O - Y \geq 0 \qquad (\delta Z / \delta \lambda) \lambda = 0 \quad (4.31)$$

As in the problem discussed in the previous section, we restrict our analysis to the case where some output is produced using both labour and the other variable input. When the aggregate demand constraint is binding on the firm such that $\lambda* > 0$, the marginal conditions in (4.29), (4.30) and (4.31) become equalities yielding three equations to solve for three unknowns, $N*$, $X*$ and $\lambda*$:

$$F_N(1 - \lambda*) = W \qquad (4.32)$$

$$F_X(1 - \lambda*) = M \qquad (4.33)$$

$$Y* = Y^O = F(N*, X*, \overline{K}) \qquad (4.34)$$

The solution to this system of equations yields the following 'weak' version of the effective demand for labour schedule:

$$N* = f(Y^O, W, M) \qquad (4.35)$$

The real wage rate enters directly into the effective demand for labour schedule since the firm can now choose the ratio of labour to other inputs in producing $Y*$ $(=Y^O)$ units of the good.

What is the responsiveness of the effective demand for labour to <u>ceteris paribus</u> changes in the real wage rate? As before, this question is answered by differentiating the marginal conditions (4.33) and (4.34) with respect to the real wage rate, yielding:

$$(1-\lambda^*)(F_{NN} N_W^* + F_{NX} X_W^*) - F_N \lambda_W^* - 1 = 0 \quad (4.36)$$

$$(1-\lambda^*)(F_{XN} N_W^* + F_{XX} X_W^*) - F_X \lambda_W^* = 0 \quad (4.37)$$

$$Y_W^O - F_N N_W^* - F_X X_W^* = 0 \quad (4.38)$$

where X_W^* represents the change in the optimal quantity of the other factor of production employed resulting from a change in the real wage rate; and F_{XN} and F_{NX} are the usual cross-partial derivatives representing the change in the marginal product of one input with respect to changes in the employment levels of the other with $F_{NX}=F_{XN}$, and both expressions are positive. Unlike the one variable factor case where the problem is solved recursively, the system made up of equations (4.36)-(4.38) must be solved simultaneously. Substituting for X_W^* in (4.36) using (4.38) and for λ_W^* using (4.37) and after rearranging, we derive the following expression for N_W^* in the two variable factor case:

$$N_W^* = [1/D][1/(1-\lambda^*)] + [1/D]$$

$$[\{(F_N F_{XX})/(F_X F_X)\} - F_{NX}]Y_W^O \quad (4.39)$$

where

$$D = [1/F_X][F_{NN} F_X - 2F_{NX} F_N + (F_{XX} F_N F_N)/(F_X)] \quad (4.40)$$

By the usual assumptions the F_{XX} and F_{NN} are negative, and since all other terms in (4.40) are positive, D is unambiguously negative. Thus in our benchmark case, where aggregate effective demand is independent of the real wage rate ($Y_W^O=0$), (4.39) shows that the effective demand for labour schedule is inversely associated with the real wage rate (since λ^* is a fraction, $(1-\lambda^*)$ must be positive). Notice as well that the coefficients on Y_W^O in (4.39) are necessarily positive (D and the terms inside the brackets are both negative). Thus if Y_W^O takes on a negative value, the inverse relationship between real wages and employment is strengthened.

However, unlike the 'strong' version of the Keynesian model, in the 'weak' version the demand for labour may still be inversely associated with the real wage rate even if Y_W^O is positive. This will depend on the relative strengths of the substitution and effective demand effects of real wage changes on the demand for labour.

A direct comparison of the 'strong' and 'weak' versions of the Keynesian demand for labour schedule are perhaps best understood using a specific example where the production function in (4.28) is of a Cobb-Douglas variety. This also allows us to compare the two versions of the effective demand for labour schedule with the corresponding notional schedule as adopted in neoclassical theory.

The firm's problem is now to maximise (4.27) subject to the production function:

$$Y = AN^{\alpha} X^{\beta} \qquad (4.28')$$

where A captures other factors of production; and α and β are positive fractions with $(\alpha+\beta)$ less than unity. The marginal and complementary slackness conditions corresponding to this problem are:

$$\delta Z/\delta N = \alpha AN^{\alpha-1} X^{\beta}(1-\lambda) - W = 0 \qquad (\delta Z/\delta N)N=0$$
$$(4.41)$$

$$\delta Z/\delta X = \beta AN^{\alpha} X^{\beta-1}(1-\lambda) - M = 0 \qquad (\delta Z/\delta X)X=0$$
$$(4.42)$$

$$\delta Z/\delta \lambda = Y^O - AN^{\alpha} X^{\beta} \geqq 0 \qquad (\delta Z/\delta \lambda)\lambda=0 \quad (4.43)$$

The marginal conditions in (4.41) and (4.42) are expressed as equalities because we only consider cases where N*, X* and Y* are non-zero.

The notional demand for labour schedule (N_N^*) is derived in this problem when $\lambda^*=0$. In this case we solve for N* and X* using the following log-linear versions of (4.41) and (4.42) when $\lambda=0$ (where lower case letters represent the logs of the variables):

$$\ln(\alpha A) + (\alpha-1)n^* + \beta x^* = w \qquad (4.44)$$

$$\ln(\beta A) + \alpha n^* + (\beta-1)x^* = m \qquad (4.45)$$

Solving for n* using (4.44) and (4.45) yields the following notional demand for labour schedule (n_N^*):

$$n_N^* = [(\beta-1)/(1-\alpha-\beta)]w - [\beta/(1-\alpha-\beta)]m - \phi \tag{4.46}$$

where

$$\phi = [(\beta-1)/(1-\alpha-\beta)][\ln(\alpha A) - (\beta/\{\beta-1\})\ln(\beta A)] \tag{4.47}$$

The responsiveness of employment to ceteris paribus changes in the real wage rate, which in the log-linear model yields the elasticity of the notional demand for labour (ε_w^N) is:

$$\delta n_N^*/\delta w = \varepsilon_w^N = (\beta-1)/(1-\alpha-\beta) \tag{4.48}$$

The notional demand for labour schedule has a real wage elasticity which exceeds unity. This elasticity takes into account both the output and substitution effects of real wage changes on the demand for labour.

The 'weak' version of the effective demand for labour schedule (N_E^*) arises in equations (4.41)-(4.43) when $\lambda^* > 0$. In this case the complementary slackness condition in (4.43) requires that the corresponding marginal condition be expressed as an equality. We can therefore solve for N^*, X^* and λ^* using the following log-linear specification of (4.41)-(4.43):

$$\ln(\alpha A) + (\alpha-1)n^* + \beta x^* + \ln(1-\lambda^*) = w \tag{4.49}$$

$$\ln(\beta A) + \alpha n^* + (\beta-1)x^* + \ln(1-\lambda^*) = m \tag{4.50}$$

$$y^* = y^O = \ln A + \alpha n^* + \beta x^* \tag{4.51}$$

An expression for n^* can be derived by solving for $(1-\lambda^*)$ and x^* in terms of n^* using (4.50) and (4.51) and substituting the results into (4.49). After rearrangement, this yields the 'weak' version of the effective demand for labour schedule (n_E^*):

$$n_E^* = \phi_1 - [\beta/(\alpha+\beta)]w + [\beta/(\alpha+\beta)]m +$$
$$[1/(\alpha+\beta)]y^O \tag{4.52}$$

where

$$\phi_1 = [-\beta/(\alpha+\beta)][\ln\beta + (1/\beta)\ln A - \ln\alpha] \tag{4.53}$$

The real wage elasticity of this version of the effective demand for labour (ε_w^{1E}), assuming that

$Y_w^0 = 0$, is:

$$\delta n^*_{1E} / \delta w = \varepsilon_w^{1E} = -\beta / (\alpha + \beta) \qquad (4.54)$$

Three major differences can be noted in comparing the 'weak' version of the effective demand for labour schedule in (4.52) with the associated notional demand for labour schedule in (4.46). First, the real wage elasticity of the effective schedule is below that of the corresponding notional schedule.[34] This occurs because this Keynesian model, while admitting the possibility of substitution effects operating on the demand for labour, does not allow for output effects of real wage changes on employment. Second, the effective demand for labour schedule allows for the level of aggregate demand, and thus output, to enter directly into the effective demand for labour schedule. As we emphasised in Section 1 above, neoclassical macromodels do not admit this possibility.[35] Third, note that the sign on the real price of the other factor of production differs between the two models. This again relates to the output effect of changes in input prices. (4.46) reveals that the notional demand for labour would fall in the event of a ceteris paribus rise in the price of the other factor of production (m). This occurs because the output of the firm would be expected to fall in such an event. When the firm is constrained by the level of demand, a rise in the price of the other factor would encourage firms to substitute labour for the other factor and, unless the rise in the price makes it unprofitable for the firm to continue to produce at current output levels (Y^0), a rise in the demand for labour would ensue.

Finally, we can use the model expressed in (4.41)-(4.43) to derive the 'strong' version of the effective demand for labour schedule by considering the case where $\beta = 0$ (the other input does not contribute to the output of the firm). The model once again becomes recursive, with (4.43) providing the solution for n* and (4.41) solving for λ*. In this case, the 'strong' version of the effective demand for labour (n^*_{2E}) is given as:

$$n^*_{2E} = (1/\alpha)y^0 - (1/\alpha)\ln A \qquad (4.55)$$

Real wages do not influence the demand for labour in this model unless Y_w^0 is non-zero.

The investigation into the effective demand

for labour schedules conducted in this section corresponds to a set of analysis generally ignored in the macroeconomic literature - that of cost minimising behaviour on the part of firms. Specifying the firm's problem as maximising profits subject to a demand constraint is formally identical to the typical problem of minimising costs at a given level of output. Both sets of analyses allow output to directly influence the effective demand for labour. Indeed, the employment function literature, where the level of employment is determined in part by the level of output, is typically motivated by considering a cost minimisation exercise.[36] Our analysis in this section suggests that such models can be considered Keynesian demand for labour schedules. These models imply that increases in the real level of expenditures would <u>directly</u> increase output and employment levels when firms are demand constrained. Furthermore, such increases in employment could occur with a rising level of real wages although, as the weak version of the model suggests, this might tend to reduce the overall expansion in employment. In contrast to neoclassical models based on the notional demand for labour schedule, the Keynesian models do not necessarily require real wage reductions to accompany increases in employment at the aggregate level. These models are also fairly pessimistic about the alleged positive employment effects that could be engineered through reductions in real wage rates, at least in the short run.

APPENDIX 4.1: MATHEMATICS OF THE NEOCLASSICAL MODEL

The real wage elasticity of the labour demand schedule based on a CES production function is derived as follows (for a given capital stock). Total differentiation of (4.2b) yields after rearrangement:

$$-(\rho/v)Q^{-[(\rho+v)/v]}\delta Q \ = \ -\rho(1-\delta)N^{-(\rho+1)}\delta N \quad (A4.1)$$

The marginal product of labour is then solved as:

$$\delta Q/\delta N \ = \ v(1-\delta)N^{-(\rho+1)}Q^{[(\rho+v)/v]} \quad (A4.2)$$

Under profit maximisation, the marginal product of labour will equal the real wage rate:

$$\delta Q / \delta N = W/P. \qquad (A4.3)$$

Combining (A4.2) and (A4.3) and taking logs:

$$\phi - (\rho-1)n + [(\rho+v)/v]q = w \qquad (A4.4)$$

where lower case letters represent the logs of the variables, and $\phi=\ln[v(1-\delta)]$. Solving for n in (A4.4) and replacing $[1/(\rho+1)]$ with the elasticity of substitution (σ) yields:

$$n = \sigma[\phi + (\{\rho+v\}/v)q - w]. \qquad (A4.5)$$

Differentiating (A4.5) with respect to w:

$$\delta n / \delta w = \sigma[(\{\rho+v\}/v)(\delta q/\delta n)(\delta n/\delta w) - 1] \qquad (A4.6)$$

Rearrangement of (A4.6) yields:

$$\varepsilon_w^D = \delta n/\delta w = -\sigma[1/\{1 - ([\rho+v]\delta q)/([\rho+1]v\delta n)\}] \qquad (A4.7)$$

Notice that by multiplying (A4.2) by N/Q yields the following expression for $\delta q/\delta n$:

$$(\delta Q/\delta N)(N/Q) = \delta q/\delta n = v(1-\delta)N^{-\rho}Q^{(\rho/v)} \qquad (A4.8)$$

Combining (A4.7) and (A4.8) we arrive at:

$$\varepsilon_w^D = -\sigma[1/\{1-([1-\delta][\rho+v]Q^{[\rho/v]})/([\rho+1]N^\rho)\}] \qquad (A4.9)$$

where N and Q are evaluated at their initial levels.

This equation forms the basis of our analysis of the permissable range for the elasticity of the labour demand curve under alternative assumptions regarding the elasticity of substitution (σ).[37] If the restriction v=1 is adopted (constant returns to scale), equation (A4.9) reduces to equation (4.5) in the text:[38]

$$\varepsilon_w^D = -\sigma[1/\{1 - (1-\delta)(Q/N)^\rho\}]. \qquad (4.5)$$

In the special case of the Cobb-Douglas production function, the elasticity of substitution equals unity (and thus $\rho=0$). In such circumstances (4.5) reduces to:

$$\varepsilon_w^D = -(1/\delta) \qquad (A4.10)$$

Static analysis

This expression is identical to that obtained in equation (4.4) in the text, where $\alpha = (1-\delta)$.

We next consider the cyclical movements in real unit labour costs (U). This analysis is conducted by deriving the elasticity of the log of U (u) with respect to changes in the real wage rate (u_w). Differentiating equation (4.6') in the text with respect to w yields:

$$u_w = \delta u/\delta w = 1 + \delta n/\delta w - (\delta q/\delta n)(\delta n/\delta w)$$
(A4.11)

By noting that $\delta n/\delta w$ defines the real wage elasticity of the demand for labour (ε_w^D), and combining the terms in ε_w^D in (A4.11):

$$u_w = 1 + \varepsilon_w^D(1 - \delta q/\delta n)$$
(A4.12)

In the case of constant returns to scale (v=1 in (4.26)), we can rewrite the expression for the elasticity of the demand for labour in (A4.7) as:

$$\varepsilon_w^D = \delta n/\delta w = -\sigma[1/(1 - \delta q/\delta n)]$$
(A4.7a)

By manipulating (A4.7a) we arrive at the following expression:

$$\delta q/\delta n = 1 + \sigma/\varepsilon_w^D$$
(A4.13)

Substitution of (A4.13) into (A4.12) yields:

$$u_w = 1 + \varepsilon_w^D[1 - 1 - \sigma/\varepsilon_w^D]$$
(A4.14)

Thus from (A4.14) we arrive at equation (4.9) in the text:

$$u_w = 1 - \sigma$$
(4.9)

NOTES

1. See Keynes (1937) for a clear exposition of this view.

2. This type of analysis is represented as the Keynesian theory in most prominent textbooks. See for example Branson (1972); Parkin and Bade (1982); and Sargent (1979). Notice, as well, that Friedman's (1968, 1975) critique of Keynesian theory only considers the synthesis model: 'Indeed the whole Keynesian argument... arose out of the supposition that it is possible to get workers... to accept lower real wages produced by inflation that they would not have accepted in

the direct form of a reduction in nominal wages' (Friedman, 1975, p.17).

3. Coddington (1976) elegantly summarises this phenomenon as follows: 'Like the interpretation of the work of any active mind, the interpretation of Keynes' writings requires the use of selection and emphasis: it requires a view as to what is central and what merely peripheral, what is essential and what merely incidental... in this way apparent inconsistencies may readily be resolved, at least to the satisfaction of those adhering to that interpretation' (p.1259).

4. X therefore consists of a vector of nominal prices multiplied by the components of K.

5. In the more general model where some (or all) other inputs are allowed to vary, the demand for labour schedule will depend on the real wage rate and the price of labour relative to the prices of these other factors of production.

6. See Sachs (1982) for example.

7. This specification is adopted by Alogoskoufis (1983) for example.

8. This is based on the familiar Le Chatelier principle in microeconomic theory (see for example Varian, 1978).

9. This specification is adopted by Lucas and Rapping (1969a) for example.

10. See Appendix 4.1 below.

11. It may appear odd that in models where labour is assumed to be the only variable factor of production, the elasticity of the labour demand curve depends on the size of the elasticity of substitution. The reason for this is that this variable influences the extent to which diminishing marginal productivity operates, and thus the extent of the output effect generated by changes in the real wage rate.

12. Sachs (1979) emphasises the importance of this variable to explain what are essentially long-run or secular movements in employment levels.

13. Stein (1982) uses this variable in his theoretical and empirical analyses of cyclical movements in output and employment.

14. Note, however, that when the labour demand curve is inelastic ($0 > \varepsilon_w^D > -1$) then the model predicts that u will move counter-cyclically.

15. See Metzler's equation 11 and the related discussion that follows (1981, p.54).

16. All page references to Keynes (1939) refer to the version of this paper reprinted as Appendix 3 in the General Theory 1973 edition.

17. Davidson accepts that consistency could be achieved by postulating that, for certain relevant regions, the neoclassical labour demand schedule is infinitely elastic with respect to the real wage rate (p.52). This implies that over this relevant range the marginal product of labour is

constant. This view is however inconsistent with Keynes' argument that 'an increase in employment can only occur to the accompanyment of a decline in the real wage rate' (1936, p.17).

18. All unspecified references refer to the General Theory.

19. His analysis could also be interpreted as implying that the labour supply schedule is kinked with respect to the money wage rate, with labour supply falling dramatically when money wages are reduced below current levels, and rising only slightly when money wages are increased above current levels.

20. Keynes discusses the price of 'wage goods' in this context since, as noted by Leijonhufvud (1968), his model of the goods market consists of two sectors, wage and investment goods. We ignore this feature of Keynes' analysis and refer the reader to Leijonhufvud.

21. Trevithic (1976) derives these propositions formally in a model which considers the supply of labour schedule to any particular industry.

22. This point is noted by Meltzer (1983) in his reply to Davidson. See his pp.73-4.

23. In a footnote to the above passage, Keynes notes further that it is particularly Chapter 2 of the General Theory 'which most needs to be revised' (1939, p.401).

24. We consider here only the case of a closed economy. Keynes also notes that the 'same conclusions hold for an open system, provided that equilibrium with the rest of the world can be secured by means of fluctuating exchange' (p.270).

25. Notice that Keynes must be assuming that the reduction in money wages reduces real wages as well. If this were not the case, his argument that workers tend to have a high relative propensity to consume would suggest that the fall in money wages might actually lead to an increased level of real consumption expenditure.

26. Dunlop himself argues that there probably exists a critical level of employment where the marginal productivity of labour begins to fall. An appropriate model, Dunlop concludes, 'would minimise the importance of cost curves except at the very peak of the boom...' (Dunlop, 1939, p.434).

27. The level of aggregate effective demand can, for our purposes, be taken as given by the intersection of the usual IS and LM curves as is typical in Keynesian analysis.

28. The case where $Y^* < Y^0$ is often referred to in the disequilibrium Keynesian literature as 'repressed inflation'. See, for example, Malinvaud (1977).

29. (W/F_N) defines the marginal cost of output.

30. This can be derived formally as follows. If $\lambda^* = 0$, the firm is on its notional demand for labour schedule with employment set such that $F_N = W$. When a demand constraint arises such that $\lambda^* > 0$, employment will be below this level.

If diminishing marginal productivity of labour is operating, this level of employment will be associated with a higher marginal product of labour than that determined on the notional schedule. Thus on the effective demand for labour schedule, $F_N > W$ and, by (4.16), λ^* is a fraction.

31. If investment expenditure is financed internally by the firm, then this analysis helps explain why investment rises when real wages fall.

32. We can also note that the marginal costs of the demand constraint in terms of profits foregone by the firm (λ^*) may rise or fall according to (4.25). The first two terms inside the second set of brackets in (4.25) are necessarily positive if $Y_W^O < 0$, thus the sign of λ_W^* will depend on whether these terms are in total greater or less than unity. The economic intuition for this is straightforward. Consider a fall in real wages. This will tend to raise the value of λ^*, since the firm's unit profits for an output level of Y^O will rise. However, the ensuing increase in output (Y_W^O) will lead to a rise in employment levels and thus a fall in the marginal product of labour, tending to squeeze unit profits. The combination of these two effects leaves the sign of λ_W^* ambiguous.

33. See Keynes (1936, pp.358-71). See also the model developed by Solow and Stiglitz (1968) in which aggregate demand and real wages are positively related.

34. In the case of a Cobb-Douglas production function, the elasticity of the effective demand for labour schedule will always be below unity as long as $Y_W^O = 0$.

35. In a critical assessment of neoclassical macroeconomic theory, Hahn (1982) argues: 'Appearances belie reality. Firms expensively engaged in forecasting the demand for, say, motor cars are really [according to neoclassical analysis] forming price expectations.... Economics, being the subject that it is, cannot easily refute all this. But there certainly is sufficient ground for thinking again' (p.46). The two versions of the Keynesian effective demand for labour schedules are, in our view, a starting point for 'thinking again' about the determinants of the demand for labour in the aggregate.

36. See for example Brechling (1965, 1975).

37. Equation (A4.9) reveals that this elasticity is fairly insensitive to the values of δ and v. The reason for this is that the term in δ and v must be a fraction in the model (see text for a discussion). Thus changes in these parameters should produce only negligible effects on the elasticity of demand for labour).

38. Notice that in (A4.9) the range of v is in fact very restricted if the term in the square bracket is to remain positive.

Chapter Five

THE DEMAND FOR LABOUR SCHEDULE: DYNAMIC ANALYSIS

In the previous chapter we analysed and compared static versions of neoclassical and alternative Keynesian models of the demand for labour schedule. In this chapter we extend the analysis to dynamic versions of these models based on the analysis of forward-looking firms conducted by Sargent (1978, 1979). Our main focus in this chapter is whether the predictions produced by the static models considered in the previous chapter survive the introduction of dynamic considerations.[1]

This chapter is organised as follows. The neoclassical analysis as developed by Sargent (1978, 1979) is considered in Section 1. This analysis is extended to capture the alternative Keynesian perspective in the next section where we introduce current and expected future demand constraints into the model. Concluding comments are offered in Section 3.

1. THE NEOCLASSICAL DYNAMIC DEMAND FOR LABOUR SCHEDULE

The intertemporal demand for labour schedule developed by Sargent (1978, 1979) is based on considering a representative forward-looking firm which does not maximise current profits but instead maximises the present value of its expected profits over time by choosing the current stock of labour employed and a contingency plan for its future employment levels. Dynamic considerations arise from the interaction of two particular factors. First, if the firm faces increasing marginal costs of adjusting its employment levels then, when warranted, the firm would be expected to adjust these levels only partially in any given period.

This is a typical argument made to justify the inclusion of lagged employment levels in the static demand for labour equations such as (4.3) of the previous chapter.[2]   However, in the context of forward-looking firms, this approach is insufficient.   Surely the firm would know that it faces such costs of adjustment, and would therefore be expected to take into account any desired future changes in its demand for labour in determining the current period's level of demand.   A forward-looking firm would therefore want to begin the adjustment process before such changes are warranted by external factors.   A second and related consideration is to uncover what factors may signal to the firm that its future desired demand for labour is expected to differ from its current desired level.   In a neoclassical context, the firm would be keenly interested in the expected future evolution of the real wage rate.[3]   Thus the expected future values of the real wage would influence the firm's demand for labour in the current period.   Within a rational expectations framework, the firm would form anticipations of the future evolution of real wages on the basis of all currently available information.   This is the problem set out by Sargent which yields a dynamic neoclassical demand for labour equation which incorporates lags in employment and real wages as well.[4]

The analysis generates two types of model, one which focuses solely on real wage movements, and a more elaborate version which allows for other variables to enter the decision-making process of firms.   The former type is derived by postulating that firms maximise the expected present value of its current and future profits by choosing its stock of labour for the current period and a contingency plan for this stock for all future periods.   This exercise is repeated by the firm every year as new information becomes available. Formally the firm's problem is to maximise:

$$E_t PV_t = \Sigma_{j=0}^{\infty} \alpha^j [Y_{t+j} - (\beta/2)(N_{t+j} - N_{t+j-1})^2$$
$$- E_t w_{t+j} N_{t+j}] \tag{5.1}$$

for the given quadratic production function:

$$Y_{t+j} = f_0 N_{t+j} - (f_1/2)(N_{t+j}^2) \tag{5.2}$$

Dynamic analysis

where E_t is an expectations operator representing the mathematical expectations formed at time t;[5] PV_t is the present value of profits in real terms (deflated by output price): α is a real discount factor ($0<\alpha<1$); Y_{t+j} is the level of real output in period $t+j$; N_{t+j} is employment in period $t+j$; $E_t w_{t+j}$ is the expected real wage rate in period $t+j$; $\beta/2$ represents a cost of adjustment parameter; and f_0, f_1 are given production parameters. The term in $(\beta/2)(N_{t+j} - N_{t+j-1})^2$ represents the quadratic costs of adjusting the level of employment which reduces the firm's real level of profits at every employment level.[6] All the coefficients in (5.1) and (5.2) are positive.

The corresponding first-order conditions for achieving an optimum are the following Euler equations ($j=0...\infty$):[7][8]

$$(\delta E_t PV_t)/(\delta N_{t+j}) = f_0 - f_1 N_{t+j} - \beta(N_{t+j}-N_{t+j-1})$$
$$+ \beta\alpha(N_{t+j+1}-N_{t+j}) = E_t w_{t+j} \qquad (5.3)$$

Notice that if $\beta=0$, the firm does not face any costs in adjusting its employment levels; then (5.3) collapses to the static model:

$$N_{t+j} = (1/f_1)(f_0 - E_t w_{t+j}) \qquad (j=0...\infty) \quad (5.4)$$

Thus the costs of adjustment play the crucial role of linking each period's (optimal) level of employment to past and future levels, thereby generating a dynamic employment equation.

Dividing all the terms in (5.3) by β and rearranging, we can rewrite this equation using the lag operator (L) as:

$$\alpha[1 - (\phi/\alpha)L + (1/\alpha)L^2)]N_{t+j+1}$$
$$= [1/\beta][E_t w_{t+j} - f_0] \qquad (5.5)$$

where
$$\phi = (f_1/\beta) + (\alpha+1) \qquad (5.6)$$

Sargent (1979, pp.197-8) shows how a second-order difference equation such as (5.5) can be factorised as:

$$\alpha[(1 - \lambda_1 L)(1 - \lambda_2 L)]N_{t+j+1}$$
$$= [1/\beta][E_t w_{t+j} - f_0] \qquad (5.7)$$

124

where:

$$\lambda_1 \lambda_2 = 1/\alpha, \text{ and } (\lambda_1 + \lambda_2) = \phi/\alpha \qquad (5.8)$$

Since it is assumed that the system described by
(5.7) converges to an equilibrium (i.e. the
transversality condition holds), we can divide all
terms in (5.7) by $(1-\lambda_2 L)$ and by applying a
'reverse' Koyck transformation we can rewrite this
equation as: [9]

$$N_{t+j} = \lambda_1 N_{t+j-1} - (\lambda_1/\beta)\Sigma_{i=0}^{\infty}(1/\lambda_2)^i$$

$$(E_{t+j} w_{t+j+i} - f_0) \qquad (5.9)$$

where λ_1 is a positive fraction and, by (5.8), λ_2
is greater than unity.

Equation (5.9) is the dynamic demand schedule
for labour which expresses current employment as
depending on the previous periods' employment level
and the current and future values of the real wage
rate. The remaining problem for the firm is to
form predictions of the future evolution of the
real wage rate given the information in the firm's
possession concerning the deterministic portion of
its dynamic path. Thus if the real wage rate
(w_{t+j}) is modelled in general as following an nth
order autoregressive process such as:

$$w_t = \rho_1 w_{t-1} + \cdots + \rho_n w_{t-n} + \varepsilon_t \qquad (5.10)$$

where ε_t is the stochastic (and unpredictable)
shock ('innovation') to the real wage rate in any
period t $[\varepsilon_t \sim NI(0, \sigma_\varepsilon^2)]$, then the firm can solve
for $E_{t+j} w_{t+j+i}$ using (5.10) if it knows the
particular values for the ρ_js (j=1...n). Combining
(5.9) and (5.10) yields the following general
specification of the dynamic demand for labour
schedule: [10]

$$N_{t+j} = \delta_N(L)N_{t+j} + \delta_w(L)w_{t+j} + \delta_0 \varepsilon_{t+j} \qquad (5.11)$$

where δ_0 is a negative constant; δ_N is restricted
to just one lag; and δ_w is of nth order. Notice
that the current values of the δ coefficients in
(5.11) are restricted to equal zero, and from (5.9)
the δ_w coefficients sum to a negative value.

Equation (5.11) expresses employment as
following a first-order autoregressive process
which is inversely related to the n lags in the
real wage rate. This equation forms the basis of

the Granger-causality tests discussed in Part Three below, with a few alterations. First, the model abstracts from trends in productivity due in part to capital accumulation by firms. Thus the model is best interpreted as capturing only the cyclical movements in employment with the variables in (5.11) expressed in deviations from any given trends. Second, the employment autoregression for the individual firm relates strictly to only a first-order process. However, assuming that (heroically) the model can meaningfully be aggregated across the entire economy consisting of many industries and firms, the autoregressive process for aggregate employment will probably be of a higher order.(11) There are two reasons for this. First, the timing of the decision-making process within any one period may differ from firm to firm within any given industry. If the decision-making period is one year, and different firms make these decisions in, say, different quarters of the year, then at the aggregate level four quarterly lags will appear in the dynamic employment equation. The second reason is a statistical point noted by Granger and Newbold (1977, pp.28-31). They show that the aggregation of two independent first-order autoregressive processes results at most in a second-order autoregressive process augmented by a first-order moving average error (an ARMA(2,1) process). This argument suggests that for our purposes aggregating across firms in different industries which are sufficiently separated in the economy will produce higher-order lags in the aggregate employment autoregression. These two sets of arguments have been typically appealed to in justifying the inclusion of further lags in employment in aggregate versions of (5.11).(12)

Before proceeding to a discussion of extensions of this analysis, we first describe briefly the operation of the model. Consider a firm in long-run equilibrium in any period (t+j). The firm observes in period (t+j) an unpredicted fall in the real wage rate it faces, which it expects to be maintained into the indefinite future.(13) Thus the new long-run equilibrium position is associated with a lower expected future real wage rate and a new higher level of employment. However, because it faces increasing marginal costs of adjusting its employment levels, the firm will move off the long-run demand for labour curve and onto a new short-run curve. Note that the short-run curve is less elastic than the corresponding long-run curve since it incorporates additional costs in employing more (or less) labour in the short run. Thus a short-run equilibrium position will be reached with employment rising above its initial level but below the eventual equilibrium position. Assuming no further shocks to the real wage rate, in subsequent periods the firm will gradually increase its employment levels to new positions which lie on new short-run labour demand curves until the eventual equilibrium position is attained.

Unlike the static analysis of the demand for labour schedule which suggests that the fall in the real wage rate generates an instantaneous change in employment levels along a given long-run demand for labour curve, the dynamic analysis predicts that the adjustment path for employment will not be observed as movements along the long-run demand for labour curve, but will follow a succession of short-run curves with employment approaching the eventual equilibrium position asymptotically. The dynamic model also generates predictions concerning the real wage-employment relationship which differ from those produced by models based on the static demand for labour schedule.

Because firms face costs in adjusting their level of employment, the real wage elasticity of the demand for labour in the short run is much lower than that presumed by the static analysis. It is only after the firm has adjusted fully to the real wage change that this elasticity will equal that predicted by the static model. Thus in terms of (5.11) the short-run real wage elasticity of the demand for labour equals $(\delta N_{t+j})/(\delta \varepsilon_{t+j}) = \delta_0$, representing the impact effect on employment of an 'innovation' in the real wage rate. The long-run real wage elasticity of employment (ε_w^D) which takes into account the distributed lags in the process of adjusting employment levels is given as:

$$\varepsilon_w^D = [\Sigma_{i=1}^n \delta_{wi}]/[1 - \Sigma_{i=1}^n \delta_{Ni}] \qquad (5.12)$$

In a time series context, then, the appropriate empirical question is the implied long-run cyclical response of employment to real wage changes rather than any contemporaneous correlation between employment and real wages.[14] Notice, however, that (5.9) combined with (5.10) implies that the sum of the δ_w coefficients will be negative. In addition, the stylised fact that fluctuations in

aggregate employment generally exceed those of real
wages implies that ε_w^D should exceed unity (in
absolute values) as in the static neoclassical
model. The model implies that once the serial
correlation in employment levels is taken into
account, when taken together, lagged real wages
will appear to be negatively associated with
current employment levels in a time series
exercise. This proposition is examined in some of
the tests reported in Part Three below.

Additional factors of production

Sargent (1979) argues that the dynamic model
captured by (5.9) represents the demand side of the
labour market which, when combined with a rational
expectations version of the Lucas and Rapping
(1969a) model of supply behaviour, yields a new
classical model of employment fluctuations
incorporating serially-correlated movements in
employment.[15] However, this dynamic demand
schedule for employment on its own is sufficiently
general to admit several alternative avenues of
analysis. In the following section we demonstrate
how this model can straightforwardly be generalised
to incorporate potential aggregate demand
constraints on the dynamic employment path as
emphasised in disequilibrium theory. For the
moment we consider here a highly simplified
extension to the model which captures the arguments
found in Sachs (1979), Kirkpatrick (1982), Layard
and Symons (1984) and Symons (1985) concerning the
influence of oil prices on aggregate employment
levels.
A simple extension to the model described in
the previous section is derived by introducing a
stochastic productivity term in the production
function. We can re-specify the production
function expressed in (5.2) as:

$$Y_{t+j} = (f_0 + E_t a_{t+j})N_{t+j} - (f_1/2)(N_{t+j}^2) \tag{5.13}$$

where a_{t+j} is a stochastic variable which shifts
the marginal product of labour at every level of
employment. a_{t+j} can be interpreted as capturing
changes in the employment levels of other variable
factors of production which are complementary to
labour. Notice that by capturing the effects of
other factors of production through the term in

a_{t+j}, we are ignoring potential substitution effects between labour and these other factors.

Introducing this stochastic productivity term into the analysis yields a dynamic employment equation which is identical to (5.9) except that an additional term must be included. Sargent (1979, pp.196-8) shows that the resulting equation will be:

$$N_{t+j} = \lambda_1 N_{t+j-1} - (\lambda_1/\beta)\Sigma_{i=0}^{\infty}(1/\lambda_2)^i$$

$$(E_{t+j}[w_{t+j+i} - a_{t+j+i}] - f_0) \qquad (5.14)$$

Equation (5.14) reveals that any observed change in the current level of labour productivity (a_{t+j}) or any expected future change in this variable ($E_{t+j}a_{t+j+i}$) will generate a response in current employment in the same direction. Further, if a_{t+j} is assumed to follow an exogenously determined dynamic pattern which includes certain predictable components, say an AR(z) model, then the forward-looking firm can utilise this information in choosing its desired employment level for the current period. Thus, as with the single dynamic model of the demand for labour, the employment path can be written as the following distributed lag equation:

$$N_{t+j} = \delta_N(L)N_{t+j} + \delta_w(L)w_{t+j} + \delta_a(L)a_{t+j}$$

$$+ \varepsilon_{t+j} + u_{t+j} \qquad (5.15)$$

where $\delta_a(L)$ includes z lags whose coefficients sum to a positive number; and u_{t+j} is a stochastic variable $[u_{t+j} \sim NI(0,\sigma_u^2)]$ representing new information available at time $t+j$ concerning current and future values of a_{t+j}. Any movements in a_{t+j} will generate shifts in the long-run demand for labour curve.

Assume that the only other factor of production is oil and that, for simplicity, the firm's technology is such that it must employ labour (N_{t+j}) and oil (O_{t+j}) in fixed proportions:

$$O_{t+j} = \gamma N_{t+j} \qquad (j=0...\infty) \qquad (5.16)$$

Equation (5.16) rules out any substitution possibilities between oil and labour. Further, it is assumed that the firm's demand for oil is inversely associated with the real price of oil (m_{t+j}) and that the firm can adjust its oil inputs without cost. In such circumstances the firm's problem is to maximise:

$$E_t PV_t = \Sigma_{j=0}^{\infty} \alpha^i [Y_{t+j} - (\beta/2)(N_{t+j} - N_{t+j-1})^2$$
$$- E_t w_{t+j} N_{t+j} - \gamma E_t m_{t+j} N_{t+j}] \quad (5.17)$$

subject to:

$$Y_{t+j} = [f_0 + (\phi/2)\gamma N_{t+j}]N_{t+j} - (f_1/2)N_{t+j}^2 \quad (5.18)$$

where we assume that:

$$a_{t+j} = (\phi/2)O_{t+j} = (\phi/2)\gamma N_{t+j} \quad (5.19)$$

Following the analysis above, the solution to this problem will be of the form:[17]

$$N_{t+j} = \lambda_1^* N_{t+j-1} - (\lambda_1^*/\beta) \Sigma_{i=0}^{\infty} (1/\lambda_2^*)^i$$
$$(E_{t+j} w_{t+j+i} + \gamma E_{t+j} m_{t+j+i} - f_0) \quad (5.20)$$

Equation (5.20) differs from the corresponding equation (5.9) derived above in that it includes terms in future expected oil prices and also has different parameters in the employment autoregression.

After imposing rational expectations, we can write the new general dynamic demand for labour schedule as:

$$N_{t+j} = \delta_N(L)N_{t+j} + \delta_w(L)w_{t+j} + \delta_m(L)m_{t+j}$$
$$+ \delta_{01}\varepsilon_{t+j} + \delta_{02}u_{t+j} \quad (5.21)$$

where δ_{01} and δ_{02} are negative; the δ_m term incorporates z lags in oil prices (m_{t+j}); and the sum of the δ_m terms is negative.

Our revised dynamic demand for labour schedule expressed in (5.21) is consistent with the view that the recent observed falls in employment are the result of the oil price shocks of 1973-4 and 1979-80. (5.21) implies that employment levels are negatively associated with a distributed lag of real oil prices. Thus if the oil price follows, say, a random walk, then a once-and-for-all increase in the price of oil will permanently reduce employment levels below what they otherwise would have been. This would be shown as a backwards shift of the long-run demand for labour curve. Further, this model is consistent with neoclassical analysis in first emphasising the importance of relative prices on employment and, second, in implying that if the dynamic path of real wages could somehow be reduced to a permanently lower average level, a (lagged) rise in employment levels would be generated. Finally, we can note that if (5.21) is the relevant equation determining employment fluctuations, then empirical results based on (5.11) may be of dubious validity. This point is emphasised in the empirical analyses conducted by Kirkpatrick (1982) and Symons and Layard (1984).

We have demonstrated in this section that dynamic neoclassical models of the demand for labour predict that current and lagged real wage rates should explain at least a large part of observed fluctuations in employment. The real wage rate is emphasised in this literature precisely because it is the relevant relative price of employing labour, and therefore enters directly into the decision-making process of firms. Furthermore, it is a variable that the firm can directly observe since it is operating simultaneously in product and labour markets. Thus neoclassical models imply that, ceteris paribus, reductions in real wages would raise the profitability of firms and thereby induce them to employ more labour and raise output levels. This employment-enhancing effect of real wage cuts will be strengthened if substitution possibilities between factors of production are considered. This raises the question of what arguments can be advanced to support the view that real wage movements are fairly unimportant in explaining fluctuations in employment over the business cycle and the associated pessimism concerning the potential employment-enhancing effects of real wage cuts. This is the subject of the next section.

2. A KEYNESIAN DYNAMIC DEMAND FOR LABOUR SCHEDULE

The analysis in Section 3 of the previous chapter investigated the choice-theoretic foundations of how output can be introduced into a demand for labour schedule. This analysis implies that a demand for labour schedule which includes output as an argument is consistent with so-called 'rational' behaviour. As in the spirit of Keynes' perspective, it is the market mechanism which appears 'irrational', according to this analysis, in the sense that flexible wages and prices do not necessarily ensure the maintenance of full employment.

This analysis could be extended in a number of directions. A first step would be to specify labour supply behaviour and combine this with the effective demand for labour schedule in deriving a partial disequilibrium model of the labour market. Of course, such an analysis would be predicated on a theory explaining real wage adjustments. The market clearing theory of price adjustment as adopted in neoclassical theory could be a first step here.[18] A model of this variety could explain fluctuations in aggregate employment but would fail to capture Keynes' notion of involuntary unemployment.[19] A further development would be to consider a multi-sectoral version of the Keynesian model which explicitly includes a goods and money market and admits flexible wages and prices. This is the path taken by Gale (1983) in a slightly different framework. However, our major concern in these pages is the specification of the aggregate demand for labour schedule and the important role that this schedule plays, on its own, in establishing propositions concerning employment fluctuations which are amenable to empirical testing. Thus rather than extending the (admittedly) primitive analysis of Chapter Four, it is more useful for our purposes to consider closely the empirical propositions derived from a model of the effective demand for labour schedule to compare with the predictions derived from the neoclassical models premised on the notional demand for labour schedule. To accomplish this task, we must incorporate dynamic considerations into the analysis. This is the topic in this section. The analysis provides an explanation of why firms may find it necessary to engage in forecasting the level of demand for its products.

The analysis is derived by considering the effects of introducing potential demand constraints on the dynamic neoclassical labour demand schedule discussed in the previous section. This allows us to differentiate between effective and notional dynamic demand for labour schedules. The dynamic effective demand for labour schedule is derived by considering a representative forward-looking firm which produces an output (Y) using two variable factors of production: labour (N) and some other factor (X). The firm maximises the expected

present value of its profits by making contingency
plans for N and X for given exogenous processes
determining the paths of real wages (w), the real
price of the other factor (m), and the real level
of demand for the firm's product (Y^0). A key
assumption of the model is that the costs of
adjusting labour far exceed those of adjusting the
other factor. We base our analysis on Sargent's
(1979) version of the neoclassical demand for
labour schedule which considers two factors of
production, each of which enters into the
production function as a separate and independent
argument.[20] This allows him to ignore potential
substitution effects between the two factors,
thereby considerably simplifying the analysis.
This particular specification is convenient for our
purposes for two reasons. First, Sargent's (1978)
two variable factor model where the marginal
product of each factor is independent of the
employment level of the other factor yields the
same dynamic demand for labour schedule as that
expressed in equation (5.9) above. The results
presented in this chapter for the dynamic effective
demand for labour schedule can therefore be
directly compared with the neoclassical model of
the previous section. Second, this specification
allows the firm to produce a level of output equal
to the level of demand even though the high
relative costs of adjusting employment levels will
lead the firm to adjust employment only sluggishly
to changes in the level of demand for its output.
    Formally, the firm's problem is to maximise
the expected present value of its lifetime profits
for exogenously-given relative prices and the
demand for its output by solving the following
lagrangian expression:

$$\text{Max } Z = \Sigma_{j=0}^{\infty} \, \alpha^j [Y_{t+j} - (\beta/2)(N_{t+j} - N_{t+j-1})^2$$
$$- E_t w_{t+j} N_{t+j} - E_t m_{t+j} X_{t+j}$$
$$+ \lambda_j E_t (Y_{t+j}^0 - Y_{t+j})] \qquad (5.22)$$

subject to the production function:

$$Y_{t+j} = F(N_{t+j}, X_{t+j}, \overline{K})$$

$$F_N, F_X > 0; \quad F_{NN}, F_{XX} < 0; \quad F_{XN} = F_{NX} > 0 \qquad (5.23)$$

where α, Y_{t+j}, $E_t w_{t+j}$ and β are defined as in the
previous section; $E_t Y_{t+j}^0$ is the expected level of

demand (in real terms) for all future periods $(t+j)$; and the λ_js are the marginal costs associated with any (potential) future demand constraint expressed in terms of foregone future discount (real) profits of the firm. The specification adopted in (5.22) states that the firm faces increasing costs of adjusting its labour force (N_{t+j}), but can adjust the employment level of the other factor costlessly.[21]

The first-order conditions associated with this problem are given by the following Euler equations and corresponding complementary slackness conditions:

$$\delta Z/\delta N_{t+j} = (1-\lambda_j)F_N - \beta(N_{t+j} - N_{t+j-1})$$
$$+ \beta\alpha(N_{t+j+1} - N_{t+j}) \leqq E_t w_{t+j}$$
$$\text{and} \quad (\delta Z/\delta N_{t+j})N_{t+j}=0 \qquad (5.24)$$

$$\delta Z/\delta X_{t+j} = (1-\lambda_j)F_X \leqq E_t m_{t+j}$$
$$\text{and} \quad (\delta Z/\delta X_{t+j})X_{t+j}=0 \qquad (5.25)$$

$$\delta Z/\delta\lambda_j = E_t Y^O_{t+j} - Y_{t+j} \geqq 0$$
$$\text{and} \quad (\delta Z/\delta\lambda_j)\lambda_j=0 \qquad (5.26)$$

where F_N and F_X are evaluated at period $t+j$. The system made up of (5.24)-(5.26) represents three j equations $(j=0...\infty)$ solving for the three j unknowns: λ_j; N_{t+j}; and X_{t+j}. We assume thoughout our analysis that N_{t+j} and X_{t+j} are positive for all periods. Thus by the complementary slackness conditions, the equations (5.24) and (5.25) must be expressed as equalities.

Consider first the case when $\lambda_j=0$ for all periods; i.e. effective demand constraints are never binding on the firm. Under these conditions the model yields the dynamic neoclassical model as derived by Sargent.[22] The neoclassical version of the notional dynamic demand for labour schedule can therefore be interpreted as a special case of this more general model when it is assumed that the demand for the firm's output does not, and will never in future periods, act as a constraint on the firm's demand for labour. All that is needed to motivate the analysis of the effective dynamic demand for labour schedule is that the firm attaches a non-zero probability that it may be constrained by the level of aggregate demand at some future date.

Consider next the other extreme where λ_j is positive in all periods.[23] This implies that (5.26) must also be expressed as an equality. We can rearrange (5.24) and (5.25) to derive expressions for λ_j as:

$$\lambda_j = 1 - (1/F_N)(\beta\Delta N_{t+j} - \beta\alpha\Delta N_{t+j+1} + E_t w_{t+j}) \tag{5.27}$$

$$\lambda_j = 1 - (1/F_X)(E_t m_{t+j}) \tag{5.28}$$

where Δ represents the first difference of the variable. Equations (5.27) and (5.28) are the dynamic counterparts of the first-order conditions derived for the static model above. As before, λ_j represents the current real costs to the firm of the demand constraints in terms of foregone profits.[24] Notice that λ_j is negatively related to $E_t w_{t+j}$, $E_t m_{t+j}$ and β.[25] As in the static model of the effective demand for labour schedule, a fall (rise) in current and future expected input prices raises (lowers) these costs in the dynamic model. In addition, the lower (higher) the costs of adjusting the inputs, the larger (smaller) are these foregone profits. This occurs because the lower the costs incurred by the firm in adjusting its inputs, the higher its overall level of profits at any output level.

To solve for the dynamic effective demand for labour schedule, we first combine (5.27) and (5.28) to eliminate λ_j, which after rearranging yields the following expression for N_{t+j}:

$$-\beta\Delta N_{t+j} + \beta\alpha\Delta N_{t+j+1} = E_t w_{t+j} - (F_N/F_X)(E_t m_{t+j}) \tag{5.29}$$

A linear approximation is required at this point to eliminate the nuisance term in $(F_N/F_X)(E_t m_{t+j})$. Consider the production function which for convenience we express without the term in the capital stock ($\overline{K}$) and without ($t+j$) subscripts as:

$$Y = F(N,X) \tag{5.23a}$$

We can write the marginal products of the two factors as:

$$F_N = g_1(N,X) \tag{5.30}$$

$$F_X = g_2(N,X) \tag{5.31}$$

An inversion of (5.30) yields an expression for the other input (X) as:

$$X = g_3(N,Y) \tag{5.32}$$

Substituting (5.32) into (5.30) and (5.31) we can therefore express the nuisance term in (5.29) as:

$$(F_N/F_X)(E_t m_{t+j}) =$$

$$\{[g_1(N,g_3\{N,Y\})]/[g_2(N,g_3\{N,Y\})]\}\{E_t m_{t+j}\}$$

$$= h(N,Y)M \tag{5.33}$$

where $E_t m_{t+j}$ is referred to as M.

Using a Taylor's expansion around an arbitrary point $\hat{N},\hat{Y},\hat{M}$, we can approximate (5.33) as:

$$h(N,Y)M \simeq h(\hat{N},\hat{Y})\hat{M} + h_N(\hat{N},\hat{Y})\hat{M}(N-\hat{N}) +$$

$$h_y(\hat{N},\hat{Y})\hat{M}(Y-\hat{Y}) + h(\hat{N},\hat{Y})(M-\hat{M}) \tag{5.34}$$

where $h_N(.)$ and $h_y(.)$ are partial derivatives of the h function in (5.33) with respect to N and Y respectively. Combining terms in N, Y and M and substituting for Y using the marginal condition (5.26) yields after rearrangment:

$$(F_N/F_X)(E_t m_{t+j}) = h(N,Y)M \simeq a_0 - a_1 N_{t+j} +$$

$$a_2 E_t Y^0_{t+j} + a_3 E_t m_{t+j} \tag{5.35}$$

where:[26]

$$a_0 = \hat{M}[h_N(\hat{N},\hat{Y})\hat{N} + h_y(\hat{N},\hat{Y})\hat{Y}] > 0;$$

$$a_1 = -\hat{M}[h_N(\hat{N},\hat{Y})] > 0;$$

$$a_2 = \hat{M}[h_y(\hat{N},\hat{Y})] > 0;$$

$$a_3 = h(\hat{N},\hat{Y}) > 0.$$

Substituting our linear approximation in (5.35) into (5.29) and after collecting terms in the different lags for N_t yields:

$$\beta\alpha N_{t+j+1} + [a_1 + \beta(1+\alpha)]N_{t+j} + \beta N_{t+j-1}$$

$$= E_t w_{t+j} - a_3 E_t m_{t+j} - a_2 E_t Y^0_{t+j} \tag{5.36}$$

Dividing all terms by β, we can rewrite this equation using the lag operator as:

$$\alpha[1 + (\phi/\alpha)L + (1/\alpha)L^2]N_{t+j+1}$$
$$= (1/\beta)[E_t w_{t+j} - a_3 E_t m_{t+j} - a_2 E_t a Y^O_{t+j}] \quad (5.37)$$

where

$$\phi = -[(a_1/\beta) + (1+\alpha)] \quad (5.38)$$

Applying the analysis provided by Sargent (1979) for the dynamic neoclassical demand for labour schedule, we can factorise (5.37) as:

$$\alpha(1-\delta_1 L)(1-\delta_2 L)N_{t+j+1}$$
$$= (1/\beta)[E_t w_{t+j} - a_3 E_t m_{t+j} - a_2 E_t Y^O_{t+j}] \quad (5.39)$$

where δ_1 is a positive fraction and δ_2 is greater than unity such that:[27]

$$\delta_1 \delta_2 = 1/\alpha \quad (5.40a)$$

$$(\delta_1 + \delta_2) = \phi/\alpha \quad (5.40b)$$

Dividing all terms in (5.39) by $(1-\delta_2 L)$ and after applying the 'reverse' Koyck transformation, we arrive at the following dynamic effective demand for labour schedule:

$$N_{t+j} = \delta_1 N_{t+j-1} - (\delta_1/\beta)\Sigma^{\alpha}_{i=0}(1/\delta_2)^i[E_{t+j}m_{t+j+i}$$
$$- a_3 E_{t+j}m_{t+j+i} - a_2 E_{t+j}Y^O_{t+j+i}] \quad (5.41)$$

Equation (5.41) defines the dynamic effective demand for labour schedule with employment depending on all future expected values of the input prices and the future expected levels of demand. Real input prices are relevant in the firm's contingency plan for employment under an effective demand constraint because at any expected output level, the firm must choose the relative intensities in which the factors are applied. This choice will be based on a comparison of the relative costs of employing each factor and the additional relative costs of adjusting the employment levels of each factor if necessary. Notice three points about the coefficients on the exogenous variables in (5.41). First, the coefficients on the price of the other factor are

137

unambiguously positive in this model, while the neoclassical model predicts that these coefficients will be negative.[28] The firm is only allowed the choice of varying the relative intensities of the factors in producing a given output level, thus a ceteris paribus rise (fall) in the price of the other factor will induce the firm to employ more (less) labour. Second, the contingency plan for employment depends positively on the future expected levels of demand. Since it faces high costs of adjusting its labour force, anticipated future changes in demand conditions induce the firm to begin changing the level of its demand for labour in the current period. Third, the expected future levels of the real wage rate exert a negative influence on the effective demand for labour due to the existence of substitution possibilities between the two factors. Notice that the real wage effect on employment in this model only reflects these substitution possibilities; the output effect of real wages on employment is denied. Thus although this is not at all clear from (5.41), the coefficient on real wages in this dynamic demand for labour schedule should in fact be far lower than than presumed by the neoclassical model.[29]

Strictly speaking, (5.41) describes the information set that firms require in determining the current level of employment. An empirical version of this equation can be derived when rational expectations are imposed to allow the firm to solve for $E_{t+j}w_{t+j+i}$, $E_{t+j}m_{t+j+i}$ and for $E_{t+j}Y^0_{t+j+i}$. If these variables can be adequately described as following independent autoregressive processes, then following the arguments made concerning the neoclassical model in the previous section, we can define the general specification of the dynamic effective demand for labour schedule as:

$$N_t = \delta_N(L)N_t + \delta_w(L)w_t + \delta_m(L)m_t$$
$$+ \delta_y(L)Y_t + \varepsilon_{it} \qquad (5.42)$$

where the lengths of the various δ_j (j = N, w, m, Y) coefficients are determined by the length of the (independent) autoregressive processes driving each of the variables; all the δ_0 coefficients are restricted to zero; and ε_{it} (i = 1, 2, 3) represent new information concerning current and future real wages, the real price of the other input, and the

138

level of real demand respectively. Notice that the sum of the δ_w coefficients are negative and the sums of the δ_m and δ_Y coefficients positive.

3. CONCLUDING COMMENTS

The theoretical investigations carried out in Parts One and Two considered aggregate demand-induced cycles in aggregate employment and output. The secular, or long-run, relationships between aggregate variables were therefore totally ignored.[30] Our analysis distinguished between two sets of perspectives.

Models based on the neoclassical, or equilibrium, perspective emphasise the role of relative price movements in generating fluctuations in aggregate employment. These models were associated with what we called the notional demand for labour schedule. The unifying theme of neoclassical models is the proposition that fluctuations in output and employment are, in general, directly associated with inverse real wage movements.[31]

Alternative Keynesian, or disequilibrium, models of employment fluctuations minimise the importance of real wages. These models are associated with what we call the effective demand for labour schedule. Two particular versions of this model were considered. The 'strong' version denies any direct effect of real wages on employment, while the 'weak' version admits substitution possibilities between labour and other factors of production, and admits a weak direct effect of real wages on employment. The unifying theme of these models is that aggregate demand, and thus output, should enter directly into (cyclical) employment equations.

All of these representative models must be considered primitive. But as Hahn recently proclaimed, most of the theory of business cycles is 'best regarded as scaffolding and not as the building' (1982, p.106). Many assumptions have been made for convenience and simplicity, and thus specific propositions derived from particular specifications cannot be taken all that seriously. The two sets of perspectives we have analysed describe two very different methodologies for considering the phenomenon of business cycles. In particular, they describe very different causal linkages by which demand impulses are transmitted

into changes in employment levels. We therefore
regard the empirical proposition concerning labour
market variables derived from these models not in
terms of specific testable hypotheses, but rather
in terms of broad propositions which are consistent
with either of the two perspectives in
macroeconomic analysis. Hahn argues, for example,
that empirical work is 'a long way from being
conclusive' and that 'the field is wide open for
thorough theoretical investigation' (1982, p.36).
Our view is less sanguine. Further theoretical
developments require an empirical knowledge of the
relevant questions that need to be asked.
Economics is a scientific half-way house, where
imperfect theory and imperfect empirical work
combine to lead us to a greater (and sometimes
lesser) knowledge of the workings of the capitalist
economies in which we live. Empirical tests of
specific models only reveal the adequacy of that
particular construction. They tell us little about
the relevance of the two different approaches in
particular. This leads us to consider the broad
presumptions of the two perspectives in the
empirical analysis reported below.

With these methodological considerations in
mind, we summarise the empirical questions raised
by our theoretical analyses. These questions form
the basis for the empirical investigations
discussed in Part Three below. The questions come
under two general headings:

1. The causal linkages between real wages, output
and employment. Neoclassical models explain
fluctuations in employment and output as arising
from inverse real wage movements. The appropriate
linkage in these models runs from the labour market
to the product market. According to these
theories, fluctuations in real wages generate
fluctuations in employment which lead to cycles in
output, with some models implying that employment
will in turn influence real wages. Output does not
directly influence employment levels in
neoclassical theory. Keynesian models, in
contrast, imply that fluctuations in employment are
generated by demand-induced fluctuations in output.
The appropriate linkage in these models runs from
output to employment with real wages playing a
subsidiary, or secondary, role in this interaction.
These models are ambiguous about the direction, if
any, of the influence of real wages on both output
and employment; the benchmark case (e.g. Barro and

Grossman, 1971) suggests independence between these variables.

2. The cyclical real wage elasticity of employment. Neoclassical models presume that this elasticity will exceed unity. Keynesian models suggest that if negative, this elasticity will be rather small. These models do admit, however, that real wages may exert a positive influence on employment.

NOTES

1. It is argued forcefully by Scarth and Myatt (1980) in a specific context, and by Gersovitz (1980) in a more general setting, that empirical propositions derived from static models will usually produce spurious predictions concerning the dynamic interaction between variables.

2. See for example Brechling (1975).

3. In an extended analysis which admits other variable factors of production, the expected future value of their relative prices would also have to be considered by the firm.

4. Sargent (1979, Chapter XVI) combines the analysis of the demand for labour schedule discussed in this section with the Lucas and Rapping (1969a) model of labour supply behaviour to arrive at a partial equilibrium dynamic model of the labour market in which real wages are determined endogenously. The predictions derived from this model are virtually identical to those generated by considering the demand for labour schedule in isolation of their labour supply factors.

5. We assume that the current information set includes the current value of the real wage rate (i.e. $E_t w_t = w_t$).

6. The model incorporates increasing marginal costs of adjustment equal to $\beta(N_{t+j} - N_{t+j-1})$.

7. Note that the term in $\beta\alpha[.]$ enters into (5.3) from the cost of adjustment expression for the next period $(t+j+1)$ which includes a term in N_{t+j}.

8. In this dynamic optimisation exercise a further condition must be satisfied to ensure that a maximum is achieved. This is the so-called transversality or terminal condition, which ensures that the chosen dynamic path for employment converges to an equilibrium in the infinite future. Sargent (1979, Chapters 9 and 14) demonstrates that this condition is satisfied by imposing restrictions which ensure that the order of the dynamic process of the exogenous variable (w_{t+j}) and the endogenous variable (N_{t+j}) is smaller than the reciprocal of the discount term (α).

9. See Sargent (1979, pp.197-8).

10. Note that the current value of the real wage rate (w_{t+j}) does not appear in (5.11) because it is replaced by its own lagged values plus the current (observable)

stochastic shock (ε_t) as in (5.10).

11. See Kirkpatrick (1982, pp.82-4) for a discussion of this point.

12. See for example Sargent (1979); Kirkpatrick (1981, 1982); and Symons and Layard (1984).

13. This implies that in the dynamic wages equation (5.10), $\rho_1 = 1$ and $\rho_j = 0$ ($j=2...n$); i.e. the real wage rate follows a random walk.

14. The question of the contemporaneous correlation between real wages and employment in this model centres on the dating of the information set. If, as we assumed in this section, firms observe the current real wage rate before employment decisions are taken for the current period, the two variables will be inversely correlated. However, if employment decisions are taken without the current real wage rate being known to firms, then the model places no restrictions on the contemporaneous relation between real wages and employment.

15. 'The model that we construct is in a fundamental sense a direct descendant of the textbook classical model, being an equilibrium model and tending to bear "classical" policy implications'. He argues further that the combination of the dynamic demand for labour schedule with the Lucas and Rapping (1969) model of labour supply behaviour provides 'an endogenous theory of persistence which is consistent with an equilibrium perspective of the economy' (Sargent, 1979, p.367).

16. This is the assumption adopted by Kirkpatrick (1982) which implies that oil is considered 'a user cost of labour in production' (p.81).

17. The λ_1^* and λ_2^* coefficients in (5.20) differ from their counterparts in (5.9) since the marginal product of labour includes an additional term in $\phi Y N_{t+j}$ over those included in (5.3). Notice that the corresponding transversality condition must also be adjusted in this case.

18. Notice, however, that such a model leaves nominal variables on a bootstrap. Some form of price or money wage rigidity would therefore be required. See note 19 below.

19. The model would, however, explain why Keynes argued that wage and price rigidity is desirable. In such a model fully flexible wages and prices would fail to ensure a return to full employment and would instead lead to dramatic oscillations in wages and prices. The chief result of flexible wages would be, according to Keynes, 'to cause a great instability of prices, so violent perhaps as to make business calcuations futile' (1936, p.269). Thus Keynes concludes 'I am now of the opinion that the maintenance of a stable general level of money-wages is, on balance of consideration, the most advisable policy for a closed system; whilst the same conclusions hold for an open system, provided that equilibrium with the rest of the world can be secured by

means of fluctuating exchanges' (p.270).

20. Sargent (1978) uses straight-time and overtime labour as the two factors.

21. This implies that the other factor (X) behaves as a shock absorber, which allows the firm to produce a level of output equal to the level of demand when the λ_js are non-zero.

22. The quadratic production function adopted by Sargent (1978) would also have to be imposed here. See his p.1016.

23. If only some λ_js are positive, then the model would require switches of regime (see Malinvaud, 1977). In such circumstances firms would still need to forecast $E_t Y^0_{t+j}$, thus allowing output to enter into an empirical demand for labour schedule.

24. The expected present value of the firm in period t is reduced by the sum of λ_js, each discounted by the appropriate factor α^j.

25. Since α is a positive fraction, the value of β exceeds that of $\beta\alpha$.

26. Note that by the (traditional) assumptions expressed in (5.23), the coefficient on N_{t+j} in (5.35) must be negative. This merely captures the proposition that a ceteris paribus increase in N leads to a fall in the marginal product of N(F_N) and a rise in the marginal product of the other factor. However, the sign on the term in $E_t Y^0_{t+j}$ is in fact ambiguous and we have assumed this to be positive. Implicit in this assumption is the proposition that $F_{NN} < F_{XX}$.

27. The stability analysis provided by Sargent (1979) applies to this model as well. This ensures that the transversality condition will hold as long as the dynamic processes of the exogenous variables and of N_{t+j} are of exponential order less than $1/\alpha$.

28. See equation (5.20) in section 1 above.

29. Our proposition on these elasticities is based on the static analysis conducted in Chapter Four above.

30. Furthermore, secular theories have little empirical content due to the almost universal collinearity between aggregate variables in the long run. It is virtually impossible to distinguish between cause and effect in such circumstances.

31. We also noted that these models do not generate any predictions concerning the cyclical movement in real unit labour costs. The relevant variable in neoclassical models of employment fluctuations is the real wage rate.

Part Three

GRANGER-CAUSALITY TESTS WITH DATA FROM THE

MANUFACTURING SECTOR OF THE UK

There is little in aggregate quarterly
data to refute the proposition that the
level of employment is determined by and
large by real factor prices.
                    Symons and Layard (1984)

Chapter Six

GRANGER-CAUSALITY TESTS AND NEOCLASSICAL THEORIES OF EMPLOYMENT FLUCTUATIONS: A REVIEW

The natural rate hypothesis has played a key role in the successful monetarist counter-revolution. Friedman (1968, 1975) and Phelps (1968) used the concept to argue that Keynesian demand management policies could not permanently alter the aggregate level of employment. The subsequent incorporation of the rational expectations mechanism in new classical macroeconomic models centred on the natural rate hypothesis (Lucas, 1972; Sargent, 1973, 1976; Sargent and Wallace, 1975; Barro, 1977, 1978) led to the more extreme proposition that systematic macroeconomic policies have no effect on the level of employment (and output) even in the short run. (See Tobin, 1980, for a critical review.)

These very strong conclusions resulted, quite naturally, in a number of investigations designed to test the validity of the natural rate hypothesis and corollary propositions. One class of test involves a time series methodology proposed by Granger (1969) and extended by Sims (1972, 1980) designed to extract empirically 'causal' relationships between key macroeconomic variables. These tests have been applied to a host of macroeconomic issues including, amongst others, the relationship between the money supply and inflation (Sargent and Wallace, 1973), the money supply and nominal income (Sims, 1972; Williams, Goodhart and Gowland, 1976; Feige and Pearce, 1979), wages and prices (Mehra, 1977), and employment and real wages (Neftci, 1978; Sargent, 1978; Kirkpatrick, 1981, 1982; Geary and Kennan, 1982).

Neftci (1978) and Sargent (1978) obtain results which appear to suggest that employment and real wage observations lie along a downward-sloping demand schedule for labour derived from microeconomic criteria (Sargent, 1978, p.1041). Sargent's claim to have tentatively identified a stable (stochastic) demand function for labour implies that there exists a unique natural rate of unemployment (for given supply factors), thus providing support for a maintained hypothesis of most neoclassical models (Hahn, 1980).

These findings also support the neoclassical view that fluctuations in employment (and output) over the business cycle arise from systematic deviations in the quantity of labour supplied. In an equilibrium model characterised by continuous labour market clearing, these systematic deviations generate changes in the real wage rate and thus the observed fluctuations in employment. The results obtained by Neftci and Sargent suggest at the very least that the equilibrium approach advocated by the new classicals, in particular, is not inconsistent with time series evidence from the US (Neftci, 1978, pp.288-9).

The aim of this chapter is to review critically the investigations into the real wage-employment relationship which apply the time series methodology proposed by Granger and Sims. In Section 1 we examine critically this methodology in a (reasonably) non-technical manner. Particular attention is given to the assumptions underlying this time series method which can often limit its usefulness.[1] Three tests for Granger-causality are examined and compared in the following Section 2. In Section 3 we review critically a set of empirical studies which applied these tests to the relationship between real wages and employment. Serious doubts are raised concerning the procedures adopted in some of these studies, which leads us to question whether the original conclusions supporting the natural rate hyothesis are warranted by the findings. In the final section we discuss a strategy in applying the time series methodology which may provide useful evidence on the question: what causes employment to fluctuate in a regular fashion?

1. METHODOLOGICAL ISSUES

The time series approach introduced by Granger (1969) applies regression analysis to test for 'causal' relationships between variables. Such an approach might at first seem surprising, since most econometricians would readily admit that regression

in general is an exercise based on finding
associations between variables. Regression differs
from correlation analysis only in so far that a
model is introduced into the analysis which assumes
that one or more variables are independent (the
exogenous variables) while another set of variables
are dependent (the endogenous variables). Thus
causality is generally assumed in the usual
classical regression analysis by stating a priori
which variables are exogenous and endogenous. The
methodology described in this section applies
regression analysis - that is, it investigates the
association between two variables - in a particular
way in order to derive tests of causal relations.
These tests are therefore in some sense logically
prior to classical regression analysis.

The ideal test of causality would involve a
controlled experiment whereby we could artificially
shock one variable (X_t) and then observe the
reaction of another (Y_t). The nature of social
science does not permit such an experiment and thus
some approximation based on actual observations of
the variables X_t and Y_t must be used. This is the
regression exercise proposed by Granger (1969) and
developed by Sims (1972), Pierce (1977) and Haugh
(1972, 1976).

The definition of 'causality' and 'feedback'
adopted by Granger relies on a linear prediction
criterion.[2] If the variable X_t 'causes' Y_t in
Granger's sense, then the prediction of Y_t is
improved (i.e. the variance of the forecast error
is reduced) when past values of X_t are added to the
prediction exercise. Here on in, we will call this
'Granger-causality'.

More formally, the methodology suggested by
Granger is based on comparing the following linear
models to predict any variable Y_t:

$$Y_t = \Sigma_{j=1}^{\infty} \alpha_j Y_{t-j} + u_t \qquad (6.1)$$

$$Y_t = \Sigma_{j=1}^{\infty} \alpha_j Y_{t-j} + \Sigma_{j=1}^{\infty} \beta_j X_{t-j} + \varepsilon_t \qquad (6.2)$$

where u_t and ε_t are classical error terms and the
α_js and β_js are regression coefficients. Granger's
definition of causation running from X_t to Y_t
implies that the variance of the prediction error
formed by predicting Y_t on the basis of equation
(6.2) should be significantly less than the
variance derived from equation (6.1). 'Feedback'
occurs in this framework if it is found that X_t
'causes' Y_t and similarly if Y_t is found to 'cause'

X_t when the regression exercise is reversed.

This methodology is based on three fundamental assumptions. It relies, first of all, on the existence of adjustment lags since a causal inference in any particular direction cannot be made from the observation of a contemporaneous correlation between X_t and Y_t. Thus the methodology relies fundamentally on the timing of movements of X_t and Y_t and, in particular, on the existence of leads and lags in their relationship. Second, the tests derived from the above definitions are mostly bivariate, relating to X_t and Y_t only, while in many circumstances the actual variables involved are taken from more complex multivariate models.[3] The applicability of this method to a number of economic issues is therefore very limited. Third, the reliance on observed leads and lags between X_t and Y_t to infer 'Granger-causality' depends on the fact that the variables are stochastic and stationary. The methodology therefore relies crucially on the existence of uncertainty because in a world of perfect foresight agents can act on the basis of future events they know will occur. Granger thus observes that 'it is difficult to find a testable alternative definition which could include the deterministic situation' (p.430). These points are elaborated below using as illustrations some recent debates in the macroeconomic literature.

Three underlying assumptions

Assumption 1

Granger-causality applies to the interaction between the variables X_t and Y_t over time. The direction of the flow of time is a central feature of the method and relies 'entirely on the assumption that the future cannot cause the past' (Granger, 1969, p.428). That is, the method assumes that there exists a direct correspondence between causal ordering and temporal ordering.[4] Thus if an investigator finds that movements in X_t generally precede those of Y_t, then the proposition that X_t Granger-causes Y_t cannot be rejected. This 'correspondence principle' is not universally accepted, and a number of investigators follow Granger and Newbold's (1977) suggestion that these causality tests indicate only that X_t and Y_t are temporally related in a particular fashion.[5] This is not a trivial matter, since counterexamples have been presented in which causal ordering and temporal ordering have been reversed.

Consider, first, the <u>deterministic</u> model used by Tobin (1970) to argue that although peaks in the money supply appear to lead those of nominal income for the US (Friedman, 1961; Friedman and Schwartz, 1963a, 1963b), this does not necessarily imply that changes in the money supply <u>cause</u> changes in nominal income. To pursue this argument Tobin develops an 'ultra-Keynesian' model in which autonomous cycles in investment (assumed to follow a sine wave) generate cycles in nominal income. Income is determined by the familiar multiplier analysis:

$$Y = m(I + G) \qquad (6.3)$$

where Y is the level of income; I is investment; G is government expenditure; and m is the multiplier (all variables in equations (6.3)-(6.14) are in nominal terms). Tobin assumes that the level of government expenditure and tax rates are held constant. Thus taking first differences we have:

$$\dot{Y} = m\dot{I} \qquad (\text{since } \dot{m} = \dot{G} = 0) \qquad (6.4)$$

where dots above the variables indicate first differences. Income therefore follows an identical (though amplified) cyclical pattern to investment. Notice that the peak in income in any cycle occurs at the same time as the peak in investment (i.e. $\dot{Y}=0$ when $\dot{I}=0$).

Since government expenditure and tax rates are constant, the government's budget deficit will decrease (increase) as investment and income rise (fall). This deficit is financed by money and bond creation in a proportion designed to keep interest rates constant. The money supply in this model is therefore totally passive; it is determined by the demand for money. This is the key equation in Tobin's model.

The demand for money has two components - an asset demand related to the (fixed) interest rate and allocatable wealth and a transactions demand proportional to income. The money demand function can be written in linear form as:

$$M = \alpha_0 W + \alpha_1 Y \qquad (6.5)$$

where M is the quantity of money; W is the value of wealth; and α_0 and α_1 are fixed parameters (all

151

variables in nominal terms).[6] Wealth (W) is made up of the capital stock and the government debt (which is determined by current and past government deficits (G-tY)). Assuming that the public borrows from the banks in fixed proportion to the capital stock (β), the public net wealth is defined as:

$$W = D + \beta K \qquad (6.6)$$

where D is the amount of accumulated government debt and K is the capital stock. Thus the money demand function in this model becomes:

$$M = \alpha_0(D + \beta K) + \alpha_1 Y \qquad (6.7)$$

We are now ready to investigate Tobin's proposition. Taking first differences of (6.7):

$$\dot{M} = \alpha_0(\dot{D} + \beta\dot{K}) + \alpha_1\dot{Y} \qquad (6.8)$$

The money supply will reach its peak and trough when $\dot{M}=0$. Notice that the following identities hold:

$$\dot{D} \equiv G - tY \qquad (6.9)$$

$$\dot{K} \equiv I \qquad (6.10)$$

Substituting (6.9) and (6.10) into (6.8) yields:

$$\dot{M} = \alpha_0[G - tY + \beta I] + \alpha_1\dot{Y} \qquad (6.11)$$

Equation (6.11) states that the <u>change</u> in the demand for money (and the money supply) depends on the <u>levels</u> of income, government expenditure and investment (all influencing the change in wealth), and the <u>change</u> in income.

Finally, if the government budget is not on average balanced, or if investment is on average positive, then wealth will be accumulating in the model and thus the demand for money will be trending upwards. To arrive at the cyclical peaks we therefore have to consider all variables in deviations around their trend values. In deviation form, equation (6.11) becomes:

$$\dot{m} = \alpha_0[-ty + \alpha i] + \alpha_1\dot{Y} \qquad (6.12)$$

where $\dot{m}=(\dot{M}-\dot{M}^e)$; $y=(Y-Y^e)$; $i=(I-I^e)$ (the superscript e refers to the average value of each variable; note that $G-G^e=0$ and $\dot{Y}^e=0$). By (6.12) we can see

152

that the only way the money supply can be at its peak is if the following holds:

$$a_0(-ty + \beta i) = 0 \qquad (6.13)$$

This condition will be valid either if the demand for money depended solely on the level of income ($a_0=0$) or if the terms in the parentheses equal zero. If we write equation (6.3) in deviations around a mean:

$$y = mi \qquad (6.3a)$$

and substituting for y in equation (6.13), we find that the money supply reaches its cyclical peak when income reaches its peak if:

$$(-tmi + \beta i) = (\beta - tm)i = 0 \qquad (6.14)$$

That is, we require $\beta = tm$. It is not obvious that this condition will hold. In fact, to arrive at his result, Tobin assumes explicitly that $\beta < tm$ (p.306). This assumption ensures that when income reaches its peak, m is negative and thus the money supply is falling (relative to trend). The peak in the money supply <u>must</u> have been reached <u>before</u> the peak in income is reached. In addition, when income and investment are at their mean values and income is growing, the money supply will be growing (relative to trend). The peak in the money supply will therefore be reached between these two positions, <u>before the peak in income</u>, even though the money supply is a passive variable in this model. Of course, Tobin's model is very stylised and he admits that it is not very realistic. But he argues that it demonstrates 'the dangers of accepting timing evidence as empirical proof of propositions about causation' (p.303).

Tobin's model provides an illustration of how the correspondence between temporal and causal ordering can break down in a deterministic setting. It helps to show why tests of causality must be based on stochastic models in which the prediction of events is subject to uncertainty. To be valid, therefore, Granger's methodology requires the use of stochastic and stationary variables; this is discussed further under assumption 3 below.

The next question that arises is whether the 'correspondence principle' will necessarily hold even in a stochastic setting. Two different arguments arise in the literature which answer this question in the negative. One argument relies on the influence of omitted variables (the 'spurious regression problem'); the other concerns the possibility that actions based on forward-looking expectations can generate inverse temporal and causal orderings.

Tobin's model can be used to examine the first of these arguments. What happens to the timing of events in this model if an unanticipated increase to investment occurs? This shock to investment would raise income but, under Tobin's assumptions, it would reduce wealth.[7] This shock would therefore have an ambiguous effect on money demand (and supply) depending on whether $\alpha_0 \dot{w}$ is greater or less than $\alpha_1 \dot{Y}$. Irrespective of the direction of this effect, the change in the money supply would occur at the same time as the change in investment and income. This contemporaneous movement in the two variables cannot help identify the causal links between these variables. Tobin's model does not, therefore, provide an alternative explanation for the results obtained by Sims (1972) which revealed that for the US shocks to the money supply historically lead those in nominal income, with no feedback.[8] Currie (1975) does present an alternative Keynesian model which could have generated such a result based on the influence of a third variable which causes both the money supply and nominal income but with a differential lag. This possibility of omitted variables influencing the results obtained in tests of causality is discussed in the next section. However, Currie is merely presenting a counterexample which attempts to explain why Sims' results may appear to support a monetarist proposition within the context of a Keynesian model. But notice that if the results obtained by Sims had suggested that shocks to the money supply do not precede those in nominal income, then this would have been very damaging to the monetarist case; Currie's counterexample would not have been needed. We return to this point below.

Schwert (1979) provides a different type of argument which allegedly undermines the validity of the 'correspondence principle' in a stochastic setting by introducing expectations explicitly into the analysis. He argues that 'the process of forming expectations about the future can change the interpretation of Granger-causality' (p.57). The critical element of this argument concerns the basis on which expectations are formed. If expectations are formed on the basis of movements of a third variable, and this influences the two variables in the model with different lags, then the argument collapses to the 'spurious regression' one discussed above. However, if the model is genuinely bivariate, then we show below that the argument is flawed and the 'correspondence principle' remains unscathed.

A striking example of Schwert's argument arises in the case of the relationship between interest rates and inflation. Fama (1976) develops a test of the Fisher hypothesis that real interest rates are independent of monetary factors by introducing rational expectations into the analysis. This efficient market hypothesis suggests that short-term interest rates predict subsequent inflation rates without making systematic forecasting errors.

Nelson and Schwert (1977) develop Fama's test by applying regression analysis which is of a form similar to that suggested by Granger. They find that the variance of the prediction errors in forecasting inflation is significantly reduced when the interest rate is included in the prediction exercise. Two regressions are carried out; one with the level of the inflation rate as the dependent variable, the other using first differences in the inflation rate:

$$\pi_t = \alpha + \beta r_t + \gamma \pi_t^e + u_t \qquad (6.15a)$$

$$(1-L)\pi_t = \alpha + \beta(r_t - \pi_{t-1}) + \gamma(\pi_t^e - \pi_{t-1}) + \varepsilon_t \qquad (6.15b)$$

where π_t is the monthly inflation rate at time t; r_t is the nominal yield on one-month Treasury bills; π_t^e is the previous period's expectation of the actual inflation rate that will arise in period t; and ε_t and u_t are white-noise errors terms (L is the lag operator). The π_t^es are derived on the basis of past inflation, using the Box-Jenkins methodology. Nelson and Schwert find that in both regressions the coefficient on the interest rate (β) is significantly different from zero at the 95 per cent level.[9] It is of critical importance to notice that although the inflation rate and the interest rate in the regression (6.15a) and (6.15b) are dated at time t, the interest rate is defined for the beginning of the period while the inflation rate is defined as the rate of change in prices that occurred during that period. Thus the interest rate at time t is observed <u>before</u> the rate of inflation in the period. Each time period (t) therefore consists of an aggregation of two moments in time - the beginning and the end. In this case, then, the significant coefficient on the interest rate suggests, at first sight, that the interest rate Granger-causes the inflation rate because the interest rate moves <u>before</u> the inflation rate. Schwert (1979) argues that this conclusion is 'misleading', since the efficient market hypothesis suggests that:

> the treasury bill rate contains an efficient assessment of the expected inflation rate, so that nominal interest rates adjust to changes in the level of <u>expected</u> inflation rates. In this scenario, predictable movements of inflation <u>cause</u> movements in the interest rate. (p.57)

Schwert claims to have found an example where the 'correspondence principle' will not hold even in a stochastic framework. His alternative scenario is based on drawing a distinction between actual and expected inflation. The latter is assumed to Granger-cause the interest rate with no feedback while actual inflation is presumed to be unaffected by the interest rate. There are two possible interpretations to this argument. The first is to assume that a third variable, presumably the rate of growth of the money supply, Granger-causes the inflation rate. Thus expected inflation should be determined by expected monetary growth. The results obtained by Nelson and Schwert could then be explained by the fact that the interest rate (r_t) contains new information on recent monetary growth (or incorporates recent announcements by the monetary authorities on future policies) which was not available when the variable π_t^e was formed. The interest rate would provide what Schwert calls 'incremental predictive content' for the rate of inflation without actually 'causing' it to move. But notice that the reason for the lack of correspondence between temporal and causal ordering lies in the fact that the relevant causal variable in this scenario - the money supply - has been totally omitted from the empirical exercise. This case therefore again provides an example of the spurious causation issue.

If Schwert's alternative scenario is based on

a truly bivariate model made up of the interest rate and the rate of inflation, then it cannot explain the results obtained by Nelson and Schwert. To see this, consider the following representation of Schwert's model:

$$r_t = a + \pi_t^e \qquad (6.16)$$

$$\pi_t = g(\pi_{t-j}) + u_t \qquad j = 1 \ldots k \qquad (6.17)$$

$$\pi_t^e = g(\pi_{t-j}) \qquad j = 1 \ldots k \qquad (6.18)$$

where a represents the constant real interest rate; and the function g(.) is left unspecified for simplicity (all other variables defined as before). Equation (6.16) states that movements in the nominal interest rate are caused by movements in expected inflation. Equation (6.17) shows how inflation follows an unspecified autocorrelated process, and equation (6.18) describes the rational expectation for inflation at any time t assuming that the process described by (6.17) is known by agents. The regression (6.15a) estimated by Nelson and Schwert would appear in the context of this model as:

$$\pi_t = \alpha + \beta r_t + \gamma \pi_t^e + u_t = a + \beta g(\pi_{t-j})$$
$$+ \gamma g(\pi_{t-j}) + u_t \qquad (6.19)$$

That is, substituting (6.16) for the nominal interest rate (r_t), and substituting equation (6.18) for inflationary expectations reveals that no additional information is provided when the interest rate is included in equations (6.15a) or (6.15b). The results obtained by Nelson and Schwert must therefore imply that the interest rate contains <u>additional</u> information in the model. The model described by equations (6.16)-(6.18) cannot be valid in light of these results. In particular, the results suggest that the interest rate influences inflation <u>over and above</u> the influence the expected inflation has on the interest rate itself. Schwert's alternative scenario could not, in a bivariate setting, have generated the results obtained by Nelson and Schwert.

This discussion suggests the following conclusions. First, the correspondence between temporal ordering and causal ordering will not necessarily hold in a deterministic system. Thus, to be valid, the tests based on Granger's

definition of causality must use variables which
are purged of most of their deterministic
components; i.e. they must be stochastic and
stationary. This point is developed further under
assumption 3 below. Second, attempts to argue that
the correspondence between temporal and causal
ordering in a stochastic setting does not hold have
not succeeded in so far as alternative models which
incorporate rational expectations have so far been
unable to offer a convincing alternative causal
linkage between any two variables which appear (on
the basis of their past movements) to be temporally
related. Until such an alternative has been
convincingly demonstrated, it seems reasonable to
presume that ordering and causal ordering do in
fact correspond. Thus if a theory suggests that a
stochastic variable X_t causes Y_t, we should find
empirically that shocks to X_t will on average have
generated subsequent shocks to Y_t. If we apply an
'appropriate' statistical technique and find a
significant relation between the timing of these
shocks, then the causal relation suggested by the
theory will not have been rejected. If, on the
other hand, we find that these shocks are
independent, then we can reject the theory in
question. We are suggesting, therefore, that the
'correspondence principle' permits the use of
Granger's methodology to develop tests of <u>necessary</u>
but not <u>sufficient</u> conditions for (non-
contemporaneous) causality to exist. It is the
rejection of a theory which posits a distinct
causal claim between variables that can, in
principle, be achieved by applying 'appropriate'
techniques generated by Granger's methodology.
These techniques are discussed in Section 2 below.

Assumption 2
The methodology developed by Granger in principle
requires a complete set of interacting variables.
<u>All</u> relevant information should be used in forming
the optimal predictors for any variable Y_t. This
of course is not usually possible and thus the
definition of causality must be made conditional on
the set of variables used. This problem is indeed
a fundamental one which can lead to incorrect
inferences; illustrations of such situations have
been presented by, amongst others, Kaldor (1970)
and Currie (1975) in a discussion of the
relationship between the money supply and nominal
income. Such problems can only 'be resolved by
widening the set of data within which causality is

defined' (Granger, 1969, p.431), which is sometimes
an impossible task in complex models.

The mostly bivariate nature of these tests can
therefore pose serious problems in a number of
areas, although this can be <u>somewhat</u> remedied by
the use of suitable 'filtering' procedures which
purge the data of some of its movements and
presumably of some of the other influences on it
(see Section 2 below). But in a number of
questions this methodology is inappropriate because
many theories propose a transmission of causal
effects between variables which is very complex.
In such circumstances empirical testing based on
Granger's definition will not lead to conclusive
results.

One of the great strengths of the neoclassical
view of employment fluctuations is the very clear
and simple causal patterns depicted. The theory
postulates that, apart from the serial correlation
in the level of employment, the real wage is the
<u>key</u> variable which determines the level of
employment and its fluctuations over the business
cycle. Both expected and unexpected changes in the
real wage rate are supposed to influence the
employment level. The theory has <u>content</u> in so far
as it places clear identifying restrictions on
<u>sequential</u> patterns between real wages and
employment, which makes it amenable to empirical
testing in a <u>bivariate</u> model. The Keynesian or
disequilibrium theories, in so far as they make a
clear causal prediction, suggest that changes in
aggregate demand and/or output are the main
variables generating changes in employment over the
cycle.

Assumption 3

Granger's definition of 'causality' and the tests
derived from it relate only to stochastic variables
(as the example in Tobin, 1970, illustrates) and in
particular to <u>stationary</u> variables.[10] A variable
is considered stationary in the wide sense
(Anderson, 1971, Chapter 7) if it has a constant
mean and variance which is independent of time. In
addition, the bivariate system made up of X_t and Y_t
must be covariance-stationary, implying that the
covariance between X_{t-j} and Y_{t-j} must also be
constant and depend only on their distance apart in
time.

The importance of this stationarity assumption
is threefold. First, the generality of the
conclusions is increased if the results of causal

tests are independent of particular trends at a particular period of time. The stationary variables used in the exercise can then be interpreted as a random sample from an infinite series rather than from a particular time period.

Second, and more important, the use of stationary variables provides a more suitable approximation to the controlled experiment situation mentioned earlier. The approximation largely involves investigating the relationship between the leads and lags in the shocks ('innovations') of each of the variables. Thus instead of artificially shocking one variable (X_t) and observing the reaction of the other (Y_t), the method is based on whether a general or consistent pattern can be observed between the leads and lags in the shocks of the two variables. Each innovation of one variable (X_t) can be interpreted as an artificial shock to that variable, and thus what we have with a stationary variable is a large number of observed shocks from which we can investigate the responses (if any) in the other stationary series (Y_t). If a consistent pattern emerges; say for example that innovations in X_t are usually followed by a similar type of shock in Y_t, then it is inferred that X_t 'causes' Y_t. A critical feature of stationary variables is that they exhibit a constant lag structure characterised by time invariant probabilities. This is a prerequisite for the appropriate detection of the temporal relationship between variables.

The use of stationary variables in the exercise is important for a third reason: macroeconomic variables tend to be highly collinear, thereby inducing the spurious correlation problem mentioned above. Stationary variables are less likely to suffer from this problem.

These then are the reasons why tests of causality are most appropriate with stationary variables. Most economic time series are not stationary, however, and thus such variables must be transformed into stationary series. Such transformations are usually undertaken in the 'first round' of the regression exercise; but these transformations can vary greatly and the actual transformation used can strongly influence the final results obtained.

160

2. THREE TESTS FOR GRANGER-CAUSALITY

Filtering techniques

An appropriate empirical application of Granger's
methodology requires that the variables X_t and Y_t
be transformed to stationarity in such a way that
causality is preserved. Many linear
transformations (de-trending the data or taking
first differences) and some non-linear
transformations (taking logarithms) satisfy this
condition (Pierce and Haugh, 1977). These are the
transformations most commonly used.

The usual procedure adopted to transform an
original series involves passing the data through a
'filter'. Very often this will consist of
regressing the first or second difference of the
variable on a time trend and (if necessary)
seasonal and other dummies. The residuals obtained
by this operation will be used as the new
stationary variable.

An important difference arises between merely
'filtering' the variables or going further and
'whitening' them. A 'whitened' series is also
stationary but is further characterised by the
absence of serial correlation. The empirical
techniques designed to test for causality differ
substantially in this respect (see Section 3.3
below); this may explain why on a number of
occasions investigators have obtained conflicting
results (Pierce and Haugh, 1977, pp.279-88). In
particular we will argue below that one of the
tests for Granger-causality, the Sims test, is
quite sensitive to the presence of serial
correlation and can on occasion wrongly suggest
that causality exists. This argument might be
understood to imply that a 'whitening' is
preferable to simple 'filtering', but this is not
obvious. Remember that any transformation applied
must be causality-preserving. The 'whitening' of a
series may be so complicated that this condition is
violated.

Thus each procedure has its relative
advantages and disadvantages; this suggests that a
careful study of causality must include a number of
different tests and in particular careful attention
must be given to the adequate treatment of
autocorrelation. One approach suggested by Pierce
and Haugh (1977, p.289) involves pre-filtering the
data to achieve stationarity (but not a 'whitened'
series) and then conducting the tests of causality

using a suitable generalised least squares procedure which post-filters the data without violating the causality-preserving condition. This may be needed if in fact the regressions run suffer from problems of autocorrelation or heteroscedasticity which may invalidate tests based on the t- and F-distributions. This approach may not, however, resolve some of the difficulties concerning the Sims test, as we show in the next section.

The tests

Three of the empirical procedures designed to test for causality as defined by Granger have been widely used.[11] In particular, these three tests were those chosen in the different investigations into the real wage-employment relationship which we review in Section 4 below. These tests include the direct Granger test (Sargent, Kirkpatrick), the two-sided Sims test (Neftci) and the Pierce-Haugh cross-correlation test (Geary and Kennan).[12]

The direct Granger test

Assume that the original variables X_t and Y_t have been suitably transformed so that the resulting stationary variables x_t and y_t can be represented as a moving average of past shocks (Sims, 1972, p.392; Pierce and Haugh, 1977, pp.269-70):

$$x_t = \Sigma_{j=0}^{\infty} \alpha_{1j}\varepsilon_{1t-j} + \Sigma_{j=0}^{\infty} \beta_{1j}\varepsilon_{2t-j} \qquad (6.20a)$$

$$y_t = \Sigma_{j=0}^{\infty} \alpha_{2j}\varepsilon_{2t-j} + \Sigma_{j=0}^{\infty} \beta_{2j}\varepsilon_{1t-j} \qquad (6.20b)$$

where ε_{1t} and ε_{2t} are mutually uncorrelated white-noise shocks relating to x_t and y_t respectively.

Given the assumption of stationarity, this system can be transformed into the following autoregressive system:

$$x_t = \Sigma_{j=1}^{\infty} \gamma_{1j}x_{t-j} + \Sigma_{j=1}^{\infty} \phi_{1j}y_{t-j} + \varepsilon_{1t} \quad (6.21a)$$

$$y_t = \Sigma_{j=1}^{\infty} \gamma_{2j}y_{t-j} + \Sigma_{j=1}^{\infty} \phi_{2j}x_{t-j} + \varepsilon_{2t} \quad (6.21b)$$

Granger's direct test involves estimating equations (6.21a) and (6.21b) with lags as long as feasible and testing, using the F-statistic, for the joint significance of the respective ϕ_{ij}s. The great advantage of this test is that it provides a direct empirical representation of Granger's definition of causality based on prediction. If y Granger-causes x then the lagged ys should be significant as a group. Another advantage with this test is that it can easily be extended to a multivariate framework though the introduction of additional explanatory variables.

This direct test has the added advantage that 'post-filtering' for autocorrelation will probably not be needed. For this to be the case, however, the distributed lag in x in equation (6.21a) must be sufficiently long to pick up any serial correlation in the xs. As Pierce and Haugh (1977, pp.288-9) point out, it is best to start with a generous lag structure and then proceed by reducing the length of the lags when insignificant Y_{ij}s and ϕ_{ij}s are obtained.

The main disadvantage with this approach and its reliance on F-tests of <u>joint</u> significance lies in the inability of such tests to distinguish between <u>temporary</u> and <u>permanent</u> Granger-causality. That is, it is possible for the F-test to suggest that x Granger-causes y but that the sum of the ϕ_{ij} coefficients sum to zero. Such a result would suggest that a permanent change in x generates a temporary fluctuation in y, but exerts no permanent influence on it. Investigators therefore need to exercise caution in interpreting the F-statistics obtained from Granger's direct test. In particular, it is useful to calculate the sum of the coefficients on the explanatory variable and the variances of the sums.

Two-sided Sims test

The test suggested by Sims is based on theorem 2 presented in his paper (and proved in his appendix). This theorem states that if the bivariate system made up of the stationary variables x_t and y_t has an autoregressive representation as in equation (6.21a) and (6.21b) above, then 'y can be expressed as a distributed lag function of current and past x with a residual which is not correlated with any values of x, past or future, if, and only if, y does not cause x in Granger's sense' (Sims, 1972, p.393). On the basis of this theorem Sims proposes a test of causality by running a regression of $x_t(y_t)$ on past and <u>future</u> values of $y_t(x_t)$:

$$x_t = \Sigma_{j=-k}^{+s} a_j y_{t-j} + u_{1t} \qquad (6.22a)$$

$$y_t = \Sigma_{j=-k}^{+s} b_j x_{t-j} + u_{2t} \qquad (6.22b)$$

If causality runs from x to y only, then the future values of x in equation (6.22b) should be insignificantly different from zero and the future values of y in equation (6.22a) should be significant as a group.[13] The F-statistic is therefore used to test whether the a_js and b_js (j=-k...-1) in equations (6.22a) and (6.22b) respectively are significantly different from zero as a group.

Notice that the text is based on a 'backwards regression'. The intuition underlying this approach is sensible. If x Granger-causes y with no feedback, then <u>future</u> values of y should be correlated with current values of x, while future values of x should not be correlated with current y. Therefore if we regress current x (the 'causal' variable) on past and future values of y (the 'caused' variable) as in equation (6.22a), the coefficients on the future values of y should be significantly different from zero as a group.

If causality is found to run only from x to y then, Sims argues, one can go further and estimate a distributed lag equation of y on x by least squares. The coefficients obtained in this manner would then be consistent. This two-stage procedure therefore surmounts the temporary versus permanent effect problem discussed above by allowing the calculation of the sum of the coefficients on the lagged xs and testing for a permanent effect of x on y by applying a t-statistic on the sum obtained.

This procedure suffers from the important drawback that the original X_t and Y_t series must be 'whitened' rather than merely 'filtered'. To see this, consider the relationship between the nominal rate of interest (r_t) and the inflation rate (π_t) discussed under assumption 1 above. The model presented in equations (6.16)-(6.18) suggests that π_t is serially correlated and independent of r_t (equation 6.17) but that expected inflation (π_t^e) determines r_t (equation 6.16). Applying the Sims test for causality running from r_t to π_t would involve estimating the following equation:

$$r_t = \Sigma_{j=-k}^{+s} b_j \pi_{t-j} + \varepsilon_t \qquad (6.23)$$

and testing whether the b_js (j=-k...-1) are significant as a group. The model described by equations (6.16)-(6.18) suggests that both r_t and the π_{t-j}s are determined by lagged values of π_t. The running of regression (6.23) is equivalent under equations (6.16)-(6.18) to regressing expected inflation on future inflation; we would therefore expect to find the $b_j (j=-k...-1)$ coefficients to be significant even though r_t does not cause π_t in this model. This result occurs because the serial correlation in the π_ts would generate a serially correlated set of π_t^es and thus a similar movement in the r_ts. The Sims test applied in this circumstance would therefore generate incorrect inferences about the causal links between r_t and π_t. This result could be avoided, however, if the serial correlation in r_t had been removed prior to estimating (6.23). In this case, the future values of the whitened inflation rate would represent the <u>unpredicted</u> movements in the inflation rate which would have been omitted from the rational forecasts of inflation (π_t^e) in equation (6.18). The rate of interest (r_t) could therefore not have predicted the future values of the innovations in the inflation rate $(\varepsilon_{t-j}, j=-k...-1)$ and thus, if the model described by equations (6.16)-(6.18) is correct, the Sims test would have led to a rejection of the hypothesis that r_t Granger-causes the rate of inflation. To be valid, therefore, the Sims test usually requires that the dependent variable in each regression be suitably filtered so that the resulting stationary variable is white noise.[14] Comparative studies by Feige and Pearce (1979), Nelson and Schwert (1982) and Weisenberger and Thomas (1981) show how the results obtained using the Sims test are extremely sensitive to the choice of filter when both variables exhibit strong cyclical patterns.

Pierce-Haugh cross-correlation test
The test developed by Pierce (1977) and Haugh (1972, 1976) differs from the Granger and Sims procedures in that (1) it is essentially a test for <u>independence</u> rather than causality; (2) it is based on cross-correlation analysis rather than regression analysis; and (3) separate filters are used for each variable and this filter is determined 'empirically' rather than in an 'ad-hoc' fashion (Pierce and Haugh, 1977, pp.279-80).

The first stage of the Pierce-Haugh test involves <u>estimating</u> the appropriate filters for X_t and Y_t to produce the <u>whitened</u> series x_t and y_t respectively. Haugh (1972) recommends the use of the Box-Jenkins methodology based on estimating ARIMA models for <u>each</u> detrended and deseasonalised variable such as:

$$\tilde{X}_t = \Sigma_{j=1}^{k_1} \alpha_{1j} \tilde{X}_{t-j} + \Sigma_{j=0}^{s_1} \beta_{1j} u_{2t-j} \qquad (6.24a)$$

$$\tilde{Y}_t = \Sigma_{j=1}^{k_2} \alpha_{2j} \tilde{Y}_{t-j} + \Sigma_{j=0}^{s_2} \beta_{2j} u_{2t-j} \qquad (6.24b)$$

where $\tilde{X}$ and $\tilde{Y}$ are the detrended etc. (and may be in differenced form) versions of X and Y but not the filtered versions; u_t is a white-noise error; and k_i and s_i ($i=1,2$) are, to a certain extent, determined empirically. Once the appropriate lags (k and s) and the α_{ij}s and β_{ij}s have been estimated, the residuals (e_{1t} and e_{2t} respectively) can be derived.

The second stage of the procedure involves calculating the cross-correlation coefficients for each lag in e_{1t} and e_{2t} respectively:

$$r_{12}(j) = \{\Sigma_{t=1}^{n} e_{1t-j} e_{2t}\} / \{[\Sigma_{t=1}^{n} e_{1t}^2]^{\frac{1}{2}}.$$

$$[\Sigma_{t=1}^{n} e_{2t}^2]^{\frac{1}{2}}\} \qquad j=1\ldots k_1 \quad (6.25a)$$

$$r_{21}(j) = \{\Sigma_{t=1}^{n} e_{2t-j} e_{1t}\} / \{[\Sigma_{t=1}^{n} e_{1t}^2]^{\frac{1}{2}}.$$

$$[\Sigma_{t=1}^{n} e_{2t}^2]^{\frac{1}{2}}\} \qquad j=1\ldots k_2 \quad (6.25b)$$

where n is the size of the data set. Equations (6.25a) and (6.25b) represent k_1 and k_2 correlation coefficients respectively. Each $r_{12}(j)$ defines the simple correlation coefficient between the jth lag in e_{1t} (the innovation in X_t) and current e_{2t} (the innovation in Y_t). The reverse is true for each r_{21}.

Consider the hypothesis that X_t and Y_t are independent. In this case the residual cross-correlation in equation (6.25a) and (6.25b) should on average be zero. In particular, Haugh (1976) shows that in the special case of independence each of the cross-correlation coefficients are asymptotically normal and independent across j. Thus the sum of the squared correlation coefficients multiplied by the sample size yields a statistic (S) which is distributed as a χ^2 statistic with (k_1+k_2) degrees of freedom:

$$S = n\Sigma_{j=1}^{k_1} r_{12}^2(j) + n\Sigma_{j=1}^{k_2} r_{21}^2(j) \qquad (6.26)$$

(The correlation coefficient for the current values of e_{1t} and e_{2t} could also be included here; the χ^2 statistic would lose an additional degree of freedom.)

The difficulty with this test is that when the

variables are causally related, the distribution of the S-statistic is not well defined (Pierce and Haugh, 1977, p.284). Thus the test _may_ have the tendency not to reject independence when causality does actually exist. Part of the problem is that the S-statistic is based on the assumption of independence in the $r(j)$s _across j_; this would probably be invalid when X_t and Y_t are indeed causally related. One might expect, for example that if X_t Granger-causes Y_t the effect of a change in X at time t would begin to have a smaller effect on Y after a certain time lag. The test is therefore _probably biased_ in favour of accepting independence.

A comparison of the tests

The above discussions on the relative strengths and weaknesses of the three techniques designed to test for Granger-causality suggests that of the three tests, the direct Granger test is probably the most reliable. The two-sided Sims test suffers from the drawback that it requires whitened variables rather than merely filtered ones, and the Pierce-Haugh cross-correlation test is based on the distribution of a statistic (S) whose properties are generally not well defined.

Geweke (1981) applies Monte-Carlo methods to compare the performance of the Pierce-Haugh S-statistic and (a variant of) the direct Granger test in an experimental situation.[15] Two experiments were undertaken in which 500 replications of two time series, x_t and y_t, were generated with 250 observations in each replication. In both experiments x_t and y_t were made to follow an autoregressive pattern.[16] In the first experiment the stochastic terms in the x_t and y_t (ε_t and u_t respectively) autoregressions were serially uncorrelated, _independent_ random variables. Independence was therefore imposed on x_t and y_t. The experiment consisted of applying the Pierce-Haugh and direct Granger tests for varying lengths of lags in the variables (13, 25 and 37 lags) and for observations of size 100 and 250, and calculating the proportion of replications in which independence was rejected. The ideal test would reject independence 5 per cent of the time if the significance level chosen was 5 per cent. In all six cases the Pierce-Haugh test rejected independence slightly _less_ than 5 per cent of the

167

time while in two cases (13 lags with 100 and 250 observations) the direct Granger test rejected independence slightly <u>more</u> than 5 per cent of the time. The reliability of the direct Granger test also appears to be sensitive to the length of the lags in the estimated relationship; it exhibits a bias towards rejecting independence in the model with the shortest lags (13) and a bias towards accepting independence when very long lags (37) are used. In general the results of the first experiment suggest that when x_t and y_t are indeed independent, the direct Granger test will reject independence only slightly more often than the Pierce-Haugh test. The differences are quite small.

In the second experiment the innovations in the x_t and y_t autoregressions were again serially uncorrelated, but this time their cross-correlations were non-zero. In this experiment, therefore, Granger-causality with feedback was imposed on the data. The outcome of this experiment was striking. With 100 observations and using the 5 per cent significance level, the Pierce-Haugh test rejected independence <u>less than 20 per cent of the time</u> (rather than 95 per cent of the time as should occur with an ideal test). With 250 observations the Pierce-Haugh test performed much better, but still the highest rejection rate was under 70 per cent. The direct Granger test rejected independence much more often: about 95 per cent of the time with 250 observations but only a maximum of 58 per cent of the time with only 100 observations. Again, the proportion of replications in which independence was rejected using the direct Granger test was inversely related to the number of lags in the model.

What conclusions can be drawn from Geweke's study? First, as might have been expected, the Pierce-Haugh test will in most cases tend to reject independence less often than the direct Granger test. This difference is only marginal when x_t and y_t are in fact independent but is quite substantial when causality does indeed exist. That is, the Pierce-Haugh statistic tends to accept the hypothesis that x_t and y_t are independent when this is false more than 80 per cent of the time with 100 observations and 30-40 per cent of the time with 250 observations. Second, both tests are extremely sensitive to the number of observations, their reliability increasing dramatically when the sample size increases from 100 to 250 observations.

Finally, the shorter the lags, the more likely it is that the direct Granger test will correctly reject independence.

It should be remembered that unfortunately these conclusions are only directly applicable to the case Geweke was studying; that is, when both x_t and y_t are serially correlated. Whether these results are robust with respect to changes in the time patterns of the variables is not known. Geweke, Meese and Dent (1983) report the results of a similar Monte-Carlo study which does suggest, however, that in a larger class of models including the case where one variable almost follows a random walk, the direct Granger test (using an F-test rather than the likelihood ratio or lagrange multiplier tests) outperforms the Sims test. In particular, 'the sampling distribution of statistics for Sims tests requiring correction for serial correlation performed very poorly and was sensitive to prefiltering...' (p.36).

These experiments, which are admittedly at an early stage, suggest that the direct Granger test is probably the most reliable of the three tests, but even its reliability in samples with less than 200 observations is not high. At the very least, therefore, attempts to test for Granger-causality should include a number of different tests and a number of different filters to assess the robustness of the results obtained.

Given this rather lengthy review of the time-series methodology underlying tests of causation and the review of the tests themselves and their relative advantages and disadvantages, we can now proceed to a discussion of the empirical studies into the real wage-employment relationship.

3. A HISTORICAL REVIEW OF THE LITERATURE

Much of the evidence amassed in recent years on the Granger-causal relationship between real wages and employment is derived from USA data. Bodkin (1969) provided the initial stimulus, presenting results based on simple static regression exercises using data from USA and Canada.[17] His results, which appeared to contradict the neoclassical theory, led to the use of the causality testing methodology described in this chapter. A lively debate ensued with USA data providing the sample for the studies by Neftci (1978), Sargent (1978), Kirkpatrick (1981) and Geary and Kennan (1982). Geary and

Kennan also examined evidence from an international comparison of twelve OECD countries, while Kirkpatrick (1982) investigated German data.

The results have in general been mixed. Probably the available evidence will not convince those holding reasonably strong priors to alter their position. Some of the results appear to be sensitive to the length of the sampling period and data from different countries sometimes produce contradictory results. Perhaps greater doubts are raised by the apparent lack of stationarity in the data employed in the studies (Geary and Kennan, 1982, p.860; and Kirkpatrick, 1982, p.88). However, in contrast with the initial optimism concerning the neoclassical theory expressed by Neftci and Sargent, the most recent evidence suggests that the relationship between real wages and employment is sufficiently weak to warrant further empirical examination.

Theory and contradiction

The recent interest in the real wage-employment relationship was stimulated by two contradictory developments in the late 1960s: one theoretical; the other empirical. At the theoretical level, the monetarist counter-revolution blossomed with Friedman's (1968) elaboration of the natural rate hypothesis. This hypothesis led to the development of equilibrium theories of employment fluctuations (Sargent, 1978; Alogoskoufis, 1983) with the real wage-employment relationship taking centre stage.(18)

As we described in Chapter Three above, Friedman's analysis is based on the divergence between actual and perceived (or anticipated) real wages, with the former determining the quantity of labour demanded while the latter determines the quantity of labour supplied. In the event of unanticipated increases in the price level, both labour demand and labour supply increase, thus generating an increase in employment in the short run. Workers' perceptions would, however, adjust over time to the new price level (or to the new inflation rate) and in the long run, when the perceived real wage rate becomes equalised with the actual real wage rate, employment would return to its original level corresponding to the natural rate of unemployment. Friedman's theory therefore presented an equilibrium theory of employment

170

fluctuations based on countercyclical movements in actual real wages. It is an equilibrium theory in the sense that at all points in time the quantity of labour demanded equals the quantity supplied. Real wage and employment observations are predicted to move along a stable real demand curve for labour.

At around the same time that the natural rate hypothesis was presented, an unrelated empirical study by Bodkin (1969) produced results which appeared to contradict Friedman's hypothesis.[19] Using Canadian and USA yearly and quarterly data, Bodkin concluded that:

> The traditional view..., that real wages
> are inversely related to the cyclical
> utilization of the labour force, receives
> little support from the data examined in
> this paper.
> (p.370)

The most interesting results presented by Bodkin were obtained by regressing the deviation of real wages around their trend on the measured unemployment rate (a proxy for the cyclical utilisation of the labour force):

$$\hat{W}_t = \alpha + BU_t + \varepsilon_t \qquad (6.27)$$

where $\hat{W}_t$ are the residuals obtained from regressing real wages on a time trend; U is the measured unemployment rate; and ε_t is a random variable.[20] Applying OLS to (6.27), Bodkin finds that the coefficient on the unemployment rate is insignificant with Canadian data, and significantly negative for the USA.[21] Estimation by instrumental variables to capture the potential effect of wage deviations on unemployment rates did not alter these conclusions.

Bodkin's results and related empirical evidence presented by Kuh (1966) generated three areas of further research. The first was the development of a disequilibrium model of income and employment by Barro and Grossman (1971), discussed and elaborated on in Chapters Four and Five of Part 2 above, which attempts to explain these findings within the context of individual maximising behaviour. In the disequilibrium model 'unemployment can coexist with "non-excessive" real wages, and a procyclical pattern of real wages is consistent with the theoretical model' (Barro and Grossman, 1971, p.92).[22]

The two other areas of research stimulated by Bodkin's study arose from an attempt to reconcile Bodkin's results with the neoclassical model's predictions of counter-cyclical real wage movements. These developments concerned two aspects of Bodkin's empirical model: (1) the appropriate definition of the 'real wage rate'; and (2) the dynamics of the real wage-employment relationship.

In his study Bodkin used <u>average earnings</u> as his wage variable. Sargent (1979, Chapter 16) builds on this fact to provide an alternative explanation of Bodkin's findings by emphasising the distinction between normal and overtime hours. If in response to an exogenous shock to real wages employers adjust their offers of overtime hours faster than straight-time hours (i.e. aggregate employment), then movements in average earnings over the cycle will reflect the greater than proportionate change in overtime premiums paid even if straight-time real wage rates move in a counter-cyclical fashion.[23] Sargent therefore explains Bodkin's results as arising from a <u>statistical artefact</u>; it is claimed to be the result of using average earnings data rather than data on wage rates which exclude overtime payments. This argument suggests that real wage rates which exclude overtime payments (and bonuses) should be used in empirical studies of the real wage-employment relationship.

Causality tests - confirmation and contradictions

A much more important question raised in response to Bodkin concerns the <u>timing</u> of the relationship between real wages and employment. The observation of a contemporaneous correlation between these two variables is only relevant in a world characterised by instantaneous adjustments. If the adjustment of employment levels is subject to increasing marginal costs (as in Lucas, 1970; and Sargent, 1978), then employment will respond to changes in the real wage rate with a time-lag. Similarly, if as in Friedman (1968, 1975) inflationary expectations (and thus money wages) adjust sluggishly to an increased demand for labour, then real wages will adjust sluggishly to fluctuations in employment. The Granger-Sims methodology is therefore an 'appropriate' tool to carry out an investigation of the real wage-employment relationship.

Neftci's (1978) study was motivated by this point. Bodkin's study, which demonstrated a positive <u>contemporaneous</u> relationship between real wages (earnings) and employment, is flawed because

> ... in the presence of distributed lags, simple regression will not, in general, detect lagged responses and thus give the erroneous impression that real wages and employment are positively correlated.
>
> (Neftci, 1978, p.283)

Neftci examines the real wage-employment relationship by applying the Sims test to monthly data from the US manufacturing sector for the years 1948-71. The employment and real wage variables he uses are, respectively, the number of employees on the payroll of manufacturing establishments, and average hourly earnings (excluding overtime) deflated by the consumer price index.

Neftci's results are at first sight striking. After filtering the raw data,[24] he applies the two-sided Sims test to the filtered real wage and employment variable using 12 monthly leads and 24 lags as right hand side variables. The F-statistics obtained strongly suggest that real wages Granger-cause employment with no feedback. The F-statistic for real wages Granger-causing employment is 3.26, significant at the 5 per cent level, while for reverse causality the statistic is only 1.25 which is insignificant even at the 25 per cent level.

On the basis of these results, Neftci proceeds to estimate a one-sided distribution lag of (filtered) employment on lagged real wages. He finds that when 12 or more monthly lags are used, the sum of the coefficients on the real wage rate is negative. For example, when 18 lags are imposed, the sum of the coefficients is -1.52 with a standard error of 0.27. In addition, Neftci was able to reconcile Bodkin's earlier results with his evidence. He finds that in the distributed lag regressions the coefficient on the current real wage is positive and significant. This provides further evidence to suggest that Bodkin's (and Kuh's) results were due to their 'ignoring the dynamics of the problem' (Neftci, 1978, p.287).[25]

Additional evidence corroborating Neftci's results are provided by Sargent (1978). He applies the direct Granger test to unfiltered quarterly USA data for the period 1948(1)-1972(4) with four lags

on each variable.[26]   The F-statistic testing for
Granger-causality running from real wages to
employment is significant at the 10 per cent level;
the F-statistic for reverse causation is
significant at only the 85 per cent level!

We note in passing, however, that although the
F-statistics confirm Neftci's results, none of the
individual coefficients on the 'causal' variables
are significant.   Indeed, in the real wage
regressions the only significant variable (apart
from the first quarter dummy) is the first lag in
the real wage rate and this coefficient is
insignificantly different from unity.   Therefore
Sargent's results with US data also suggest that
the real wage rate follows a random walk.   As
Altonji and Ashenfelter (1980) demonstrate, it is
difficult to reconcile the equilibrium theory of
employment fluctuations with essentially random,
and permanent, real wage fluctuations.   This is a
worrying feature of Sargent's results.

Further empirical work by Kirkpatrick (1981)
and Geary and Kennan (1982) casts doubts on the
results obtained by Neftci and Sargent.   Two
important sets of evidence are presented by these
authors.   First, both sets of investigators find
that, by extending the estimating period for the US
to 1977, the results obtained by both Sargent and
Neftci are overturned.[27]   This is a worrying
result, suggesting that the real wage-employment
relationship is unstable.   One popular explanation
for this, examined with UK data by Symons (1985),
with German data by Kirkpatrick (1982) and with
data from six OECD countries by Symons and Layard
(1984), concerns the oil price shocks of 1973-4 and
the alleged backwards shift in the demand for
labour curve.[28]   If real wage and employment
observations for the longer data period lie along
two different demand curves for labour, then it is
not surprising that empirical results may suggest
that real wages and employment are independent.

Applying a multivariate version of the direct
Granger test to quarterly German data, Kirkpatrick
(1982) shows however that when raw material prices
(deflated by the wholesale price index) are
included in the tests, the results are
significantly different for the 1960s and 1970s.
For the period 1960(1)-1979(4) the F-statistic for
real wages Granger-causing employment is
significant at only the 17 per cent level of
significance.   For the shortened data period from
1960(1)-1969(4), this statistic is insignificant at

the 30 per cent level, while for the years 1970(1)
-1979(4) the F-statistic becomes significant at the
5 per cent level.[29] Thus even when a variable
which captures the influence of the oil price shock
is introduced into the analysis, the real wage-
employment relationship still appears to be
unstable.

An alternative explanation for this
instability concerns the acceleration of inflation
during the 1970s. If wages tend to respond to
price changes with a time lag as in Friedman (1968)
and Lucas and Rapping (1969a), or if the duration
of wage contracts exceed those of prices, then the
larger the change in prices in any given period,
the larger will be the observed oscillations in the
real wage rate. This would generate
heteroscedasticity in the real wage rate. This
lack of stationarity in the data, noted by Geary
and Kennan (1982, p.860) may explain why different
results are obtained when the data sets are
extended to include periods of rapid inflation (the
1970s).

The second set of evidence presented by Geary
and Kennan (1982) and Kirkpatrick (1981) is based
on using an alternative price deflator than that
employed by both Neftci and Sargent. Both Geary
and Kennan and Kirkpatrick re-estimated the models
deflating the nominal wage rate by the whoelsale
price index (WPI) rather than the consumer price
index (CPI) used by Neftci and Sargent. With the
WPI deflator, which it is claimed 'provides a
better measure of the firm's demand price of
labour' (Geary and Kennan, 1982, p.855), the
causality tests suggest that employment is
independent of the real wage rate.[30]

Further evidence

Geary and Kennan (1982) also present evidence on
the (WPI-deflated) real wage-employment
relationship using quarterly data from around the
late 1950s to the mid-1970s for the manufacturing
sector of twelve OECD countries (including the US).
They apply three tests to the data. These are: the
Pierce-Haugh S-statistic (with ten lags on each
variable); a regression F-statistic suggested by
Geweke (1980); and tests based on pooling the S-
and F-statistics obtained from each country.[31]
The two S-statistics calculated for each
country provide little evidence to support the

175

neoclassical theory. In no case is the statistic significant at the 5 per cent level, and in only three out of 24 cases is it significant at the 10 per cent level. Only New Zealand, Ireland and Belgium provide even limited support (both S-statistics take on values at about, or below, the 15 per cent level of significance) for the theory. On the other hand, six of the countries produce S-statistics which are below the 50 per cent significance level! The results with the F-statistics were fairly inconclusive, mostly because there were serious conflicts between the different F-statistics calculated for each country, suggesting that these 'tests are misspecified' (p.860). Thus it seems that the S-statistics, which exihibit less volatility, are the more reliable in this study. Nevertheless the authors point out that although six of the twelve countries 'show critical levels above 10 per cent on all tests; no country shows critical levels below 10 per cent on all tests' (p.859). Thus the authors conclude that real wages and employment appear to be independent over the business cycle.

The results from the pooled tests, however, provide some evidence against this conclusion. The pooled test based on the F-statistic rejects independence in five out of twelve cases at the 5 per cent level, and in eight out of twelve cases at the 10 per cent level. The pooled test based on the S-statistic rejects independence at just outside the 5 per cent level with undifferenced data, and at almost the 2½ per cent level with differenced data. Although they present a good deal of evidence which is inconsistent with the neoclassical theory, there is sufficient evidence reported by Geary and Kennan to suggest that strong conclusions cannot be drawn from their international study.

As a final point, we note that Geary and Kennan include in their study data from the UK covering the years 1955-77. Both the S- and F-statistics strongly reject the neoclassical model with the UK data. It is of interest to investigate whether their results for the UK are robust to changes in the sample period and causality test adopted. The length of their sample period may be very important because near the end of their sample period the real wage variable they use exhibited dramatic oscillations which may have played an important role in the results they obtained. This issue is discussed in more detail in Chapter Seven below.

4. SUMMARY AND OUTLINE

The main concern of the empirical work described in this chapter has been on two (essentially neoclassical) propositions. The first is that most macroeconomic models predict a counter-cyclical movement in real wage rates. Bodkin (1969) presents evidence which appears to contradict this proposition. Lucas (1970) and Sargent (1979) point out, however, that such results, based on average earnings data, are not incompatible with a counter-cyclical movement in real wage rates when the pro-cyclical movement in overtime hours is taken into account. Further, Neftci (1978) argues that Bodkin's evidence is misleading because it fails to consider the dynamics of the real wage-employment relationship.

The second proposition investigated in the literature concerns the causal relationship between real wages and employment. Both orthodox Keynesian and neoclassical macroeconomic theories postulate that real wage movements generate or 'cause' inverse movements in employment levels. Further, the specifically monetarist analysis of Milton Friedman (1968) suggests that fluctuations in employment will generate or 'cause' lagged adjustments in real wages. Neftci (1978) and Sargent (1978) investigate these propositions by applying tests for Granger-causality to US employment and real wage data from the late 1940s to the early 1970s. Both authors find a significant and and negative unidirectional causal pattern running from real wages to employment.

These results, however, have been questioned by empirical work by Kirkpatrick (1981, 1982) and Geary and Kennan (1982). Their empirical results drawn from data from a variety of countries suggest that, in contrast to Neftci and Sargent, real wages and employment appear to be independent. A further point raised by these authors concerns the apparent lack of stationarity in the variables. The evidence presented by Neftci and Sargent does not stand up to an extension of the data set to include the mid-1970s. However, non-stationarity is observed even in the extended data sets. It is for this reason that we claim that the previous empirical work on the real wage-employment relationship is inconclusive.

One area of empirical analysis which has been neglected in the causality literature is the alternative disequilibrium, or Keynesian, approach to employment fluctuations - the quantity to quantity relation. There have not been any studies undertaken which investigate the dynamic relationship between output and employment using the methodology described in this chapter. Further, since neoclassical model theory places exclusion restrictions on output in the determination of employment fluctuations, the multivariate direct Granger test can be used to test these propositions using data from the UK.

In the following two chapters we apply Granger-Sims methodology to investigate the relationship between real wages, output and employment. In Chapter Seven we investigate, using a bivariate model, the real wage-employment relationship with quarterly data from the UK manufacturing sector from 1952(1)-1981(2). We pay particular attention to the issue of stationarity in the data and investigate whether the results reported by Geary and Kennan are influenced by the apparent lack of stationarity in the data. In Chapter Eight we report the analysis of the output-employment relationship, using the same data set. Finally we apply a multivariate version of the direct Granger test to examine the exclusion restrictions of the competing theories. These tests can be interpreted as an investigation into the necessary assumptions of the alternative approaches to explain the repeated fluctuations in employment observed in advanced capitalist countries.

NOTES

1. Technical reviews of the techniques are available in Feige and Pierce (1979) and Pierce and Haugh (1977).
2. This linear prediction criterion is precisely the one used in the formulation of optimal predictors in rational expectations models. This time series methodology is therefore closely associated with new classical macroeconomic models and explains in part why these tests of causality have played an important role in tests of these models. See the introduction to Lucas and Sargent (1981), and Feige and Pearce (1979).
3. The inclusion of a disturbance term in (6.2) might be interpreted as reflecting the influence of additional

variables which influence Y_t. Under this interpretation, the use of a bivariate model is predicated on the assumption that these additional variables are independent of Y_{t-j} and X_{t-j} ($j=1...\infty$), and that they influence the dependent variable in a non-systematic or random fashion.

4. This 'correspondence principle' has played a key role in the history of social science. In particular it represents a modern version of the Humian view of causation which maintained that causality can be inferred from observations of temporal succession and regularity. See Keat and Urry (1975, Chapters 1-2) for a discussion. I would like to thank Simon Mohun for raising this point.

5. See for example the discussion by Schwert (1979).

6. If the rate of interest were allowed to vary, then α_0 and α_1 would not be fixed but would depend on the interest rate. See Tobin (1970, pp.308-9).

7. Wealth is reduced because if $\beta<tm$, the reduction in the government debt outweighs the increase in the stock of capital.

8. Further statistical studies based on Granger's methodology by Feige and Pearce (1976, 1979) for the US and by Williams, Goodhart and Gowland (1976) using UK data did raise statistical questions concerning the robustness of Sims' results. Slight changes in statistical techniques do appear to reverse the results obtained by Sims, and so the results on this particular debate appear to be somewhat inconclusive.

9. The results suggest that the efficient market hypothesis is also rejected since β is also significantly different from unity.

10. 'Considering nonstationary series, however, takes us farther away from testable definitions and this tack will not be discussed further' (Granger, 1969, p.429).

11. See Pierce and Haugh (1977) and Feige and Pearce (1979) for a review of these and other tests of causality.

12. Feige and Pearce (1979) and Weisenberger and Thomas (1981) use all three techniques in their empirical investigations of the relationship between the money supply and nominal income; and the money supply, prices and real income, respectively.

13. As in the Granger test, the future and past lags (k and s) must be sufficiently long to include all significant coefficients. The asymmetrical truncation is discussed in Feige and Pearce (1979).

14. Charles Nelson has pointed out to me that if both variables are whitened, the Sims test becomes equivalent to the Pierce-Haugh test (discussed below).

15. Geweke's F-statistic is derived from testing for $h(L)=0$ in the following regression: $y_t=g(L^*)y_t+h(L)x_t+n_t$ where $g(L^*)$ is a polynomial in the lead operator and $h(L)$ a polynomial in the lag operator. This test appears,

therefore, to be a synthesis of the Sims and Granger tests. Since both y_t and x_t variables are included in the relationship, we define this test as consisting in the class of direct Granger tests.

16. The time series followed the following patterns: $x_t = 0.95x_{t-1} + \varepsilon_t$; $y_t = 1.6y_{t-1} - 0.64y_{t-2} + u_t$.

17. Kuh (1966) is also quoted as stimulating this literature. See Barro and Grossman (1971), Neftci (1978) and Geary and Kennan (1982).

18. Lucas (1981) describes this development in the introduction to his volume of collected essays.

19. Bodkin's stated aim was to 'have a fresh look at the issue of whether real wages tend to fall or rise... over the course of the business cycle' (Bodkin, 1969, p.356). The natural rate hypothesis does not appear in his discussion.

20. Seasonal dummies were included in the filtering regression when quarterly data was used.

21. Bodkin used both economy-wide averages and data from the manufacturing sector. The real wage rate variable was created by deflating nominal average earnings (including overtime payments) by the consumer price index. Some of the equations for manufacturing were re-estimated using the wholesale price index as the wage deflator.

22. The attempt by Scarth and Myatt (1980) to amend the synthesis Keynesian model by allowing pro-cyclical real wage movements was also motivated by Bodkin's work. The Scarth and Myatt paper suffers from a serious drawback, however. It relies on prices taking on the role as a jump variable, such that when aggregate demand falls, prices fall initially. The model is therefore unsatisfactory as it relies on price adjustments taking place before quantities adjust.

23. See Sargent (1979, pp.388-93) for a discussion.

24. Neftci's filter consists of taking the logarithms of the raw data (x_t) and passing them through the filter $(1-0.9L)x_t$, where L is the usual lag operator. He then regresses this new variable on a constant, a linear trend, and a set of seasonal dummies. The residuals generated by this regression were then transformed further by spectral methods (he applies a Fourier transform in order to smooth the data and then reverses the procedure). Neftci also explores the effects of choosing different filters and simpler methods to remove seasonality. He reports (in the appendix) that his results were only 'trivially different' in each case (pp.289-90), suggesting that the results obtained are robust to changes in the filtering technique adopted.

25. Neftci obtains almost identical results when he substitutes the unemployment rate for the level of employment in the distributed lag regressions (see his table 2).

26. Sargent's regressions include a trend term and seasonal dummies. All variables were in log form.

27. Geary and Kennan re-estimate Neftci's distributed lag regression while Kirkpatrick obtains his results using the direct Granger test.

28. See Sachs (1982) for a review of this argument.

29. We also note in passing that Kirkpatrick's results also suggest that raw materials prices Granger-cause employment only for the latter period.

30. Kirkpatrick re-estimates Sargent's regressions; Geary and Kennan re-estimate Neftci's distributed lag regressions and Sargent's regressions as well as estimating the Pierce-Haugh S-statistic. All these tests suggest that employment is independent of real wages, although one test suggests that employment Granger-causes the real wage rate (see Geary and Kennan, 1982, table 3). Further, the results obtained by Geary and Kennan with the WPI deflator also appear to be sensitive to the sample period used.

31. Geary and Kennan calculate the S-statistic for differenced and undifferenced data, and calculate versions of the F-statistic for different lag lengths, sample sizes, and the dependent variable in the regression (also for differenced and undifferenced data).

Chapter Seven

GRANGER-CAUSALITY, REAL WAGES AND EMPLOYMENT: A REAPPRAISAL WITH UK DATA

The recent empirical literature on the dynamic relationship between real wages and employment was motivated by a class of neoclassical dynamic demand for labour schedules developed by Sargent (1978, 1979). As we derived in Chapter Five above, this analysis generates two testable propositions which have been focused upon in previous investigations. First, real wages 'cause' employment in the sense of Granger (1969). Introducing lagged values of real wages into an employment auto-regression should result in a significant reduction in the size of the unexplained variation in employment. Second, no restriction is placed on the extent and direction of the correlation between any particular lagged real wage term and the current employment level. The model does predict, however, that the sum of the coefficients on the lagged real wage terms should be negative. A permanent increase in real wages should eventually result in a permanent reduction in employment.

The amendment to Sargent's model considered in Chapter Five, where following Kirkpatrick (1982), Symons (1985) and Symons and Layard (1984) real materials prices are introduced into the analysis, yields two additional propositions amenable to empirical testing. The amended neoclassical model predicts, firstly, that real materials prices should Granger-cause and, secondly, that the sum of coefficients on the lagged prices of raw materials should be negative.

In this chapter we investigate the empirical validity of these four propositions with real wage, real materials, and employment data from the manufacturing sector of the UK for the postwar period using the three tests for Granger-causality discussed in the previous chapter. This chapter is

organised as follows. The data and testing
procedures used are discussed in Section 1. In
Section 2 we report the empirical results of a
battery of bivariate tests for Granger-causality
between real wages and employment. In Section 3 we
report the results of examining the performance of
the amended neoclassical model by applying a
trivariate version of the direct Granger test to
our UK data set. Concluding comments are offered
in Section 4.

1. DATA AND ECONOMETRIC SPECIFICATION

The employment, real wage and real materials prices
variables used for this study, presented in Figure
7.1, are taken from the UK manufacturing sector.
The real wage series is identical to that used by
Geary and Kennan (1982) and is created by deflating
the straight-time hourly money wage rate (excluding
overtime and bonuses) by the wholesale price index
(WPI), which covers the factory gate price of
domestically produced manufactured goods. This
series runs from 1957(1)-1981(2) and determines the
basic sample period for the regressions. The real
materials price variable is created by deflating
the sterling price of material inputs purchased by
manufacturing industry by the WPI (see appendix 7.2
for data definitions).
    The test procedures applied in this study
require the data to be filtered to produce
stationary variables. The regressions therefore
used detrended and deseasonalised proportionate
rates of change of each of the variables. We note,
however, that the rate of change of real wages
exhibits a significant degree of
heteroscedasticity. It has a coefficient of
variation of 1.63 for the period up to 1969(4)
which increases to 7.07 in the following period.
The movements between 1976 and 1978 are
particularly pronounced. The real wage fell by a
cumulative total of approximately 15 per cent
between 1976(3) and 1977(3), and increased by a
similar amount in the following year. These
movements coincide with the implementation of the
Callaghan incomes policies and their collapse in
1978. An analysis of their effect on the results
obtained is provided below.
    The three widely used bivariate tests for
Granger-causality discussed in the previous chapter
are applied to the data set. The first, the direct

Tests: the neoclassical model

Figure 7.1.

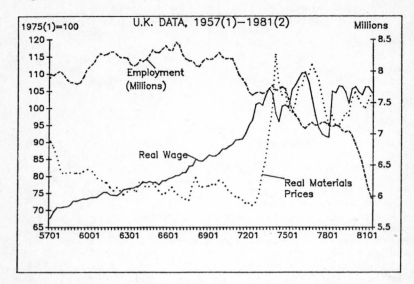

Granger test applied by Sargent (1978) and Kirkpatrick (1981) to US data, involves estimating the following bivariate vector autoregressions:

$$N_t = a_0 + \Sigma_{j=1}^{k_1} a_{0j} N_{t-j} + \Sigma_{j=1}^{k_2} a_{1j} w_{t-j} + e_{1t} \quad (7.1a)$$

$$w_t = b_0 + \Sigma_{j=1}^{k_3} b_{0j} N_{t-j} + \Sigma_{j=1}^{k_4} b_{1j} w_{t-j} + e_{2t} \quad (7.1b)$$

where the e_{it}s are in principle white-noise variables; N_t and w_t are the filtered employment and real wage variables respectively; and the k_i terms are the lengths of the lags used, which are chosen empirically. The direct Granger test involves calculating F-statistics on the joint significance of the lags of the relevant explanatory variables. When these are significant at the 10 per cent level, suggesting that the explanatory variable Granger-causes the dependent variable, we calculate the sum of the coefficients on the lags of the explanatory variables to assess the permanence and direction of the effect of the explanatory variable on the dependent variable.

The second test we apply is the Sims (1972) test used by Neftci with USA data. This test is based on estimating the following regression:

$$N_t = \alpha_0 + \Sigma_{j=-l_1}^{12} \alpha_{0j} w_{t-j} + u_{1t} \qquad (7.2a)$$

$$w_t = \beta_0 + \Sigma_{j=-l_1}^{12} \beta_{0j} N_{t-j} + u_{2t} \qquad (7.2b)$$

where l_1 and l_2 are the lengths of the leads and lags, respectively, which again are chosen empirically; and the u_{it} terms represent white-noise error terms. The Sims test is based on calculating F-statistics on the <u>leads</u> of the right hand side variables and is designed as a backwards regression. F-statistics significant at the 10 per cent level are taken to imply that the <u>dependent</u> variable Granger-causes the <u>explanatory</u> variable. In such circumstances we calculate the sum of the coefficients on the lead values of the explanatory variable.

The third test used in this study, the cross-correlation test developed by Haugh (1976) and Pierce and Haugh (1979), was used by Geary and Kennan in their international comparison. This test is based on fitting ARIMA models to the variables and calculating cross-correlation coefficients between the current innovation in one variable and current and lagged innovations of the other. The Pierce-Haugh S-statistic is defined as the sum of the squared cross-correlation coefficients multiplied by the sample size:

$$S_{(2k+1)} = n\Sigma_{j=-k}^{k} r(k)^2 \qquad (7.3)$$

where $r(k)^2$ is the squared cross-correlation between the current innovation in one series and the kth lag of the other; n is the sample size; the number in parenthesis defines the degrees of freedom; and k was chosen to equal 10 (as in Geary and Kennan). The S-statistic is distributed as a χ^2 variable under the null hypothesis of independence between the variables.

Finally, we assess the robustness of the results obtained in the bivariate exercises to the introduction of real materials prices into the analysis by estimating a trivariate version of the direct Granger test. This test, applied by Kirkpatrick (1982) to German data, consists of estimating the following three equations:

$$N_t = a_0 + \Sigma_{j=1}^{n1} a_{0j} N_{t-j} + \Sigma_{j=1}^{n2} a_{1j} w_{t-j}$$
$$+ \Sigma_{j=1}^{n3} a_{2j} m_{t-j} + \varepsilon_{1t} \qquad (7.4a)$$

$$w_t = b_0 + \Sigma_{j=1}^{n_4} \, b_{0j} \, N_{t-j} + \Sigma_{j=1}^{n_5} \, b_{1j} \, w_{t-j}$$
$$+ \, \Sigma_{j=1}^{n_6} \, b_{2j} \, m_{t-j} + \varepsilon_{2t} \qquad (7.4b)$$

$$m_t = c_0 + \Sigma_{j=1}^{n_7} \, c_{0j} \, N_{t-j} + \Sigma_{j=1}^{n_8} \, c_{1j} \, w_{t-j}$$
$$+ \, \Sigma_{j=1}^{n_9} \, c_{2j} \, m_{t-j} + \varepsilon_{3t} \qquad (7.4c)$$

where m_t are the filtered real materials prices; ε_{it} are white-noise error terms; and the lengths of the lags (n_i) are chosen empirically. As with the bivariate tests, we calculate the relevant F-statistics to test for Granger-causality on each of the equations and, when appropriate, the sum of coefficients on the lags of the relevant explanatory variables.

2. BIVARIATE TESTS

Preliminary estimates

Table 7.1 reports the results of the Sims and Granger regressions with the real wage rate (basic wages deflated by either the RPI or WPI) using a model with ten leads and lags.[1] The LM(8) statistics (column 6) test for up to eighth-order serial correlation.[2] In cases where this statistic was significant at the 5 per cent level, the equation was re-estimated by autoregressive least squares (ALS) of an appropriate order. We only report the results of the final equations estimated.

Both the Sims and Granger tests produce F-statistics (column 4) which strongly suggest that real wages Granger-cause employment with little (RPI) or no (WPI) feedback.[3] There is some suggestion, however, that the RPI-deflated real wage rate does respond to employment movements although there is some conflict about this: the Granger test accepts the hypothesis of independence while the Sims test rejects this hypothesis only at the 10 per cent level of significance.

Consider next the sum of the coefficients on the future values of the explanatory variable in the Sims test and the lagged values of the explanatory variable for the Granger test. These are presented in column 5 of Table 7.1. Two points should be noted here. First, although the Sims test does suggest that the RPI-deflated real wage rate does respond to innovations in employment (row 5), the insignificant sum of coefficients suggests that this response is temporary.

Second, the sum of the coefficients in the case where real wages Granger-cause employment appear to be significant when the WPI-deflated real wage rate is used. Notice, however, that this sum is far greater in the Sims test than in the Granger test. This reflects the fact that in the Sims test we are investigating the effect of one real wage rate on future values of employment, while in the Granger test we investigate the <u>joint</u> effect of lagged real wages on employment for any given period. Solving both equations for the long-run effect of a real wage innovation on employment yields quite similar results. The Sims test (row 2) gives a value of -0.56, while for the Granger test (row 4) this value is -0.20. Thus these first-round tests produce reasonably similar elasticities of employment with respect to innovations in real wages.

The results in Table 7.1 provide initial support for the first two propositions provided by the neoclassical model. Innovations in real wages appear to generate inverse movements in employment, although the response in employment is extremely sluggish, taking up to ten quarters to be completed. However, we also note that the estimated long-run innovation elasticities of employment are way below that predicted by this theory.

How robust are these results? First, the results obtained using the Sims test do not appear to be robust; they are sensitive to the choice of filter. When we apply a filter similar to that used by Neftci (1978), the Sims test produces a smaller (though still significant) F-statistic when the WPI deflator is used. More importantly, the sum of coefficients has become insignificant in this case (see Table A7.1).

Second, Table 7.2 below shows that the Pierce-Haugh cross-correlation tests for the full data period generate results which are inconsistent with those reported above. The S-statistic when the RPI deflator is used is way below the 50 per cent critical value (row 1). With the WPI deflator this statistic is significant at only around the 20 per cent level (row 2). Notice however that a small reduction in the sample period generates dramatic changes in the S-statistics. Rows 3 and 4 present the S-statistics when data up to 1977(4) are used,

Table 7.1. Bivariate Sims and Granger tests, 1952(1)-1981(2)

Test	Years[a]	Wage deflator	F-test[b]	Sum of coefficients[c]	LM(8)[d]	Estimation method
Real wages (w) to employment (N)[e]						
1. Sims	1954(4)-1978(4)	RPI	$F(10,76)=2.35$*	-1.43^{Δ} (0.39)	4.26	OLS
2. Sims	1959(4)-1978(4)	WPI	$F(10,56)=3.80$*	-1.88^{Δ} (0.99)	6.34	OLS
3. Granger	1954(4)-1981(2)	RPI	$F(10,87)=1.90^{\Delta}$	-0.15 (0.09)	13.01	OLS
4. Granger	1959(4)-1981(2)	WPI	$F(10,51)=3.84$*	-0.22* (0.07)	6.51	ALS(8)[f]
Employment (N) to real wages (w)[e]						
5. Sims	1954(4)-1978(4)	RPI	$F(10,75)=1.94^{\Delta}$	0.33 (0.30)	10.93	ALS(1)[f]
6. Sims	1959(4)-1978(4)	WPI	$F(10,55)=1.38$		5.69	ALS(1)[f]
7. Granger	1954(4)-1981(2)	RPI	$F(10,87)=1.65$		13.99^{Δ}	OLS
8. Granger	1959(4)-1981(2)	WPI	$F(10,67)=0.64$		9.19	OLS

Note: All equations fitted with ten lags on explanatory variables and a constant term. Sims test includes ten leads (plus current) as well.
* Statistically significant at 5 per cent level.
Δ Statistically significant at 10 per cent level.
(a) Years define sample period for dependent variable. Note that for the Sims test ten quarterly leads are used for the explanatory variable.
(b) Test for significant contribution of ten future values of explanatory variable in Sims test, and ten lagged values of explanatory variable in Granger test. Figures in parentheses are degrees of freedom.
(c) Sums of coefficients on ten future values of explanatory variable for Sims test, and the sum of coefficients on ten lags of explanatory variable for Granger test. Figures in parentheses are standard errors of sum. Figures not presented when F-test accepts null hypothesis of no causality at 10 per cent level of significance.
(d) Lagrange multiplier test for eighth-order serial correlation. This statistic is distributed as a χ^2 with eight degrees of freedom (critical values are: 5 per cent = 15.51; 10 per cent = 13.36).
(e) All variables pre-filtered by regressing the percentage rate of change of the variable on a constant, a time trend, and three seasonal dummies.
(f) Autoregressive least squares (nth order), estimated using Cochrane-Orcutt iterative technique.

188

corresponding to the sample period used by Geary and Kennan with similar data. The S-statistic for the RPI deflator has increased sharply (row 3), while with the WPI deflator the S-statistic is now way below the 50 per cent level of significance, a result similar to that obtained by Geary and Kennan.[4] Thus not only does the cross-correlation test produce results which conflict with those reported in Table 7.1, they also indicate that a small change in the sample size generates quite substantial changes in the reported test statistics. There appears to be instability in the real wage-employment relationship during the mid to late 1970s.[5]

Finally, as with earlier studies using USA data, the results obtained are strikingly different when the Sims and Granger tests are conducted for the period up to 1971(4), before inflation accelerated. As shown in the Appendix Table A7.2, the results for the shortened data period show no influence of real wages on employment while the Sims test suggests that employment may be influencing the WPI-deflated real wage rate.

All these results suggest that the observations for the latter part of our sample period have unduly influenced the F-statistics and sum of coefficients obtained in both the Sims and Granger tests. In the following two sections we report the results of re-estimating the Sims and

Table 7.2. Cross-correlation tests[a]

| Years[c] | Deflator | ARIMA models fitted to: | | S-statistic[b] |
		Real wage (w)	Employment (N)	
1954(1)-1981(2)	RPI	(5,0,0)	(6,1,0)	15.02
1959(1)-1981(2)	WPI	(5,0,0)	(6,1,0)	27.09
1954(1)-1977(4)	RPI	(4,0,0)	(6,1,0)	26.14
1959(1)-1977(4)	WPI	(10,0,0)	(6,1,0)	15.88

(a) The cross-correlograms include current and ten lagged values for each variable.
(b) The S-statistic is distributed as a χ^2 variable with 21 degrees of freedom. Critical values are: 10 per cent = 29.6; 25 per cent = 24.9; 50 per cent = 20.3.
(c) Original series filtered using full data set for rows 1 and 2, and using data up to 1977(4) for rows 3 and 4.

Granger regressions when adjustments are made to counteract this heteroscedasticity problem.

GLS estimation

The original filtered real wage variables, and the residuals obtained in the OLS regressions when the real wage rate is the dependent variable (rows 1, 2 7 and 8 of Table 7.1) all exhibit a marked increase in their variances during the 1970s.

We investigate two hypotheses which might explain this observed heteroscedasticity:
(1) the acceleration of inflation during the 1970s; and
(2) the effects of government-imposed incomes policies between 1976 and 1978.

In this section we report the results of conducting the Granger and Sims tests by generalised least squares (GLS) based on the hypothesis that the variance of the residuals is related to the quarterly inflation rate. This will occur if, as in Friedman's (1968, 1975) analysis, nominal wages adjust to price increases with a time lag.[6] In such circumstances, as prices rise real wages will at first fall and then will increase when nominal wages begin to adjust. The higher the inflation rate, the larger will be the oscillations in the real wage rate. Our proposition that the variance in the real wage rate is related to the inflation rate is thus based on the assumption of sluggish nominal wage adjustment.

A typical approach to removing heteroscedasticity amongst residuals is based on the assumption that the residual variance is a linear function of the square of an appropriate exogenous variable; in our case the quarterly inflation rate:

$$\hat{\sigma}_t^2 = \sigma_u^2 \ \pi_t^2 \qquad\qquad (7.5)$$

where $\hat{\sigma}_t^2$ is the variance of the residuals at time t; σ_u^2 is the variance of the true unobserved error term; and π_t^2 is the quarterly rate of inflation (using the RPI for the regression with the RPI-deflated real wage rate and the WPI for the WPI-deflated real wage rate).[7]

Park (1966) suggests a procedure for the elimination (or reduction) of heteroscedasticity which does not rely on such a restrictive assumption as expressed in equation (7.5). This

190

procedure involves estimating the precise nature of the relationship between the residual variance and the relevant exogenous variable using the following equations:

$$\hat{\sigma}_t^2 = \sigma_u^2 \; \pi_t^{\gamma} \; e^{vt} \tag{7.6}$$

or, taking logs:

$$\ln \hat{\sigma}_t^2 = \ln \sigma_u^2 + \gamma \ln \pi_t + v_t \tag{7.7}$$

where v_t is a white-noise error term; e is the natural exponent; and ln is a natural logarithm. An estimate of the parameter γ in equation (7.7) is obtained by a least squares regression of the log of the squared residuals from each of the original Sims and Granger tests on the log of the quarterly inflation rate. The GLS estimates are obtained by taking the estiamte of γ from the OLS regressions and re-running the tests with each variable divided by π_t raised to the power $[\gamma/2]$.

The results of applying GLS to the initial Sims and Granger tests are presented in Table 7.3.

Table 7.3. Causality tests adjusted for non-stationarity[a]

Test	Years	Wage deflator	F-test	Sum of coefficients	LM(8)	Estimation method[b]
Real wages (w) to employment (N)						
1. Sims[c]	1954(4)-1978(4)	RPI	F(10,76)=2.91*	-1.661* (0.77)	5.20	GLS
2. Sims	1959(4)-1978(4)	WPI	F(10,56)=3.08*	-1.454 (0.99)	4.43	GLS
Employment (N) to real wages (w)						
7. Granger	1954(4)-1981(2)	RPI	F(10,87)=1.08		11.48	GLS
8. Granger	1959(4)-1981(2)	WPI	F(10,67)=0.38		8.88	GLS

(a) For definitions see Table 7.1.
(b) The coefficients on the inflation rate terms produced by the Park test and used as weights for the GLS estimation are: Row 1: -0.37; Row 2: -0.27; Row 7: -0.62; Row 8: 0.94. The last two coefficients were significant at the 99 per cent level.

Tests: the neoclassical model

Apart from the Sims test using the RPI-deflated real wage rate, the other tests generated smaller F-statistics than those produced by OLS estimation. In addition, the sum of the coefficients for the Sims test using the WPI-deflated real wage rate is now insignificant.

These results suggest that when the variation in real wages during the 1970s is reduced, there is a greater tendency to reject the proposition that Granger-causality exists in either direction. These changes are fairly marginal, however. As will be discussed at length in the next section, the incomes policies of the mid to late 1970s appear to play a much more important role in the results obtained with the original Granger and Sims tests.

Callaghan incomes policies and the observed relationship

In this section we report the results of applying a set of dummy variables to the period 1976(3) to 1978(4), when real wages exhibited the largest sustained fall (1976(3)-1977(3)) and subsequent rise (1977(4)-1978(4)) during our sample period. The empirical question raised is whether these particular observations, which represent extreme outliers in the movement of real wages, unduly influenced the results obtained in our initial Granger and Sims tests.

The quarters in which the dummy variables were applied were chosen empirically. These movements are associated, however, with the implementation of phase three of the Callaghan incomes policies - a policy of stern wage controls - and its subsequent collapse in the so-called 'winter of discontent'. In the third quarter of 1976 the government in the United Kingdom, with trades union agreement, imposed a strict percentage nominal wage norm while relaxing previously-used price controls.[8] The dramatic rise in real wages between 1977(4) and 1978(4) corresponds to the breakdown of the Callaghan government's agreement with the Trades Union Council (TUC), with the TUC withdrawing from its commitment to support the government's incomes policies.[9]

Our approach was to assume that the incomes policies applied during this period had a temporary effect on real wages. Laidler (1982) argues that in certain circumstances incomes policies lead to a

192

reduction in real wages rather than a fall in
inflation rates.[10] Tarling and Wilkinson (1977)
present evidence to this effect. However, they
also note that, when dismantled, these policies are
usually followed by a wage explosion and thus a
return of real wages to previous levels or growth
rates. To capture this proposition we adopted a
procedure used by Gordon (1981, 1982) with US data
by adding a dummy variable into the equation used
to filter the real wage series which takes on a
value of -1 during the period 1976(3) to 1977(3), a
value of +1 during 1977(4) to 1978(4), and 0 in
every other quarter.[11] This procedure therefore
imposes the assumption that the rate of change of
real wages was only temporarily influenced by
Callaghan's policies.

The results obtained using this procedure are
presented in Table 7.4. They show the importance
of the wide variation in real wage movements during
the period 1976(3) to 1978(4) in generating the
original results. When these movements are dummied
out of the tests, we find little evidence of any
inverse effects of real wage innovations on
employment. Although the F-statistics testing for
causality running from real wages to employment
remain significant, the sums of the coefficients
are now insignificantly different from zero. In
fact, the Granger tests (rows 3 and 4) produce sums
of coefficients which are positive. Finally, we
note that these tests provide some evidence to
suggest that once the effect on real wages of the
Callaghan incomes policies is removed, employment
appears to Granger-cause real wages. There is,
however, some conflict in the results produced by
the tests reported in rows 5 to 8, and thus strong
conclusions on this issue should perhaps not be
drawn from this evidence.

These tests reveal that the results reported
in Table 7.1, providing support for the
neoclassical proposition that real wage innovations
generate inverse innovations in employment, are
crucially dependent on the movement of real wages
when the Callaghan incomes policies were
implemented and then dismantled during 1978. On
empirical grounds, this conclusion is perhaps not
very surprising. The large fall in real wages
between mid-1976 and mid-1977 is associated with
the levelling-off of employment between 1976 and
1978 (see Figure 7.1). Because the trend in
employment was mostly downwards throughout our
sample period, the rate of change of employment was

Table 7.4. Causality tests incorporating Callaghan incomes policy[a]

Test	Years	Wage deflator	F-test	Sum of coefficients	Coefficient on dummy variable	LM(8)	Estimation method
Real wages (w) to employment (N)							
1. Sims[b]	1954(4)-1978(4)	RPI	F(10,75)=1.50		2.12* (0.81)	10.69	OLS
2. Sims[b]	1959(4)-1978(4)	WPI	F(10,55)=2.37*	-0.31 (1.24)	2.25* (1.04)	11.44	OLS
3. Granger[c]	1954(4)-1981(2)	RPI	F(10,87)=1.87$^\Delta$	0.15 (0.11)	n.a.[d]	10.62	OLS
4. Granger[c]	1959(4)-1981(2)	WPI	F(10,67)=2.15*	0.19 (0.13)	n.a.	10.10	OLS
Employment (N) to real wages (w)							
5. Sims[c]	1954(4)-1978(4)	RPI	F(10,75)=1.36		n.a.	9.10	ALS(1)
6. Sims[c]	1959(4)-1978(4)	WPI	F(10,55)=1.97$^\Delta$	-0.57* (0.21)	n.a.	7.22	ALS(1)
7. Granger[b]	1954(4)-1981(2)	RPI	F(10,70)=1.97$^\Delta$	-0.24 (0.46)	2.76* (0.70)	2.47	ALS(8)
8. Granger[b]	1959(4)-1981(2)	WPI	F(10,50)=0.85		3.66* (0.90)	8.71	ALS(8)

(a) See Table 7.1 for all definitions.
(b) The incomes policy dummy (see text) is included in the final regressions when real wages are the dependent variable (rows 1, 2, 7, 8).
(c) The incomes policy dummy is included in the filtering procedure when employment is the dependent variable (rows 3, 4, 5, 6).
(d) Not applicable, real wage variables filtered for incomes policy effect.

above trend during these years. Similarly, the return of real wages during 1978 to their early 1976 levels generated large positive rates of change of real wages in 1978. This movement in real wages is associated with the dramatic drop in manufacturing employment that began in the following year (1979(4)). The results presented in Table 7.1 suggest that these movements can be attributed to the oscillations in the real wage rate during the period 1976-78. However, alternative arguments have been advanced suggesting that the movements in employment during these periods were influenced by factors omitted from our analysis such as the relative tightening of fiscal and monetary policies in late 1979 to 1982 and the substantial appreciation of the UK effective exchange rate between 1977 and 1980.[12]

The empirical approach adopted in this section is not designed to help adjudicate between these two views; rather our intention is to highlight the importance of developments during these periods in determining the initial results reported in Table 7.1. However, these results do in fact raise a problem with the first view that the fluctuations in employment observed between 1977 and 1981 resulted from movements in the real wage rate between 1976 and 1978. Such a view is not easily reconciled with the neoclassical model outlined in Chapter 5 above. Our empirical analysis was based on the assumption that the Callaghan incomes policies only had a temporary effect on real wages. The adjustment cost story suggests that firms making the same assumption would probably not respond to the real wage fall of 1976-7 by increasing employment since they would have anticipated a corresponding rise in the near future. Rather than strengthening the inverse real wage to employment relationship as suggested by our results, the observations during this period should in fact have worsened it according to the theory. Consistency between these results and the adjustment cost theory could be achieved if firms assumed that the effect of the incomes policies were permanent. Alternatively, the view that real wages were important during this period could be reconciled with the evidence presented in Tables 7.1 and 7.4 if the adjustment cost theory were abandoned in favour of an intertemporal substitution theory (Lucas and Rapping, 1969). However, this theory, which suggests that a temporary fall in real wages induces firms to employ more labour in the current period, rests uneasily with the evidence reported above suggesting that employment responds sluggishly, if at all, to real wage movements.

3. INTRODUCING REAL MATERIALS PRICES – TRIVARIATE TESTS[13]

Does the introduction of real materials prices into the tests for Granger-causality improve the performance of the neoclassical model? This question is addressed by applying trivariate vector autoregressions (equations 7.4 above) to our filtered data series (using the WPI deflator only) with filtered real materials prices added. As before, the regressions were applied to detrended and deseasonalised proportionate rates of change of the variables.

Table 7.5 reports the results of estimating equations (7.4) over the full sample period with four lags each on employment and real materials prices and ten lags on real wages.[14] They suggest that real wages and real materials prices Granger-cause employment with no feedback (column 1), confirming the prediction of the neoclassical model. The inverse real wage effect on employment does appear to increase somewhat when real materials prices are included in the analysis. The long-run real wage elasticity of employment has increased from -0.43 to -0.76 (see Table 7.6, columns 1 and 2), and the F-statistic testing the joint significance of the lagged real wage terms in the employment equation is now significant at the 95 per cent level. However, the sum of the lagged real material price terms is positive; the long-run elasticity is estimated to equal 0.15. This is a disturbing feature of these results, suggesting perhaps that the substitution effect induced by changes in real materials prices dominates the output effect. This is certainly not consistent with the neoclassical model.[15]

Although the introduction of real materials prices into the employment equation increases somewhat the estimated real wage elasticity of the demand for labour, it does not however remove other unsatisfactory features of the equation noted in previous sections. The model still suffers from sample period instability. Table A7.3 of the Appendix reveals that over the shortened data period only real materials prices Granger-cause employment. Thus real wages and employment appear not to Granger-cause each other over this shorter sample period; this result is robust to the inclusion of real materials prices in the analysis. In addition, the results for the employment equation in the trivariate model reported in Table 7.5 are again extremely sensitive to the movements of the real wage rate during the late 1970s. Estimating the equation up to the year 1977(4), corresponding to the Geary and Kennan sample period, yields results suggesting that real wages

Table 7.5. Trivariate Granger tests, full sample period

Dependent variable	Employment (N)	Real wages (w)	Real materials prices (m)
F-statistics:			
Four lags in N	-	F(4,68)=0.49	F(4,68)=0.29
Ten lags in w	F(10,68)=2.44*	-	F(10,68)=1.54
Four lags in m	F(4,68)=2.70*	F(4,68)=0.87	-
Sum of coefficients:			
Four lags in N	-	-0.05 (0.54)	0.03 (0.66)
Ten lags in w	-0.35* (0.11)	-	1.63* (0.76)
Four lags in m	0.07* (0.03)	-0.23 (0.18)	-
LM(8)	12.44	11.18	18.99*

Note: See Table 7.1 for all definitions. All equations estimated by OLS.

and raw materials prices fail to Granger-cause employment.[16] These results are almost identical to those obtained in our bivariate exercises over the same sample period, and confirm our earlier results that the Geary and Kennan independence results were not due to their omitting real materials prices. Finally, as with the bivariate results, the apparent inverse effect of real wages on employment arising in the trivariate model disappears when real wages are filtered for the effects of the Callaghan incomes policies (column 4, Table 7.6 below).

The performance of the original bivariate employment equation can be compared with that of the amended version using Table 7.6 which provides a more detailed account of the results obtained for this equation over our full sample period. Columns 1 and 2 present coefficient estimates and other diagnostic statistics for the two equations with unadjusted data, and columns 3 and 4 present these results with the real wage filtered for incomes

Table 7.6. The employment vector autoregressions, full sample period

Wages filtered for incomes policies[a]

	(1)	(2)	(3)	(4)
Explanatory variables				
N_{t-1}	0.83*	0.76*	0.76*	0.76*
N_{t-2}	-0.03	-0.01	-0.07	-0.06
N_{t-3}	0.18	0.20	0.23	0.24
N_{t-4}	-0.39*	-0.40*	-0.22^Δ	-0.24^Δ
Typical s.e. (N)	(0.13)	(0.13)	(0.13)	(0.13)
w_{t-1}	0.002	-0.01	0.04	0.03
w_{t-2}	-0.04	-0.06*	0.01	-0.01
w_{t-3}	-0.02	-0.04^Δ	0.03	0.02
w_{t-4}	0.01	-0.01	0.06*	0.06*
w_{t-5}	0.02	-0.003	0.07*	0.07*
w_{t-6}	-0.06*	-0.07*	0.01	0.01
w_{t-7}	-0.02	-0.04^Δ	0.04	0.04
w_{t-8}	-0.02	-0.03	0.01	0.02
w_{t-9}	-0.02	-0.02	-0.01	-0.002
w_{t-10}	-0.05*	-0.06*	-0.04	-0.03
Typical s.e. (w)	(0.02)	(0.02)	(0.03)	(0.03)
m_{t-1}		0.05*		0.02
m_{t-2}		0.03		-0.0003
m_{t-3}		-0.003		-0.02
m_{t-4}		-0.01		-0.01
Typical s.e. (m)		(0.02)		(0.02)
Diagnostic statistics				
R^2	0.73	0.77	0.75	0.75
RSS	13.20	11.39	12.53	12.19
LM(8)	6.69	12.44	6.13	7.68
F_w	$F(10,72)=1.85^\Delta$	$F(10,68)=2.44*$	$F(10,72)=2.33*$	$F(10,68)=1.84^\Delta$
F_m	-	$F(4,68)=2.70*$	-	$F(4,68)=0.47$
Sum of w coefficients	$-0.17^\Delta(0.09)$	-0.35*(0.11)	$0.23^\Delta(0.13)$	0.20(0.14)
Sum of m coefficients	-	0.07*(0.03)	-	-0.01(0.03)
Long-run w elasticity	-0.43	-0.76	0.76	0.65
Long-run m elasticity	-	0.15	-	-0.03

Note: See Table 7.1 for all definitions. The results presented in column 1 correspond to those reported in Table 7.1 row 4; column 2 corresponds to Table 7.5 column 1; column 3 to Table 7.4 row 4.
(a) Real wages filtered for the effects of incomes policies.

policies. Turning to columns 1 and 2, we see that
the coefficients on the real wage rate lagged two,
six and ten periods are in the main significant.
As we noted above, the introduction of real
materials prices into the employment vector
autoregression increases the estimated wage
elasticity of employment rather markedly. Almost
all the coefficients on the lagged real wage terms
have increased, though the effect on the first four
lags is particularly pronounced. Notice as well
that the sign on all the real wage terms is
negative once real materials prices are included in
the regression. Finally, only the first lag in
real materials prices is significant in the
equation. This was also the case for the model
with ten lags on real materials prices (the 4-10-10
model). However, as revealed in columns 3 and 4 of
Table 7.6, the negative real wage effect on
employment disappears entirely when the incomes
policies filter is applied to the real wage rate,
regardless of whether real materials prices are
included in the exercise or not.

4. CONCLUDING COMMENTS

The results presented in this chapter are
essentially negative. The original and amended
versions of the neoclassical model of the dynamic
demand for labour schedule, where the employment
autoregression is conditioned primarily by lagged
values of real wages and real materials prices,
receive little support in our tests. These results
therefore contradict the comment by Symons and
Layard (1984) quoted at the beginning of Part Three
above. Indeed, even when support for this model is
indicated, disturbing features arise. Notable
amongst these is the prediction that innovations in
real materials prices tend to generate positive
innovations in employment, thus contradicting a key
element of the model. Our investigation also
reveals that Geary and Kennan's (1982) results for
the UK depend critically on the sample period they
used. The results for our full sample period
(1957(1) to 1981(2)) suggest that real wages
Granger-cause employment with little or no
feedback. These results appear to be largely
independent of whether or not real materials prices
are included in the analysis, although the
estimated real wage elasticity of employment does
appear to increase when real materials prices are

added to the exercise. However, the relationship between real wages and employment is exceedingly unstable, with the length of the sample period used for the exercise playing a critical role in determining the results obtained. Estimates of the vector autoregression for employment using data up to 1971(4), with and without real materials prices included, suggest that real wages and employment are independent. The same is true for estimates using data up to 1977(4). Such instability was also observed with US data by Geary and Kennan and might be interpreted as implying that the models underlying this empirical literature are seriously misspecified.[17][18]

Finally, all the results obtained in the bivariate and trivariate exercises are extremely sensitive to the dramatic movements of the real wage rate between 1976 and 1978, a period when a stern incomes policy was first implemented and then dismantled during what has become known popularly as the 'winter of discontent' in 1978. In particular, the evidence suggesting that innovations in real wages generate innovations in employment relies crucially on the inclusion of these observations. Filtering out these observations, which constitute extreme outliers in the UK real wage series, totally eliminates the observed inverse effect of real wages and employment.

APPENDIX 7.1. ADDITIONAL TABLES

Table A7.1. Sims tests using Neftci filter[a][b]

Test	Years	Wage deflator	F-test	Sum of coefficients	LM(8)	Estimation method
Real wages (w) to employment (N)						
1. Sims[c]	1954(4)-1978(4)	RPI	F(10,76)=2.30*	-0.907 (0.53)	3.22	OLS
2. Sims	1959(4)-1978(4)	WPI	F(10,56)=2.59*	-0.633 (0.71)	5.96	OLS
Employment (N) to real wages (w)						
5. Sims	1954(4)-1978(4)	RPI	F(10,75)=2.09*	-0.123 (0.28)	9.60	ALS(1)
6. Sims	1959(4)-1978(4)	WPI	F(10,55)=1.29		5.70	ALS(1)

(a) See Table 7.1 for definitions.
(b) Neftci's (1978) version of Sims test adopts an alternative filter: he regresses ln x_t - 0.9ln x_{t-1} on seasonal dummies and a time trend to obtain x_t^*.
(c) Rows correspond to those in Table 7.1.

Table A7.2. Sims and Granger tests for shortened data periods, 1951(2)-1971(4)[a]

Test	Years	Wage deflator	F-test	LM(8)	Estimation method
Real wages (w) to employment (N)					
1. Sims	1954(4)-1969(2)	RPI	$F(10,38)=0.20$	12.61	OLS
2. Sims	1959(4)-1969(2)	WPI	$F(10,18)=0.41$	24.29*	OLS
3. Granger	1954(4)-1971(4)	RPI	$F(10,49)=0.53$	14.79$^\Delta$	OLS
4. Granger	1959(4)-1971(4)	WPI	$F(10,29)=0.68$	25.31*	OLS
Employment (N) to real wages (w)					
5. Sims	1954(4)-1969(2)	RPI	$F(10,37)=0.85$	14.31$^\Delta$	ALS(1)
6. Sims	1959(4)-1969(2)	WPI	$F(10,17)=2.15^\Delta$	12.63	ALS(1)
7. Granger	1954(4)-1971(4)	RPI	$F(10,49)=0.96$	17.87*	OLS
8. Granger	1959(4)-1971(4)	WPI	$F(10,29)=1.22$	28.86*	OLS

[a] See Table 7.1 for all definitions.

Table A7.3. Trivariate Granger tests, shortened sample period

Dependent variable:	Employment (N)	Real wages (w)	Real materials prices(m)
F-statistics:			
Four lags in N	-	$F(4,30)=0.62$	$F(4,30)=1.82$
Ten lags in w	$F(10,30)=0.53$	-	$F(10,30)=0.39$
Four lags in m	$F(4,30)=2.31^{\Delta}$	$F(4,30)=1.00$	-
Sum of coefficients:			
Four lags in N	-	-0.52 (0.42)	-1.62* (0.77)
Ten lags in w	0.31 (0.30)	-	-0.83 (1.02)
Four lags in m	0.35* (0.12)	0.03 (0.22)	-
LM(8)	12.92	22.64*	11.51

Note: See Table 7.1 for all definitions. All equations estimated by OLS.

APPENDIX 7.2. DATA AND SOURCES

Basic wage

Basic   hourly   wages,   manual   workers,   UK
manufacturing (spliced by authors):
1948(1)-1955(4): British   Labour   Statistics,
                 Historical Abstract, Table 30;
1956(1)-1972(4): Economic Trends, Supplement 1975,
                 Table 90;
1973(1)-1981(2): Department of Employment Gazettes,
                 various years, Table 131.

Retail price index

All goods, UK: Economic Trends, Annual Supplement.

Wholesale price index

Prices of goods leaving factory gates, UK
manufacturing: Economic Trends, Annual Supplement,
1982, Table 115.

Employees in employment

All employees in manufacturing sector, Great
Britain,   covering   Standard   Industrial
Classification groups 3-19. The series changes on
a number of occasions because of changed basis for
calculations: national insurance cards were used
until 1971; after that time calculations were based
on Census of Employment. Alterations in the
calculations also due to changes in weights of the
industrial classification. Figures presented were
spliced by authors. The reported data set is
comparable to currently reported figures in the
Gazette.

Materials prices

Prices of materials and fuels purchased by
manufacturing industry in £ sterling, Economic
Trends, Annual Supplement, 1982, Table 115.

NOTES

1. We experimented with models incorporating four, six, eight, ten and twelve quarterly leads and lags. The tests for causality running from real wages to employment suggested that real wage innovations lagged up to ten quarters were significantly influencing current innovations in employment (see the discussion in Section 3 and Tables 7.1 and 7.2). Adding two additional leads and lags did not alter this result. For the remainder of the chapter we report only the results using the ten lead and lag models.

2. We also calculated LM(4) statistics to test for up to fourth-order serial correlation. However, in some circumstances (e.g. row 4 of Table 7.1) the serial correlation in the residuals extended further than four quarters and thus higher-order ALS models were needed. We therefore only report the LM(8) statistics.

3. The regressions with the RPI-deflated real wage rate were re-run for the sample period corresponding to the regressions using the WPI-deflated real wage rate (1957(1)–1981(2)). The results were quite similar; the F-statistics were 2.75 (row 1); 1.82 (row 3); 2.15 (row 5); and 1.11 (row 7). It appears that the different lengths of the sample period for the RPI- and WPI-deflated real wages were not responsible for the different results obtained.

4. The ARIMA models used for the tests are presented in columns 3 and 4 in Table 7.2. Geary and Kennan (1982) fitted somewhat different models to their variables. However, our results are quite similar to theirs for the period up to 1977(4), so it appears that their results were fairly robust to changes in the actual filtering procedure.

5. This instability is also evident in the data from twelve OECD countries used by Geary and Kennan (1982, p.860).

6. Lucas and Rapping (1969a) present evidence with annual US data on this wage lag hypothesis.

7. In the empirical work reported below, we could not use the actual quarterly rate of change in the RPI or WPI because in certain quarters these figures were equal to zero. We therefore used the average quarterly inflation rate in each year.

8. See Tarling and Wilkinson (1977) for a review and analysis of these policies.

9. This was made official on 7 September 1977 when at its annual Congress the TUC voted for a return to free collective bargaining. See Tarling and Wilkinson (1977).

10. Pages 183–4.

11. Because lags (and leads) of up to ten quarters were used, the incomes policy dummy would have had to have been lagged by up to ten quarters when employment is the dependent variable. We therefore decided to adopt the pre-filtering method in these regressions. We also re-ran the regressions

with real wages as the dependent variable with the incomes policy dummy introduced in the filtering exercise only. The results obtained were virtually identical to those reported in rows 1, 2, 7 and 8.

12. See Buiter and Miller (1981) for some evidence. In a similar vein, Symons (1985) attributes the fall in employment at the beginning of the 1980s to the substantial rise in real interest rates during that period.

13. See Drobny and Gausden (1988) for a further analysis and discussion.

14. We experimented with models including up to ten lags on all variables with the 4-4-10 model being the preferred specification for the employment equation (column 1) in particular. The $F(6,62)$-statistic testing for the joint significance of six additional lags in real materials prices was only 0.30 with no coefficient beyond the first lag being significant (see Table 7.6), while the F-statistic testing for the inclusion of the six additional lags in real wages was 3.21, significant at the 99 per cent level. The preferred specification of the real wage equation was with only four lags on all variables; the F-statistics testing for the joint significance of additional lags on each of the variables were always below unity. The real materials price equation always suffered from a significant degree of serial correlation and, since this equation only plays a peripheral role in our discussion, we ignore it but include the results for completeness.

15. Such a result is inconsistent, however, with a disequilibrium or quantity-constrained demand for labour schedule as derived in Chapters Four and Five.

16. The F-statistics are: $F(10,54)=0.75$ for the real wage rate (the sum of coefficients is -0.01 with a standard error of 0.16); and $F(4,54)=1.02$ for real materials prices (with a sum of coefficients of 0.03 and a standard error of 0.03).

17. The critiques by Engle, Hendry and Richard (1983) and Cooley and Leroy (1985) of the time-series methodology adopted in this chapter might be appealed to in attributing this instability to the statistical techniques applied and not to issues of model choice and specification. We do not find this argument persuasive, particularly since such instability features in Symons' (1985) analysis using conventional structural equation methods.

18. See Nickell and Andrews (1983), Layard and Nickell (1985) and Symons (1985).

Chapter Eight

OUTPUT, EMPLOYMENT AND REAL WAGES: GRANGER-CAUSALITY TESTS OF THE KEYNESIAN MODEL

The disequilibrium approach to macroeconomics emphasises the direct quantity to quantity interaction operating through spillover effects from one market to another. Clower's (1965) dual decision hypothesis shows how the traditional Keynesian consumption function can be derived from a choice-theoretic framework when households experience involuntary unemployment. The analysis in Part Two above developed the analysis of Patinkin (1965) and Barro and Grossman (1971) to derive an effective demand for labour schedule in which output, itself determined by the level of aggregate effective demand, is the main variable directly determining the level of aggregate employment. Two versions of the model were considered. The strong version denies any influence of real wages on aggregate employment levels. The weak version, which admits substitution possibilities between variable factors of production, suggests that real wages can somewhat influence employment levels in addition to the influence of output.

The effective demand for labour schedule formulated for a dynamic setting in Section 2 of Chapter Five suggests that a direct linkage exists between lagged values of employment and output and current employment levels. Profit-maximising forward-looking firms operating in an uncertain environment in which adjusting input levels is costly would include these variables in their information sets in determining their preferred employment path for current and future periods. Unlike neoclassical models of employment fluctuations, the demand-constrained model of employment fluctuations suggests that output Granger-causes employment with little or no feedback. Further, the weak version of the model suggests that real wages will also be included in firms' information sets, and thus should also Granger-cause employment.

The notion of such an employment function has a long tradition in labour economics rather than in macroeconomics. The theoretical derivation and empirical implementation with UK data of an employment function is typified by Brechling (1965). His model, developed and extended by others,[1] is based on firms minimising costs where output and relative prices are assumed to be exogenous. The strong links between these employment functions and the disequilibrium literature in macroeconomics has not been widely recognised. Perhaps this is the result of the dominance of the neoclassical literature in macroeconomics and the consequent attention given to real wages in the determination of employment.[2]

In this chapter we first investigate the empirical validity of the disequilibrium approach by applying the direct Granger test to postwar quarterly output and employment data from the UK manufacturing sector. The results obtained from this exercise are then compared with those obtained in tests of the neoclassical model (Chapter Seven). In the second part of the chapter a multivariate version of the direct Granger test is applied to output, employment and real wage data from the manufacturing sector of the UK. This permits us to examine more closely the validity of disequilibrium Keynesian models of employment fluctuations. As argued in Part Two above, the dynamic disequilibrium Keynesian model admits the possibility that real wages Granger-cause employment, although the presumption is that their influence should be rather small.

This chapter is organised as follows. In Section 1 the data and estimating equations are presented. Section 2 presents the results of bivariate tests for Granger-causality between output and employment. The results of the multivariate tests are presented in Section 3. Concluding remarks are made in Section 4.

1. DATA AND ESTIMATING EQUATIONS

The employment and real wage (basic wage deflated by the wholesale price index, WPI) data used are

the same as those in the previous chapter. To this
data set we have added the index of manufacturing
production. The long-run trend in the output
series has been upwards, increasing from 54.9 in
1952(1) to 90.2 in 1981(2) (average 1975=100); a
rise of just over 60 per cent. However, the peak
in output was achieved in 1973; the index reached
112.6 in the fourth quarter of that year. Since
that time the output level has fallen slightly.
The rate of change of output therefore exhibits a
slight downward trend over the period.[3] We note
as well a substantial seasonal variation in output.
The oscillations in output are in general four to
five times greater than that of employment. The
large seasonal variation in output relative to
employment presumably reflects variations in hours
worked in different seasons due to workers taking
paid holiday leave and perhaps seasonal variations
in overtime hours worked. As in the previous
chapter, the actual variables used in the direct
Granger regressions are the deseasonalised,
detrended rates of change of the variables.

The bivariate relationship between filtered
output (Y_t) and employment (N_t) is estimated using
the direct Granger test:

$$N_t = \alpha_{10} + \Sigma_{j=1}^{m} \alpha_{1j} N_{t-j} + \Sigma_{j=1}^{m} \alpha_{2j} Y_{t-j} + \varepsilon_{1t}$$
$$(8.1a)$$

$$Y_t = \beta_{10} + \Sigma_{j=1}^{m} \beta_{1j} Y_{t-j} + \Sigma_{j=1}^{m} \beta_{2j} N_{t-j} + \varepsilon_{2t}$$
$$(8.1b)$$

where ε_{1t} and ε_{2t} are independent random variables
and the lengths of the lags, m, are determined
empirically. The multivariate versions of these
equations which include the filtered real wage rate
(w) are:

$$N_t = \alpha_{10} + \Sigma_{j=1}^{m} \alpha_{1j} N_{t-j} + \Sigma_{j=1}^{m} \alpha_{2j} Y_{t-j}$$
$$+ \Sigma_{j=1}^{n} \alpha_{3j} w_{t-j} + e_{1t} \qquad (8.2a)$$

$$Y_t = \beta_{10} + \Sigma_{j=1}^{m} \beta_{1j} Y_{t-j} + \Sigma_{j=1}^{m} \beta_{2j} N_{t-j}$$
$$+ \Sigma_{j=1}^{n} \beta_{3j} w_{t-j} + e_{2t} \qquad (8.2b)$$

$$w_t = \gamma_{10} + \Sigma_{j=1}^{n} \gamma_{1j} w_{t-j} + \Sigma_{j=1}^{m} \gamma_{2j} N_{t-j}$$
$$+ \Sigma_{j=1}^{m} \gamma_{3j} Y_{t-j} + e_{3t} \qquad (8.2c)$$

where e_{it} $(i=1,2,3)$ are independent random variables; and n is the length of the lag in the real wage rate. Notice that the length of the lags in output and employment are permitted to differ from that for the real wage rate. This arises from the results presented in Chapter Seven suggesting that ten lags in the real wage rate are required to obtain any significant effect of real wages on employment. As we demonstrate in the next section, the output-employment equations require much shorter lags. In fact, we argue below that our preferred representation of equations (8.2a)-(8.2c) uses $m=4$ and $n=10$.

2. RESULTS WITH OUTPUT AND EMPLOYMENT

Table 8.1 presents the results of estimating equations (8.1a) and (8.1b) by OLS over the period 1952(2)-1981(2) with four lags on both variables (columns 1 and 3 respectively) and, for comparative purposes, the corresponding estimates using ten lags on both variables are presented in columns 2 and 4.[4] The coefficients on each variable are presented along with typical standard errors and other relevant diagnostic statistics including the Breusch and Pagan (1980) Lagrange multiplier (LM) test for serial correlation. The first F-statistic in the table tests for the joint contribution of the lags in the explanatory variables (Granger-causality); the second F-statistic (reported in columns 2 and 4 only) tests the joint significance of the additional six lags in both variables (dynamic specification). The sum and significance of the coefficients on the lagged values of the explanatory variables are also presented.

The F-statistics testing for Granger-causality suggest a strong and significant two-way relationship between output and employment which appears to be subject to very short lags. Innovations in output or employment exert a significant effect on the other variable after at most a three quarter year lag. Introducing lags in both variables beyond four quarters does not significantly improve (at the 95 per cent level) the forecast of the dependent variables (see the bottom F-statistics in columns 2 and 4). Thus, unlike the real wage-employment relationship which is subject to much longer lags (see for example Table 7.6), employment (output) responds to

Table 8.1. Output (y) and employment (N), Granger tests 1952(2)-1981(2)[a]

Dependent variable:	Employment		Output	
	(1)	(2)	(3)	(4)
N_{t-1}	0.70*	0.60*	2.05*	1.60*
N_{t-2}	-0.23Δ	-0.05	-0.10	0.32
N_{t-3}	0.16	0.13	-0.65	-0.82
N_{t-4}	-0.09	-0.07	-1.49*	-1.35Δ
N_{t-5}	-	-0.28Δ	-	-0.89
N_{t-6}	-	-0.11	-	-0.40
N_{t-7}	-	-0.04	-	-0.68
N_{t-8}	-	0.25Δ	-	0.93
N_{t-9}	-	-0.03	-	0.50
N_{t-10}	-	-0.28*	-	-0.66
Typical standard error (N_{t-j})	(0.13)	(0.14)	(0.63)	(0.75)
Y_{t-1}	0.05*	0.06*	-0.34*	-0.31*
Y_{t-2}	0.07*	0.04	-0.15	-0.18
Y_{t-3}	0.04Δ	0.02	-0.04	-0.06
Y_{t-4}	-0.01	-0.02	0.06	0.07
Y_{t-5}	-	0.03	-	0.20
Y_{t-6}	-	0.02	-	0.24
Y_{t-7}	-	0.01	-	0.07
Y_{t-8}	-	0.00	-	0.14
Y_{t-9}	-	0.03	-	-0.05
Y_{t-10}	-	0.01	-	0.03
Typical standard error (Y_{t-j})	(0.02)	(0.03)	(0.12)	(0.15)
Diagnostic statistics:				
R^2	0.68	0.74	0.22	0.31
RSS	18.082	14.389	440.331	391.699
LM(4)[b]	6.13	5.69	4.05	3.19
F-test[c]	2.58*	1.25	6.41*	2.51*
Sum of coefficients[d]	0.15*(0.07)	0.14(0.12)	-0.20(0.57)	-1.44(1.15)
F-test[e]	-	1.84Δ	-	0.89
Observations	107	107	107	107

(a) * Significant at 5 per cent level; Δ significant at 10 per cent level. All models estimated by ordinary least squares.

(b) Lagrange multiplier test for fourth order autocorrelation (critical values: 5 per cent = 9.49; 10 per cent = 7.78). LM(8) statistics were also calculated. These were all insignificant (at the 10 per cent level).

(c) Test of significant contribution of lagged values of explanatory variable. This statistic has degrees of freedom (4,98) for the four-lag model and (10,86) for the ten-lag model.

(d) Sum of coefficients of lagged values of explanatory variable (standard error of sum in parentheses).

(e) Test of significant contribution of additional six lags in both variables. This statistic has (12,86) degrees of freedom.

211

innovations in output (employment) very quickly indeed.

Next consider the sum of coefficients on the lagged values of the explanatory variables. Our preferred equations, which include four lags in both variables (columns 1 and 3), suggest that innovations in output exert a permanent effect on employment but not the other way around. The sum of the lagged output coefficients in the employment equation (column 1) is 0.15, significant at the 95 per cent level. The sum of the lagged employment coefficients in the output equation (column 3), on the other hand, is not significant at reasonable levels. These results are therefore not inconsistent with the strong version of the Keynesian effective demand for labour schedule.

The individual coefficients produced by the four-lag model provide evidence on the time profiles of the effect of output innovations on employment (column 1). These show the consistently positive effect of lagged output on employment. The significant coefficient on the first lag of output of 0.05 suggests that a 1 per cent innovation in output growth is accompanied, ceteris paribus, by only a 0.05 per cent innovation in employment growth. However, this initial innovation in output appears to generate significant innovations in employment in the subsequent three quarters, yielding a long-run or permanent output 'innovation elasticity' of employment equal to 0.27.[5]

Evidence of the stability of the stochastic output-employment relationship is provided by estimates of equations (8.1a) and (8.1b) for a shortened data period from 1957(2)-1971(4). These results for the four-lag model are presented in Table A8.1 of Appendix 8.1 below. In both equations the F-statistics testing for Granger-causality, the sum of the coefficients on the lagged explanatory variables, and most of the coefficients on the individual variables, are unchanged when the estimation period excludes most of the 1970s. Thus, unlike the linkage running from real wages to employment which appears to be unstable with UK data, the linkage running from output to employment is very robust to changes in the observation period.[6]

The postive lagged adjustment of employment to output fluctuations as predicted by the dynamic effective demand for labour equation derived in Section 2 of Chapter Five is confirmed by these

results. In addition, these results are robust to
changes in the sample period. The model in which
employers adjust to an increase in demand by
adjusting employment levels only sluggishly can at
least not be rejected on the basis of these
results.

3. MULTIVARIATE GRANGER TESTS WITH OUTPUT, EMPLOYMENT AND REAL WAGES

The dynamic neoclassical model of employment
fluctuations as derived by Sargent (1978) predicts
that lagged values of employment and real wages
will be significant in predicting the current
levels of employment. The tests reported in
Chapter Seven provide some confirmation of these
predictions, although it was shown that these
results are particularly sensitive to the removal
of extreme outliers in real wages between 1976 and
1978. Further, the time pattern of real wage
effects on employment do not conform with the
predictions of the neoclassical model.

As demonstrated in Chapter Five, introducing
demand constraints in Sargent's model yields
dramatically different propositions. The resulting
dynamic disequilibrium model of employment
fluctuations predicts that lagged values of output
should also be significant in an employment
autoregression. Further, although lagged values of
real wages are permitted to enter significantly in
the employment autoregression, the disequilibrium
model predicts that their overall influence
(measured by the sum of the real wage coefficients)
should be rather small (below unity). Tests of
these propositions using equations (8.2a)-(8.2c)
are reported in this section.

The results of estimating these equations and
conducting tests for Granger-causality over the
full data period are presented in Table 8.2 for our
preferred equations, which include four lags in
output and employment and ten lags in the WPI-
deflated real wage rate (the 4-4-10 model). The
table provides the F-statistics testing for the
significant contribution of the lagged explanatory
variables, the sum (and significance) of
coefficients on these variables, and relevant
diagnostic statistics. These results provide the
strongest evidence to support the neoclassical
model against the disequilibrium hypothesis.[7] It
is therefore of interest to analyse these results

Table 8.2. Output (Y), employment (N) and real wages (w), multivariate Granger tests, 1957(2)-1981(2)[a]

4-4-10 model[b]

Dependent variable:	Employment (N) (1)	Output (Y) (2)	Real wages (w) (3)
F-statistics[c]			
F_Y (4,68)	1.53	–	0.64
F_W (10,68)	1.89Δ	1.33	–
F_N (4,68)	–	4.91*	0.54
Sum of coefficients[d]			
Y	0.14Δ(0.08)	–	0.29(0.45)
w	-0.20Δ(0.10)	-0.41(0.49)	–
N	–	-0.43(0.69)	-0.38(0.76)
Diagnostic statistics			
R^2	0.76	0.37	0.24
RSS	12.108	308.931	370.635
LM(4)[e]	1.30	7.19	3.36
Observations	87	87	87

(a) See Table 8.1 for all definitions. Real wages created by deflating basic wage by WPI.
(b) 4-4-10 model includes four lags on output and employment and ten lags on real wages.
(c) F_j-test for significant contribution of lags of variable j (degrees of freedom in parentheses).
(d) Sum of lagged coefficients on each variable (standard error in parentheses).
(e) LM(8) statistics were also calculated for all equations. These were insignificant except for the output equation.

in detail.

The F-statistics reported in rows 1-3 of Table 8.2 suggest that only real wages Granger-cause employment (with no feedback), while only employment Granger-causes output (with no feedback). In particular, the F-statistics reject the proposition that output Granger-causes employment. Finally, notice that real wages appear to be independent of both output and employment.

However, the sum of coefficients reported in rows 4-6 of Table 8.2 reveal that both the sum of the output and real wage coefficients are significant at the 90 per cent level. This suggests that innovations in both output and real wages exert a permanent influence on employment. The long-run output and real wage 'innovation elasticities' of employment are 0.27 and -0.40 respectively (see column 1 of Table 8.4 below). These are virtually identical to those reported for the bivariate output-employment and real wage-employment regressions reported in Table 8.1 of this chapter and Table 7.6 in Chapter Seven. The results for the employment autoregression in general provide evidence in favour of the neoclassical model, although the significant sum of the output coefficients in this regression is in direct conflict with the F-statistic testing for Granger-causality running from output to employment. This conflict between the F-test and the t-test (sum of coefficients) suggests that further investigation into this model is warranted. Again it must be re-emphasised that only the 4-4-10 model produced significant real wage coefficients in the employment autoregression. The results obtained using only four lags of the real wage rate (4-4-4 model) suggest that employment is independent of real wages. The 4-4-10 model therefore provides the strongest support in favour of the neoclassical model.

Before proceeding to a further analysis of the employment autoregression itself, we mention briefly two other results presented in Table 8.2. The F-statistics and sum of coefficients obtained in the multivariate exercise reject the possibility that real wages and output Granger-cause each other. The result that real wages are not Granger-caused by either output or employment confirms the results presented in Chapter Seven suggesting that automatic adjustments of real wages to fluctuations in output and employment cannot be relied upon to correct such fluctuations.

Second, the suggestion that real wages do not Granger-cause output has implications for interpreting the influence of real wages on employment. In particular, the results in Table 8.2 suggest that real wages Granger-cause employment but do not Granger-cause output. This implies that the reported real wage 'innovation elasticity' of employment only represents a substitution effect and denies any output effect of real wage movements on employment.

Bivariate Granger tests between real wages and output, reported in Table A8.2 of the appendix to this chapter, confirm these results. While a model incorporating four lags on both variables produced totally insignificant F-statistics and sums of coefficients, the model with ten lags on both variables suggests that real wages may Granger-cause output (the F-statistic in column 2 of Table A8.2 is significant at the 90 per cent level), but the insignificant sum of real wage coefficients imply that this effect is only temporary. Further, when the effects of the Callaghan incomes policies are filtered out of the real wage variable, real wages appear to exert a positive influence on output (see the sum of the real wage coefficients in column 3 or Table A8.2). These results certainly do not support neoclassical propositions.[8] Thus the results reported in Table 8.2, while providing some support for the neoclassical model (indeed, this is the strongest support for the neoclassical perspective obtained with the data set), reveal a number of empirical inadequacies with this perspective.

Consider next the performance of the 4-4-10 model for the shortened data period, 1957(2)-1971(4). These results, presented in Table 8.3, show how the demand-constrained or disequilibrium model of employment fluctuations outperforms the neoclassical model for this earlier period. Output appears to Granger-cause employment on the basis of the F-statistic, and the significant sum of the output coefficients in the employment autoregression suggests that this effect is permanent. In contrast, employment appears to be independent of real wages during this period. Further, the results for the output and real wage autoregressions confirm our earlier results which rejected both the proposition that real wages are Granger-caused by output and employment, and that output is Granger-caused by real wages. Notice that it once again appears that employment Granger-

Table 8.3. Output (Y), employment (N) and real wages (w), multivariate Granger tests for shortened data period, 1957(2)-1971(4)[a]

4-4-10 model[b]

Dependent variable:	Employment (N) (1)	Output (Y) (2)	Real wages (w) (3)
F-statistics			
F_Y (4,30)	2.96*	-	0.70
F_w (10,30)	0.84	0.37	-
F_N (4,30)	-	2.08Δ	0.56
Sum of coefficients			
Y	0.34*(0.13)	-	-0.03(0.45)
w	-0.09(0.32)	0.92(1.55)	-
N	-	-2.27(1.11)	-0.56(0.45)
Diagnostic statistics			
R^2	0.67	0.25	0.45
RSS	4.939	75.618	19.133
LM(4)	2.82	5.14	4.90
Observations	49	49	49

(a) See Table 8.1 for all definitions.

causes output, but that the sum of the employment
coefficients in the output autoregression are
significant and negative. This result is simply
not believable, and adds further evidence to our
view that the output equation is misspecified.

The results for the shortened data period
confirm our earlier results concerning the output
and real wage autoregressions. However, the
results for the employment autoregression are not
consistent over the two sample periods. The
apparent contradiction between the results obtained
for the full data period which provide some support
for the neoclassical explanation of employment
fluctuations, and for the shortened data period
which reject the neoclassical view in favour of the
demand-constrained view, suggests that observations
during the mid to late 1970s are exerting a strong
influence on the inferences drawn from the
analysis. Note that a similar problem arose in the
bivariate analysis of real wages and employment
reported in the previous chapter. We thus need to
investigate the employment autoregression itself in
more detail.

This analysis is presented in Table 8.4. The
first and third columns provide the individual
coefficients for the employment autoregressions for
the full sample period (corresponding to the
results presented in column 1 of Table 8.2) and for
the shortened data period (presented in column 1 of
Table 8.3) respectively. The second column
reproduces the full sample period results when the
effects of the Callaghan incomes policies are
filtered out of the real wage series. The table
presents the individual coefficients, typical
standard errors, relevant diagnostic statistics,
and reproduces the F-statistics reported in Tables
8.2 and 8.3 testing for the joint significance of
the lagged values of output (F_Y) and real wages
(F_w). The sums of lagged output and real wage
coefficients are also presented.

Consider the individual coefficients presented
in column 1 of Table 8.4. The first two lagged
values of the output innovations are positive and
significant (at the 90 per cent level), diminishing
in size as the length of the lags increases.
Notice in addition that the values of these
coefficients are almost identical to those produced
in the bivariate output-employment model (column 2
of Table 8.1) although they are now less
significant individually and as a group. Notice as
well that the coefficients on the lagged real wage

Table 8.4. Output (Y) and real wages (w) causing employment (N): multivariate Granger tests[a]

Dependent variable:	Employment		
	(1) Original model (b)	(2) Incomes policy model (c)	(3) Shortened data period (d)
N_{t-1}	0.63*	0.66*	0.16
N_{t-2}	-0.07	-0.07	-0.07
N_{t-3}	0.17	0.27△	0.19
N_{t-4}	-0.25△	-0.14	0.02
Typical standard error (N_{t-j})	(0.15)	(0.15)	(0.20)
Y_{t-1}	0.05△	0.03	0.10*
Y_{t-2}	0.06△	0.03	0.14*
Y_{t-3}	0.04	0.01	0.08△
Y_{t-4}	-0.01	-0.04	0.01
Typical standard error (Y_{t-j})	(0.03)	(0.03)	(0.04)
w_{t-1}	-0.01	0.04	0.01
w_{t-2}	-0.04△	0.00	-0.15
w_{t-3}	-0.02	0.04	-0.07
w_{t-4}	0.01	0.07*	0.00
w_{t-5}	0.02	0.08*	-0.08
w_{t-6}	-0.06*	0.01	-0.02
w_{t-7}	-0.03	0.03	0.01
w_{t-8}	-0.02	0.03	0.07
w_{t-9}	-0.01	-0.00	0.09
w_{t-10}	-0.05△	-0.03	0.18*
Typical standard error (w_{t-j})	(0.02)	(0.03)	(0.09)
Diagnostic statistics			
R^2	0.76	0.77	0.67
RSS	12.108	11.545	4.939
LM(4) (e)	1.30	1.36	2.82
F_Y (f)	1.53(4,68)	1.44(4,68)	2.96*(4,30)
F_w (g)	1.89△(10,68)	2.31*(10,68)	0.84(10,30)
Sum of lagged Y coefficients (h)	0.14△(0.08)	0.03(0.08)	0.34*(0.13)
Sum of lagged w coefficients (h)	0.020△(0.08)	0.03(0.08)	0.34*(0.13)
Observations	87	87	49

(a) See Table 8.1 for all definitions. Real wage created using WPI deflator.
(b) Corresponds to results presented in Table 8.2, column 1.
(c) Real wage filtered for incomes policy effect.
(d) Corresponds to results presented in Table 8.3, column 1.
(e) LM(8) statitics were also calculated. These were all insignificant.
(f) F-test on significant contribution of lagged Y (degrees of freedom in parentheses).
(g) F-test on significant contribution of lagged W (degrees of freedom in parentheses).
(h) Standard error in parentheses.

variables are similar in size and significance to those obtained in the bivariate real wage-employment regressions reported in Table 7.6 in the previous chapter. The only major change that occurs when the Granger tests are conducted in a multivariate setting is that the standard errors on the lagged output variables have somewhat increased when real wages are introduced into the employment autoregression. This might explain why the F-test for Granger-causality does not reject the hypothesis that output does not Granger-cause employment. However, the size of the individual coefficients on the lagged output variables and the significance (at the 90 per cent level) of the sum of these coefficients suggest that the F-test is perhaps misleading. Furthermore, the long-run real wage innovation elasticity of employment provided by these results (-0.40) is well below unity. Thus although the results presented in column 1 of this table provide the strongest evidence in favour of the neoclassical explanation for employment fluctuations, this evidence is in fact fairly weak. Notice as well that the strength of this evidence appears to rely on the later observations of the data set. The results for the shortened data period presented in column 3 of Table 8.4 decisively reject the neoclassical explanation in favour of the demand-constrained view. The question that remains is whether the effects of the Callaghan incomes policies on real wages are responsible for these differing results, as we found to be the case in the previous chapter with the bivariate analysis of real wages and employment.

The results of estimating the employment autoregression with real wages filtered for the effects of the Callaghan incomes policies are presented in the second column of Table 8.4. What is striking about these results is that they are inconsistent with <u>both</u> those obtained for the original model covering the entire data set and for the shortened data set. The F-statistics testing for Granger-causality imply that real wages Granger-cause employment but output does not. The sum of the output coefficients are now insignificant, while the sum of the real wage coefficients are significantly positive. Thus when the effects of the Callaghan incomes policies are filtered out of the real wage series, both the neoclassical and demand-constrained explanations of employment fluctuations appear to be rejected.

What potential explanations can be advanced for this result? First it could be argued that the employment equation is in fact misspecified due to the omission of a relevant explanatory variable. The theoretical analysis of the dynamic effective demand for labour schedule in Chapters Four and Five was derived by assuming that the adjustment of the demand for labour in the event of an actual or expected fall in aggregate demand would be relatively sluggish. This implies that the demand for some other variable factor of production must adjust relatively quickly if the level of the firm's production is to always equal the demand for its products. This other factor has been omitted from the empirical analysis. A key candidate might be oil in this case, given the considerable theoretical and empirical attention paid to the oil price shocks during the mid to late 1970s as potentially explaining the recently-observed falls in employment levels in a number of OECD countries. It may be the case that introducing the price of oil into the employment autoregression will improve the performance of the disequilibrium model. This model suggests that employment and oil prices should be positively associated since the model denies any output effects of change in real factor prices. Note that it was pointed out at the end of Chapter Five that recent (preliminary) results obtained for the neoclassical model which adds oil prices to the set of regressions in the employment autoregression confirms this positive association. It would therefore be of considerable interest to investigate the performance of an expanded version of the disequilibrium model.

A second potential explanation for this result is provided by the results for the bivariate output and real wage autoregressions presented in Table A8.2 of the Appendix (column 3). When the incomes policy period is filtered out of the real wage series it appears that real wages Granger-cause employment (with no feedback) with a significantly positive sum of coefficients. Thus the results presented in column 2 of Table 8.4 may reflect the possibility that the real wage filtered for the effects of incomes policies are in fact capturing the effects of output on employment. Both these suggested explanations for this result suggest that further empirical analysis into the disequilibrium model of the determination of employment fluctuations is needed. However, the results

presented in Table 8.4 provide little support for
the neoclassial model.

5. CONCLUSIONS

The results from the UK manufacturing sector
presented in this chapter provide reasonable
support for the disequilibrium demand-constraint
model of employment fluctuations, and appear to
reject the neoclassical model which focuses on real
wage movements to explain employment fluctuations.
The version of the bivariate direct Granger test
conducted with output and employment data for the
period 1957(2)-1981(2) suggests that a strong
causal link exists running from output to
employment. Lagged values of output innovations
contribute significantly in predicting innovations
in employment. In addition the results suggest
that the adjustment of employment to output
fluctuations is extremely rapid, taking up to four
quarters to be completed. These results are very
robust to changes in the observation period. It is
particularly striking that virtually identical
results are obtained when the model is estimated
for the period up to 1971(4). Such stability is
certainly not observed for the real wage-employment
relationship in the UK manufacturing sector. The
results presented in Section 2 above represent the
rediscovery of a <u>stable</u> employment function in a
stochastic setting.
    The multivariate version of the direct Granger
test undertaken with employment, output, and real
wage data provides conflicting results, however.
Although the disequilibrium model receives strong
support when data up to 1971(4) are used, the
results for the longer sample period are not as
clear. In particular, the results obtained are
particularly sensitive to the removal of the
effects on real wage movements of the Callaghan
incomes policies. A further empirical
investigation of the disequlibrium model which
allows for the influence of oil prices on
employment is suggested by these results.
    Nevertheless, the results presented in this
chapter provide a further refutation of the
neoclassical explanation of employment
fluctuations. The results providing the strongest
support for this perspective (column 1 of Table
8.4) suggest a long-run real wage 'innovation
elasticity' of only -0.40, a value which is far

lower than that predicted by this model. Furthermore, the results suggest either that output is independent of real wages or that the two variables are positively associated (Table A8.2). The results therefore reject unambiguously the proposition that real wages exert a negative <u>output</u> effect on employment.

APPENDIX 8.1. ADDITIONAL TABLES

Table A8.1. Output (Y) and employment (N), Granger tests for shortened data period, 1957(2)-1971(4)[a]

Dependent variable:	Employment (N)	Output (Y)
	(1)	(2)
N_{t-1}	0.26	0.19
N_{t-2}	0.07	0.04
N_{t-3}	0.29^{Δ}	-0.21
N_{t-4}	0.11	-1.87*
Typical standard error (N_{t-j})	(0.17)	(0.65)
Y_{t-1}	0.08*	-0.11
Y_{t-2}	0.10*	-0.08*
Y_{t-3}	0.04	-0.14
Y_{t-4}	-0.003	0.33*
Typical standard error (Y_{t-j})	(0.04)	(0.17)
Diagnostic statistics:		
R^2	0.57	0.26
RSS	6.318	128.812
LM(4)[b]	4.18	5.75
F-test[c]	2.52^{Δ}	2.87*
Sum of coefficients	0.23*(0.10)	-1.85*(0.82)
Observations	49	49

(a) See Table 8.1 of text for definitions.
(b) LM(8) statistics were also calculated. These were all insignificant.
(c) Test of significant contribution of lagged values of explanatory variable.

Table A8.2. Output (Y) and real wages (w), bivariate Granger tests, 1957(2)-1981(2)[a]

Ten-lag model[b]

Dependent variable:	Output (Y) (1)	Real wages (w) (2)	Output (Y) (3)[c]	Real wages (w) (4)[c]
F-statistics				
F_w (10,66)	1.67^Δ	-	2.10*	-
F_Y (10,66)	-	0.83	-	1.15
Sum of coefficients				
w	-0.28(0.47)	-	1.42*(0.71)	-
Y	-	0.27(0.44)	-	-0.47(0.44)
Diagnostic statistics				
R^2	0.31	0.27	0.35	0.24
RSS	337.398	355.898	320.757	289.304
LM(4)[d]	12.87*	4.13	6.33	4.35
Observations	87	87	87	87

(a) See Table 8.1 for all definitions.
(b) Ten lags on both variables. A model with four lags on both variables was also estimated. All F-statistics and estimated sums of coefficients were insignificant.
(c) Granger tests with real wages filtered for the effects of incomes policies (see Chapter Seven for a discussion).
(d) LM(8) statistics were also calculated. These were significant at the 90 per cent level in columns 1, 2 and 3.

NOTES

1. See Muellbauer (1980) for a review and an extension of these models.

2. The collection of papers in Greenhalgh, Layard and Oswald (1983) provides a stark example of this dominance. The real wage-employment relationship is the focal point of virtually all the papers in the book.

3. The regression used to de-trend and de-seasonalise the rate of change of output produced a coefficient on the linear time trend equal to -0.02 (significant at the 99 per cent level). In addition, the seasonal dummies were all highly significant in the regression (unlike the employment and real wage regressions which exhibited little or no seasonal variation).

4. These equations were estimated with four, six, eight, ten and twelve lags on both variables. All equations were re-estimated using the unfiltered data in rates of change and introducing seasonal dummies and a time trend in the final regressions. In both cases the four-lag model was preferred. Re-estimating the equations over the period 1957(2)-1981(2), corresponding to the sample period used in Chapter Seven, produced similar results.

5. Similar results were obtained by Brechling (1965) using a quasi-structural form equation with quarterly data from the UK manufacturing sector covering the years 1950(1)-1963(4).

6. Notice, however, that the sum of the lagged employment coefficients in the output equation (column 2) is now significant at the 95 per cent level. However, as with the results reported in columns 3 and 4 of Table 8.1, this sum of coefficients is negative. This is an implausible result, suggesting that the output equation is mis-specified, providing further evidence in favour of the demand-constrained view of the determination of employment.

7. The model with four lags on all the variables yielded results consistent with those reported in the previous chapter and in Table 8.1 of this chapter. In particular, real wages were totally insignificant in the employment autoregression, while output was significant with coefficients similar to those reported in Table 8.1 above.

8. These results should be interpreted with caution since there is some suggestion of serially-correlated residuals in these regressions.

Chapter Nine

CONCLUDING COMMENTS

1. A THEORETICAL SUMMARY

The inheritors of what Keynes called 'classical'
economic theory emphasise the importance of real
wage movements in generating, and subsequently
correcting, fluctuations in aggregate employment
levels in advanced capitalist countries. This
analysis is derived by considering the behaviour of
atomistic agents maximising objective functions in
the face of resource constraints. The analysis
assumes that these rational agents operate in a
rational marketplace where relative price movements
ensure the maintenance of an equality between the
demands and supplies of commodities. Thus in terms
of the labour market this theory supposes that the
real wage rate is the main determinant of
employment levels.
    Two propositions emerge when this theory is
applied to real-world problems. First, business
cycles are in the main generated or caused by real
wage movements. Thus if it is believed that demand
management policies do indeed influence aggregate
output and employment levels, the theory suggests
that this effect must be due to the covert effect
of such policies on real wage levels. Second, this
theory suggests that the solution to the problem of
mass unemployment lies in finding some mechanism to
reduce real wages. This view provides the
underpinnings for Minford's (1983) proposals which
are designed to place downward pressure on real
wages by reducing the power of trade unions and the
level of unemployment benefits in the UK.
    The theoretical analysis conducted in Part Two
above suggests that these views are derived from an
analysis of the notional demand schedule from
employment. If firms are never constrained by the

226

level of aggregate effective demand and if the
marginal product of labour depends (in the short
period) only on given technological conditions and
employment levels themselves, then reductions in
real wages should be expected to encourage firms to
employ more labour and expand their output levels.
However, if the output of firms is on some
occasions constrained by the level of aggregate
effective demand, the resulting effective demand
for labour schedule suggests that real wage
movements will be relatively unimportant in the
determination of employment levels. The analysis
of the demand-constrained firm conducted in Chapter
Four provides a potential justification for the
unimportance of real wages argument.

Such considerations yield two propositions
which differ dramatically from those derived from
neoclassical analysis. First, changes in aggregate
effective demand can exert a <u>direct</u> influence on,
or cause, fluctuations in employment. Output,
itself determined by the level of sales by firms,
will be a direct determinant of employment levels.
This suggests that models of the demand for labour
should on theoretical grounds include the level of
the firm's output (or variables capturing aggregate
demand conditions). Second, the influence of real
wages on employment will depend on two forces at
work. The first is the output effect: the
influence of real wages on the level of aggregate
effective demand and thus on the output of firms.
The second is the substitution effect: the
influence of real wages on the factor proportions
chosen by firms in producing given levels of
output. It is important to notice that this
alternative Keynesian analysis does not in
principle deny the influence of real wages on
employment. It merely distrusts it. In
particular, the output effect of real wages on
employment is questioned by this perspective. Thus
in terms of Minford's (1983) policy proposals, this
alternative perspective implies that if real wages
were in fact reduced after the implementation of
such policies, these reductions would have only a
marginal impact on aggregate employment levels and
little or no effect on aggregate output levels.

As we have attempted to show, the two
perspectives cannot, and should not, be
differentiated in terms of their respective views
of the rationality of individuals. The
perspectives differ in terms of their overall
visions of the operation of the market mechanism

itself.   The models we have used to describe these
two   perspectives   are   undoubtedly   primitive   and
abstract from numerous and important considerations
in   the   analysis   of   fluctuations   in   aggregate
employment levels.   Aggregation was ignored.   The
amount of hours worked and the heterogeneity of the
labour   force   were   ignored.   The   structure   and
distribution of production across different sectors
of the economy using different forms of technology
were   ignored.   Finally,   we   only considered price-
taking firms and ignored the important question of
who   sets   prices   and   the   determinants   of   pricing
decisions.   However,   these   simplifications help to
isolate the fundamental differences between the two
perspectives - namely their respective views of the
operation of the marketplace in advanced capitalist
economies.   Neoclassical   models   presume   that
flexible prices will always ensure the automatic
movement of aggregate output and employment levels
towards levels dictated by resource constraints.
Any failure of such movements implies some rigidity
in   prices   due   to   the   explicit   or   implicit
resistance of agents to allow (relative) prices to
adjust.   Notional   and   effective   demands   and
supplies are assumed to always be equal in this
analysis.
     The alternative Keynesian analysis developed
in Chapter Four presumes that rational optimising
agents   work   in   an   irrational   environment   where
demand   constraints   operate   to   create   a   wedge
between notional and effective demand and supplies.
According to this view, the binding constraint on
individual behaviour is the operation of markets
themselves   in   an   unplanned   and   atomistic
environment.   In   such   circumstances,   rational
behaviour dictates that agents will have to take
into account current and potential future quantity
constraints in the determination of their current
economic decisions and plans.   In sum, neoclassical
analysis is based on the premise that markets work;
the alternative view is derived from the view that
markets fail to perform their allocative role.
Both   views   are   consistent   with   individual
rationality.[1]

2. IMPLICATIONS OF THE EMPIRICAL RESULTS

The tests for Granger-causality carried out with UK
data in Part Three above suggest the following
conclusions.   First, the evidence does not support

the view that real wages adjust automatically to fluctuations in either output or employment. Second, the evidence as a whole fails to provide strong support for the view that employment is permanently influenced by permanent changes in real wages (as measured by the real wage 'innovation elasticity' of employment). There is, however, some evidence implying a permanent real wage effect on employment, but this effect appears to arise only from observations based on the mid- to late 1970s. Furthermore, the investigation into the real wage-output relationship suggests that even if real wages do in fact influence employment, this reflects substitution effects and not output effects. Output appears to be independent of real wages. Third, the evidence suggests that output does determine employment levels, although again this effect appears to be somewhat unstable. Thus although the results obtained in the empirical exercises cannot be considered conclusive, they do suggest that the overwhelming reliance on a stable inverse real wage-employment relationship in modern macroeconomic analysis is misplaced. Models of the labour market, and the determination of the demand schedule for employment in particular, should at the very least include aggregate demand variables in the analysis.

As a final point we mention briefly the implications of our results in considering the role for incomes policies within an overall Keynesian-type strategy of an expansion in aggregate demand. As was shown in Chapter Seven, the Callaghan incomes policies had a dramatic and unprecedented effect on real wage rates. In the context of an economy which is constrained by the level of aggregate effective demand such policies, if required, need not be based on reducing <u>real</u> wage rates. Indeed, it may be the case that real wage-<u>increasing</u> incomes policies may not have damaging consequences on employment and may also prove to be acceptable to workers and their trades unions.(2) Furthermore, real wage-increasing incomes policies based, say, on keeping the functional distribution of income constant in a capitalist economy might permit the implementation of longer-term planning of incomes through the incomes policy mechanism. Such forms of planning may prove acceptable to capitalists and workers alike.

NOTES

1. Notice as well that the notion of sticky prices appears as 'irrational' behaviour in terms of the neoclassical vision but can be seen to be 'rational' in terms of the alternative Keynesian vision where relative price movements serve to redistribute income rather than inducing changes in output levels.

2. This argument is further enhanced if productivity is growing along some trend path.

REFERENCES

Akerlof, G. (1979), 'The Case Against Conservative Macroeconomics: An Inaugural Lecture', Economica, August

Akerlof, G. (1982), 'Labor Contracts as Partial Gift Exchange', Quarterly Journal of Economics, November

Alogoskoufis, G. (1983), 'The Labour Market in an Equilibrium Business Cycle Model', Journal of Monetary Economics, January

Altonji, J. and O. Ashenfelter (1980), 'Wage Movements and the Labour Market Equilibrium Hypothesis', Economica, August

Anderson, T. (1971), The Statistical Analysis of Time Series, New York, John Wiley and Sons

Arrow, K. (1959), 'Toward a Theory of Price Adjustment', in M. Abramowitz (ed.), The Allocation of Economic Resources, Stanford, Stanford University Press

Backus, D. and J. Driffill (1985), 'Rational Expectations and Policy Credibility Following a Change in Regime', Review of Economic Studies, April

Barro, R. (1977), 'Unanticipated Money Growth and Unemployment in the United States', American Economic Review, March

Barro, R. (1978), 'Unanticipated Money, Output and the Price Level in the United States', Journal of Political Economy, July

Barro, R. and H. Grossman (1971), 'A General Disequilibrium Model of Income and Employment', American Economic Review, March

Benjamin, D. and L. Kochin (1979), 'Searching for an Explanation of Unemployment in Interwar Britain', Journal of Political Economy, June

Benjamin, D. and L. Kochin (1982), 'Unemployment and Unemployment Benefits in Twentieth Century Britain: A Reply to our Critics', Journal of Political Economy, April

Beveridge, W. (1944), Full Employment in a Free Society, London, George Allen and Unwin

Blinder, A. and R. Solow (1973), 'Does Fiscal Policy Matter?', Journal of Public Economics, November

Bodkin, R. (1969), 'Real Wages and Cyclical Variations in Employment: A Re-examination of the Evidence', Canadian Journal of Economics, August

Branson, W. (1972), Macroeconomic Theory and Policy, New York, Harper and Row

Brechling, F. (1965), 'The Relationship Between Output and Employment in British Manufacturing Industries', Review of Economic Studies, July

Brechling, F. (1975), Investment and Employment Decisions, Manchester, Manchester University Press

References

Breusch, T. and A. Pagan (1980), 'The Lagrange Multiplier Test and its Application to Model Specification in Econometrics', Review of Economic Studies, vol.47.
Buiter, W. and M. MIller (1981), 'The Thatcher Experiment: The First Two Years', Brookings Papers on Economic Activity, 2
Clower, R. (1965), 'The Keynesian Counterrevolution: A Theoretical Appraisal', in Hahn, F. and F. Brechling (eds), The Theory of Interest Rates, London, Macmillan
Coddington, A. (1976), 'Keynesian Economics: The Search for First Principles', Journal of Economic Literature, December
Collins, M. (1982), 'Unemployment in Interwar Britain: Still Searching for an Explanation', Journal of Political Economy, April
Cooley, T. and S. Leroy (1981), 'Identification and Estimation of Money Demand', American Economic Review, December
Cooley, T. and S. Leroy (1985), 'A-theoretical Macroeconometrics: A Critique', Journal of Monetary Economics, vol.16, November
Cross, R. (1982), 'How Much Voluntary Unemployment in Interwar Britain', Journal of Political Economy, April
Currie, D. (1975), 'Money, Income and Causality - A Comment', Queen Mary College Working Paper, no.7, February
Currie, D. (1985), 'Macroeconomic Policy Design and Control Theory - A Failed Partnership', Economic Journal, June
Davidson, P. (1983), 'The Dubious Labour Market Analysis in Meltzer's Restatement of Keynes' Theory', Journal of Economic Literature, March
Drobny, A. (1983), 'Rational Expectations and the Challenge to Monetarism: A Review', British Review of Economic Issues, Spring
Drobny, A. and R. Gausden (1988), 'Granger-Causality, Real Factor Prices and Employment: A Re-appraisal with UK Data', European Economic Review, forthcoming
Dunlop, J. (1939), 'The Movement of Real and Money Wage Rates', Economic Journal, September
Engle, R., D. Hendry and F. Richard (1983), 'Exogeneity', Econometrica, March
Fama, E. (1975), 'Short Term Interest Rates as Predictors of Inflation', American Economic Review, June
Feige, E.L. and D. Pearce (1976), 'Economically Rational Expectations: Are Innovations in the Rate of Inflation Independent of Innovations in Measures of Monetary and Fiscal Policy?', Journal of Political Economy, June
Frazer, W. and L. Boland (1983), 'An Essay on the Foundations of Friedman's Methodology', American Economic Review, March
Frenkel, J. and H.G. Johnson (1976), The Monetary Approach

to Balance of Payments Theory, London, George Allen and Unwin

Friedman, M. (1953), Essays in Positive Economics, Chicago, University of Chicago Press

Friedman, M. (1956), 'The Quantity Theory of Money: A Restatement', reprinted in Mueller (1971)

Friedman, M. (1957), A Theory of the Consumption Function, Princeton, Princeton University Press

Friedman, M. (1959), 'The Demand for Money - Some Theoretical and Empirical Results', Journal of Political Economy, June

Friedman, M. (1962), Capitalism and Freedom, Chicago, University of Chicago Press

Friedman, M. (1968), 'The Role of Monetary Policy', American Economic Review, March

Friedman, M. (1975), 'Unemployment Versus Inflation?', Institute of Economic Affairs, Occasional Paper, no.44

Friedman, M. and A. Schwartz (1963a), A Monetary History of the United States, 1867-1960, Princeton, Princeton University Press

Friedman, M. and A. Schwartz (1963b), 'Money and Business Cycles', Review of Economics and Statistics, February

Gale, D. (1983), 'Competitive Models with Keynesian Features', Economic Journal, Conference Papers

Geary, P. and J. Kennan (1982), 'The Employment-Real Wage Relationship: An International Study', Journal of Political Economy, August

Gersovitz, M. (1980), 'Mis-specification and Cyclical Models: The Real Wage and the Phillips Curve', Economica, November

Geweke, J. (1980), 'Inference and Causality in Economic Time Series Models', in Griliches, Z. and M. Intrilligator (eds), Handbook of Econometrics, Amsterdam, North-Holland

Geweke, J. (1981), 'The Approximate Slopes of Econometric Tests', Econometrica, November

Geweke, J., R. Meese and W. Dent (1983), 'Comparing Alternative Tests of Causality in Temporal Systems: Analytic Results and Experimental Evidence', Journal of Econometrics, February

Goldfeld, S.M. (1973), 'The Demand for Money Revisited', Brookings Papers on Economic Activity, 3

Gordon, D., T. Weiskopf and S. Bowles (1983), 'Long Swings and the Nonreproductive Cycle', American Economic Review, May

Gordon, R.J. (1981), 'Output Fluctuations and Gradual Price Adjustment', Journal of Economic Literature, June

Gordon, R.J. (1982), 'Why US Wage and Employment Behaviour Differs from that in Britain and Japan', Economic Journal, March

References

Gorman, W. (1953), 'Community Preference Fields', Econometrica, January

Grandmont (1977), 'Temporary General Equilibrium Theory', Econometrica, July

Granger, C. (1969), 'Investigating Causal Relations by Econometric Models and Cross-Spectral Methods', Econometrica, July

Granger, C. and P. Newbold (1977), Forecasting Economic Time Series, New York, Academic Press

Greenhalgh, C.A., P.R.G. Layard and A.J. Oswald (1983), The Causes of Unemployment, Oxford, Clarendon Press

Grossman, H. (1979), 'Why Does Aggregate Employment Fluctuate?', American Economic Review, May

Grubb, D., R. Jackman and R. Layard (1982), 'Causes of the Current Stagflation', Review of Economic Studies, Special Edition

Hagen, E. (1949), 'The Classical Theory of the Level of Output and Employment', reprinted in Mueller (1971)

Hahn, F. (1978), 'On Non-Walrasian Equilibria', Review of Economic Studies, January

Hahn, F. (1980), 'Monetarism and Economic Theory', Economica, February

Hahn, F. (1982), Money and Inflation, Oxford, Basil Blackwell

Haugh, L. (1972), 'The Identification of Time Series Interrelationships with Special Reference to Dynamic Regression', Ph.D. dissertation, University of Wisconsin

Haugh, L. (1976), 'Checking the Independence of Two Covariance-Stationary Time Series: A Univariate Residual Cross Correlation Approach', Journal of The American Statistical Association, June

Hicks, J. (1932), The Theory of Wages, 2nd edition, Oxford, Clarendon Press, reprinted 1974

Hicks, J. (1937), 'Mr Keynes and the "Classics": A Suggested Interpretation', reprinted in Mueller (1971)

Hicks, J. (1939), Value and Capital, 2nd edition, Oxford, Clarendon Press, reprinted 1974

Hoover, K. (1984), 'Two Types of Monetarism', Journal of Economic Literature, March

Kahn, L. (1980), 'Bargaining Power, Search Theory and the Phillips Curve', Cambridge Journal of Economics, September

Kaldor, N. (1970), 'The New Monetarism', Lloyds Bank Review, July

Kaldor, N. (1972), 'The Irrelevance of Equilibrium Economics', Economic Journal, December

Kalecki, M. (1969), Studies in the Theory of Business Cycles, English edition, Warsaw, Polish Scientific Publishers

Keat, R. and J. Urry (1975), Social Theory as Science, London, Routledge and Kegan Paul

Keynes, J.M. (1936), The General Theory of Employment, Interest and Money, London, Macmillan, reprinted in 1973

234

Keynes, J.M. (1937), 'The General Theory of Employment', Quarterly Journal of Economics, February

Keynes, J.M. (1939), 'Relative Movements of Real Wages and Output', reprinted as Appendix 3 in Keynes (1936)

Kirkpatrick, G. (1981), 'Further Results on the Time Series Analysis of Real Wages and Employment for US Manufacturing, 1948-1977', Weltwirtschaftliches Archiv, vol.117, no.2

Kirkpatrick, G. (1982), 'Real Factor Prices and German Manufacturing Employment: A Time Series Analysis, 1960(1)-1979(4)', Weltwirtschaftliches Archiv, vol.118, no.1

Kuh, E. (1966), 'Unemployment, Production Functions and Effective Demand', Journal of Political Economy, June

Kuhn, T.S. (1970), The Structure of Scientific Revolutions, 2nd edition, Chicago, University of Chicago Press

Laidler, D. (1981), 'Monetarism: An Interpretation and an Assessment', Economic Journal, March

Laidler, D. (1982), Monetarist Perspectives, Oxford, Philip Allan

Lawson, N. (1984), 'The British Experiment', The Fifth Mais Lecture, delivered at the City University Business School, 18 June

Leamer, E. (1983), 'Let's Take the Con Out of Econometrics', American Economic Review, March

Leibenstein, H. (1966), 'Allocative Efficiency Versus X-Efficiency', American Economic Review, June

Leijonhufvud, A. (1968), On Keynesian Economics and the Economics of Keynes, New York, Oxford University Press

Leijonhufvud, A. (1969), 'Keynes and the Classics', Institute of Economic Affairs, Occasional Paper no.30

Leontief, W. (1937), 'The Fundamental Assumption of Mr Keynes' Monetary Theory of Unemployment', Quarterly Journal of Economics, November

Lipsey, R. (1960), 'The Relation Between Unemployment and the Rate of Change of Money Wage Rates in the United Kingdom, 1862-1957: A Further Analysis', Economica, February

Lucas, R.E. (1970), 'Capacity, Overtime and Empirical Production Functions', American Economic Review, May

Lucas, R.E. (1972), 'Expectations and the Neutrality of Money', Journal of Economic Theory, April

Lucas, R.E. (1973), 'Some International Evidence on Output-Inflation Tradeoffs', American International Review, June

Lucas, R.E. (1975), 'An Equilibrium Model of the Business Cycle', reprinted in Lucas (1981)

Lucas, R.E. (1977), 'Understanding Business Cycles', reprinted in Lucas (1981)

Lucas, R.E. (1981), Studies in Business-Cycle Theory, Oxford, Basil Blackwell

References

Lucas, R.E. and L. Rapping (1969a), 'Real Wages, Employment and Inflation', Journal of Political Economy, September/October

Lucas, R.E. and L. Rapping (1969b), 'Price Expectations and the Phillips Curve', American Economic Review, June

Lucas, R.E. and T. Sargent (1981) (eds), Rational Expectations and Econometric Practice, London, George Allen and Unwin

Malinvaud, E. (1977), The Theory of Unemployment Reconsidered, Oxford, Basil Blackwell

Marshall, A. (1979), Principles of Economics, 8th edition, London, Macmillan

McCallum, B. (1979), 'The Current State of The Policy Ineffectiveness Debate', American Economic Review, May

McDonald, I. and R. Solow (1981), 'Wage Bargaining and Employment', American Economic Review, December

Mehra, Y. (1977), 'Money Wages, Prices and Causality', Journal of Political Economy, December

Meltzer, A. (1981), 'Keynes' General Theory: A Different Perspective', Journal of Economic Literature, March

Meltzer, A. (1983), 'Interpreting Keynes', Journal of Economic Literature, March

Metcalf, D., S. Nickell and N. Floros (1982), 'Unemployment in Interwar Britain', Journal of Political Economy, April

Minford, P. (1984), 'Response to Nickell', Economic Journal, December

Minford, P. with D. Davies, M. Peel and A. Sprague (1983), Unemployment: Cause and Cure, Oxford, Martin Robertson and Co.

Modigliani, F. (1944), 'Liquidity Preference and the Theory of Interest and Money', Econometrica, January

Modigliani, F. (1977), 'The Monetarist Controversy Or Should We Forsake Stabilization Policies?', American Economic Review, March

Mueller, M. (1971) (ed.), Readings in Macroeconomics, Illinois, Dryden Press

Muth, J. (1960), 'Optimal Properties of Exponentially Weighted Processes', Journal of the American Statistical Association, June

Muth, J. (1961), 'Rational Expectations and the Theory of Price Movements', Econometrica, May

Neftci, S. (1978), 'A Time Series Analysis of the Real Wages-Employment Relationship', Journal of Political Economy, April

Nelson, C. and G. Schwert (1977), 'On Testing the Hypothesis that the Real Rate of Interest is Constant', American Economic Review, June

Nelson, C. and G. Schwert (1982), 'Tests for Predictive Relationships Between Time-Series Variables: A Monte Carlo Investigation', Journal of The American

Statistical Association, March

Nickell, S. (1984), 'Review of Unemployment: Cause and Cure', Economic Journal, December

Nickell, S. and M. Andrews (1983), 'Unions, Real Wages and Employment in Britain 1951-1979', Oxford Economic Papers, Supplement, November

Ormerod, P. and G. Worswick (1982), 'Unemployment in Interwar Britain', Journal of Political Economy, April

Park, R. (1966), 'Estimation with Heteroscedastic Error Terms', Econometrica, October

Parkin, M. and R. Bade (1982), Modern Macroeconomics, Oxford, Philip Allan

Patinkin, D. (1951), 'Price Flexibility and Full Employment', reprinted in Mueller (1971).

Patinkin, D. (1965), Money, Interest and Prices, 2nd edition, New York, Harper and Row

Patinkin, D. (1983), 'New Perspectives or Old Pitfalls? Some Comments on Alan Meltzer's Interpretation of the General Theory', Journal of Economic Literature, March

Phelps, E. (1968), 'Money Wage Dynamics and Labour Market Equilibrium', Journal of Political Economy, July/August

Phelps, E. and J. Taylor (1977), 'Stabilizing Powers of Monetary Policy Under Rational Expectations', Journal of Political Economy, February

Phillips, A.W. (1958), 'The Relation Between Unemployment and the Rate of Change of Money Wage Rates in the United Kingdom, 1861-1957', reprinted in Mueller (1971)

Pierce, D. (1977), 'Relationships - and the Lack Thereof - Between Economic Time Series with Special Reference to Money and Interest Rates', Journal of The American Statistical Association, March

Pierce, D. and L. Haugh (1977), 'Causality in Temporal Systems: Characterizations and a Survey', Journal of Econometrics, May

Pigou, A.C. (1933), The Theory of Unemployment, London, Macmillan

Pigou, A.C. (1943), 'The Classical Stationary State', Economic Journal, December

Ritter, L. (1963), 'The Role of Money in Keynesian Theory', reprinted in Mueller (1971)

Robinson, J. (1971), Economic Heresies, Some Old-Fashioned Questions in Economic Theory, New York, Basic Books

Rowthorn, R. (1977), 'Conflict, Inflation and Money', Cambridge Journal of Economics, September

Sachs, J. (1979), 'Wages, Profits and Macroeconomic Adjustment: A Comparative Study', Brookings Papers on Economic Activity, 2

Sachs, J. (1982), 'Stabilization Policies in the World Economy: Scope and Skepticism', American Economic Review, May

References

Samuelson, P. (1970), Economics, 8th edition, New York, McGraw-Hill

Samuelson, P. and R. Solow (1960), 'Analytical Aspects of Anti-Inflation Policy', reprinted in Mueller (1971)

Sargent, T. (1973), 'Rational Expectations, the Real Rate of Interest and the Natural Rate of Unemployment', Brookings Papers on Economic Activity, 2

Sargent, T. (1976), 'A Classical Macroeconomic Model for the United States', Journal of Political Economy, April

Sargent, T. (1978), 'Estimation of Dynamic Labor Demand Schedules Under Rational Expectations', Journal of Political Economy, December

Sargent, T. (1979), Macroeconomic Theory, London, Academic Press

Sargent, T. and N. Wallace (1973), 'Rational Expectations and the Dynamics of Hyperinflation', International Economic Review, June

Sargent, T. and N. Wallace (1975), 'Rational Expectations, the Optimal Monetary Instrument, and the Optimal Money Supply Rule', Journal of Political Economy, April

Scarth, W. and A. Myatt (1980), 'The Real Wage-Employment Relationship', Economic Journal, March

Schwert, G. (1979), 'Tests of Causality', in Brunner, K. and A. Meltzer (eds), Three Aspects of Policy and Policymaking: Knowledge, Data and Institutions, Amsterdam, North-Holland

Shackle, G. (1972), Epistemics and Economics, Cambridge, Cambridge University Press

Sheffrin, S. (1983), Rational Expectations, Cambridge, Cambridge University Press

Sims, C. (1972), 'Money, Income and Causality', American Economic Review, September

Sims, C. (1974), 'Distributed Lags', in Intrilligator, M. and D. Hendrick (eds), Frontiers of Quantitative Economics, Amsterdam, North-Holland

Sims, C. (1980), 'Macroeconomics and Reality', Econometrica, January

Solow, R. (1979), 'Another Possible Source of Wage Stickiness', Journal of Macroeconomics, Winter

Solow, R. (1980), 'On Theories of Unemployment', American Economic Review, March

Solow, R. and J. Stiglitz (1968), 'Output, Employment and Wages in the Short Run', Quarterly Journal of Economics, November

Stein, J. (1982), Monetarist, Keynesian and New Classical Economics, Oxford, Basil Blackwell

Stiglitz, J. (1976), 'The Efficiency Wage Hypothesis, Surplus Labour and the Distribution of Income in LDCs', Oxford Economic Papers, July

Symons, J. (1985), 'Relative Prices and the Demand for Labour in British Manufacturing', Economica, February

Symons, J. and P.R.G. Layard (1984), 'Neoclassical Demand for Labour Functions for Six Major Economies', *Economic Journal*, December

Tarling, R. and F. Wilkinson (1977), 'The Social Contract: Postwar Incomes Policies and Their Inflationary Impact', *Cambridge Journal of Economics*, December

Tarshis, L. (1939), 'Changes in Real and Money Wages', *Economic Journal*, March

Taylor, J. (1979), 'Staggered Wage Setting in a Macro Model', *American Economic Review*, May

Tobin, J. (1951), 'Money Wage Rates and Employment', reprinted in Mueller (1971)

Tobin, J. (1970), 'Money and Income: Post Hoc Ergo Propter Hoc?', *Quarterly Journal of Economics*, May

Tobin, J. (1975), 'Keynesian Models of Recession and Depression', *American Economic Review*, May

Tobin, J. (1980), *Asset Accumulation and Economic Activity*, Oxford, Basil Blackwell

Trevithic, J. (1976), 'Money Wage Inflexibility and the Keynesian Supply Function', *Economic Journal*, June

Varian, H. (1978), *Microeconomic Analysis*, London, W.W. Norton & Co

Weisenberger, E. and J. Thomas (1981), 'The Causal Role of Money in West Germany', mimeo

Weitzman, M. (1982), 'Increasing Returns and the Foundations of Unemployment Theory', *Economic Journal*, September

Williams, D., C. Goodhart and D. Gowland (1976), 'Money, Income and Causality: The UK Experience', *American Economic Review*, June

Yellen, J. (1984), 'Efficiency Wage Models of Unemployment', *American Economic Review*, May